Voicing Concerns

Voicing Concerns: sociological perspectives on contemporary education reforms

Edited by
Madeleine Arnot & Len Barton

Triangle Books

Triangle Books Ltd
PO Box 65, Wallingford, Oxfordshire OX10 0YG, United Kingdom

Published in the United Kingdom, 1992
© Triangle Books Ltd, 1992

ISBN 1 873927 00 2

Text composition in Palatino by Triangle Books Ltd
Printed and bound in the United Kingdom by
Cambridge University Press

Contents

Introduction   *vii*

1   **Miriam David**. Parents and the State: how has social research informed education reforms?   **1**

2   **Liz Kelly.** Not in Front of the Children: responding to right wing agendas on sexuality and education   **20**

3   **Madeleine Arnot**. Feminism, Education and the New Right   **41**

4   **Len Barton & Mike Oliver**. Special Needs: personal trouble or public issue?   **66**

5   **Ahmed Gurnah**. On the Specificity of Racism   **88**

6   **Andrew Pollard**. Teachers' Responses to the Reshaping of Primary Education   **104**

7   **David Halpin**. Staying On and Staying In: comprehensive schooling in the 1990s   **125**

8   **Tony Edwards, Sharon Gewirtz & Geoff Whitty**. Whose Choice of Schools? Making Sense of City Technology Colleges   **143**

9   **John Furlong**. Reconstructing Professionalism: ideological struggle in initial teacher education   **163**

10   **Geoffrey Walford**. The Reform of Higher Education   **186**

11   **Roger Dale**. Recovering from a Pyrrhic Victory? Quality, Relevance and Impact in the Sociology of Education   **201**

Contributors

MADELEINE ARNOT, Department of Education, University of Cambridge, 17 Trumpington Street, Cambridge CB2 1QA

LEN BARTON, Division of Education, University of Sheffield, Sheffield S10 2TN

ROGER DALE, Education Department, University of Auckland, Auckland, New Zealand

MIRIAM DAVID, Social Science Department, Polytechnic of the South Bank, Borough Road, London SE1 0AA

TONY EDWARDS, School of Education, University of Newcastle upon Tyne, Newcastle upon Tyne NE1 7RU

JOHN FURLONG, Department of Education, University College of Swansea, Hendrefoilan, Swansea SA2 7NB

SHARON GEWIRTZ, Centre for Educational Studies, Kings College, University of London, Chelsea Campus, 522 Kings Road, London SW10 0UA

AHMED GURNAH, Education Department, Sheffield City Council, Sheffield S1 1RJ

DAVID HALPIN, Department of Education, University of Warwick, Westwood, Coventry CV4 7AL

LIZ KELLY, Child Abuse Studies Unit, Polytechnic of North London, Ladbroke House, 62-66 Highbury Grove, London N5 2AD

MIKE OLIVER, Thames Polytechnic, Avery Hill Campus, Bexley Road, Eltham, London SE9 2PQ

ANDREW POLLARD, Faculty of Education, Bristol Polytechnic, Redland Hill, Bristol BS6 6UZ

GEOFFREY WALFORD, Aston Business School, Aston University, Aston Triangle, Birmingham B4 7ET

GEOFF WHITTY, Goldsmith's College, University of London, New Cross, London SE14 6NU

Introduction

MADELEINE ARNOT & LEN BARTON

This book has been produced during a period of major changes in education. Many but not all of these changes have been the result of Conservative Party reforms during the 1980s, culminating in the 1988 Education Reform Act and its implementation. The driving force behind these developments have been supporters of a market ideology with an emphasis on choice, competition and 'modernisation'. Alongside these can also be found supporters of a radical form of conservatism with its commitment to sustaining the social order through family, 'nation' and a new morality. These influences have encouraged the establishment of new priorities, objectives and intended educational outcomes, coupled with a fundamental concern with where and how the system of provision is to be managed.

Teacher education is not unfamiliar with the demands for change emanating from various sources including government. Indeed, for over a decade it has been the subject of serious criticism. These have included critiques of the contribution of sociology of education within initial and in-service teacher education courses. The political attacks of the Black Papers in the late 1960s and early 1970s focussed not just on schools or the teaching profession. By the mid 1970s sociology of education courses were being attacked for their political bias. The Gould Report (1977) examined sociology of education courses, helped by lecturers such as Caroline Cox who were themselves engaged in teaching the discipline. They challenged the right of sociology of education to offer a critique of existing educational policies and provision arguing that such analyses were dangerous rather than inaccurate. Sociological critiques of liberalism, of the role which education played within capitalism and of the continuing reproduction of social inequality encouraged teachers and student teachers to criticise basic social values, the educational system and its premises.

The reaction of those in the discipline at the time included hearkening back to the concept of a sociological imagination and the valuable role that the social sciences could play in delving behind the taken-for-granted world of practitioners and policy makers. Sociologists could, through their research, investigate the structures and processes involved in education in such a way as to inform genuine attempts at social reform. As Dale has argued in his overview of the chapters of this volume, sociologists despite their critical stance were committed to the project of social redemption/emancipation through universal provision. They allied themselves to the pursuit of egalitarianism and excellence in education for all children. In this sense, they were not out of line with the mainstream educationalists, nor indeed the expressed goals of policy makers in the post war period.

Increasingly, however, sociological research raised more and more challenging questions about the real purposes of schooling, and the motivations and commitment of politicians to the principles of equality of opportunity for all. The range of options available to teachers and schools, and to policy makers to encourage social reform through educational reforms, became increasingly narrow. Attention had already been drawn to the political and economic assumptions behind the selection and organisation of knowledge, the principles underlying school organisation and the negative experiences of working class, black and female pupils within state education. Thus strategies for educational reform by the 1980s were becoming, according to Dale (Chapter 11), increasingly utopian rather than optimistic. Significantly Paulo Freire's work which was taken up by sociologists in the 1970s and by feminists in the 1980s encouraged the development of utopian thought as functional to political action.

By the early 1980s criticisms of sociology of education from the Right had become increasingly outspoken and given more credibility within the new political framework. When Conservative party politicians focussed attention on raising the quality of schooling, sociology of education was represented as one of the causes of low teacher morale as well as an over-politicised teaching profession; it was blamed for setting up diversionary attempts in schools to promote racial harmony and to challenge sexism, without getting down to the real business of improving the quality of teaching and the raising of standards. Equality was counterposed with quality of schooling as two different political goals, with sociology clearly seen as obsessed with social rather than genuine educational concerns. Critics also alleged that sociology of education as an academic subject was characterised by political bias, subversion, irrelevance and weak intellectual scholarship (Dawson, 1981; Cox & Marx, 1982).

In a paper in which Dawson argues for the removal of sociology of education from all courses for student teachers, he maintains that:

> ...at a time of retrenchment, when luxuries have been discarded and necessities are threatened, it is unwise to spare an unnecessary, costly and

harmful ideology. Sociology of education should be cut out of courses for student teachers, not primarily as a means of reducing the Public Sector Borrowing Requirement (important though that is) but to improve the intellectual and moral environment in which would be teachers are taught (p. 60).

This type of discourse needs to be engaged with critically both for its dogmatism and the unsupported generalisations which constitute much of its substance. However, a great deal has now happened which has markedly influenced the extent and nature of the discipline.

The restructuring of in-service teacher education and its funding which was transferred away from local educational authorities towards schools has had major consequences for sociology of education courses. Funding was clearly linked to the new priorities of improved school management, leadership, curriculum planning and evaluation. Teachers were encouraged not to elect to study sociological courses as part of their professional development, defined increasingly in terms of improved classroom skills and school development.

Conservative government policies have also resulted in the closure of many initial teacher education institutions and courses; other institutions have amalgamated or set up associations. A major change has been the introduction in 1984 of the Council for the Accreditation of Teacher Education (CATE). All initial courses must gain CATE approval in order for their students to receive qualified teacher status. This involves meeting particular criteria as defined by the CATE committee; for example, the time given to subject specialism, teaching practice, mathematics, science and information technology. In order to achieve these and other requirements extensive changes have needed to be made. Many traditional educational studies elements within such courses have been removed or given greatly reduced time with an added applied emphasis. Thus, many sociology of education courses have become the victims of these events. The recent announcement of the proposed changes to teacher training will no doubt be viewed as a further attack on the discipline (Clarke, 1992).

Given the somewhat hostile climate in which sociology of education is now operating, it is somewhat unusual to publish a text which explicitly addresses the discipline. Although there have been a number of sociological texts commenting on, for example, the Education Reform Act (Bash & Coulby, 1989; Flude & Hammer, 1990) these have tended to offer sociological insights into the possible implications of the legislation rather than debate the relevance of sociological research and teaching to the new climate. Such analyses have tended to assume that the discipline can find a role for itself in developing a model of policy studies which is different from the mainstream somewhat management oriented models of policy analysis (Ozga, 1987).

Our project is somewhat different. This book represents a commitment to the importance of sociology of education and to its continuance within higher education courses and research. The key role which the discipline has played in the decades after the war cannot be abandoned. For, within an educational system designed according to the principles of a market economy, sociology of education will have an increasingly important part to play in assessing its impact on particular social groups and in contributing to more effective alternative approaches within education. The battle over state education alone has yet to be fought.

We have therefore invited a range of sociologists to contribute to this collection. We gave them a difficult task. First, we asked them to consider the record of sociological research in their particular area and to consider whether and how such research could help us make sense of the current climate and educational reforms of the last decade. What had we already learnt about the processes and structures of schooling and its social relations that could contribute to our understanding of the origins, nature or impact of the Conservative Party's restructuring of education? We asked sociologists in the 1990's to remember the corpus of sociological research that had been halted dramatically in its development by the electoral victory of the Conservative Party in 1979.

Secondly we asked our authors to assess from a sociological perspective a selected range of contemporary educational reforms or debates about reform. The reforms they could select were not necessarily the most obvious ones, such as the Education Reform Act, but were those seen as significant within the context of each chapter theme. We encouraged authors to move away from the list of reforms identified by Conservative government as 'radical' and hence of greatest importance in the restructuring of education. All too often we find the agenda of sociological analyses set by politicians who have much to gain by the increased attention granted to such structural reforms as 'opting out', financial management, the National Curriculum, open enrolment etc.

Thirdly, we had challenged our authors to consider the future direction of sociological research in education. We asked for, and were delighted to receive, a range of different research agendas which attempt to recapture even if only in an initial sortie, some of the specifically sociological questions which have shaped the discipline in the past. We hoped through such requests to reject Conservative party rhetoric of the need to 'break with the past' which would have meant losing our own roots and rationales for our existence as members of a discipline. We hoped also to begin to construct a future for sociology of education within the reconstructed educational world.

For many of our authors, including ourselves, this exercise proved to be incredibly difficult. The new structures in which we work had constructed the 'irrelevance' of our pasts to such an extent that it was even painful to remember it. As authors we were almost too embarrassed to refer back to theories of social and cultural reproduction in a period where individual advancement and material concerns have hegemonic force. Could we really retrieve the findings of a discipline whose concepts had been jettisoned not just by its opponents but also by its members - concepts such as social class conflict, the capitalist economy, ideological and social formations, agents and agencies, state apparatuses, gender relations? For many of us, now attempting to find new relevance in the world of policy making, the language and concepts of sociology of education appeared more of a hindrance than an aid. We had all experienced in effect what Bourdieu once called 'genesis amnesia' - the collective loss of memory concerning the origins of our social perceptions.

It was therefore, with some difficulty that textual references to sociological theories and research were inserted into each chapter. However for some of the authors in this collection, the process represented a first step in recognising yet again the value of 'old' debates about, for example, the relationship of structure and agency, the relationship of public and private spheres or the debates between principles of liberal education and social reconstruction.

For others, the exercise has provided a good opportunity not just to remember but also to assess in retrospect the tradition of sociological research in education. There is no special pleading for the value of sociology *per se*, rather the analyses seek to identify the weakness of past and existing work. The critiques are not hostile to the tradition but they are sharp. They reveal, for example, inadequacies in the agenda set for sociology of education by the social democratic traditions of policy making in the post war period and the failure to respond adequately to the winds of change in the late 1970s and 1980s.

In the space of this introduction it is impossible to do justice to the critical analyses offered by each chapter. Instead we hope to identify some of the lessons we have learnt as editors in reading through the drafts of these chapters and reflecting on the messages which emerge from them. We were aware from the start that this reassessment of both sociology of education and contemporary educational reforms would be affected by the selection and organisation of chapters in the collection. We felt it important to keep a mixture of chapters which dealt with particular phases of education and those which tackled particular themes. In the first category therefore are chapters on primary education by Andy Pollard, secondary education by David Halpin; teacher education by John Furlong and higher education by Geoffrey Walford. In the latter category are chapters by Miriam David, Liz Kelly, Ahmed Gurnah, Tony Edwards, Sharon Gerwitz & Geoff Whitty, Len Barton & Mike Oliver, and Madeleine Arnot analysing parents and the state, sexuality, the education of black people, the pursuit of excellence, special needs and feminism respectively. This selection, although unfortunately not comprehensive, offers us the chance to explore some of the existing concerns of sociology of education and to consider new issues which were not tackled by sociological research in any great depth in the 1970's but which now have assumed considerable significance in the 1990s.

A number of themes recur in the various articles. The significance of the change in political climate has clearly been experienced by sociologists as marking a major break in the influence of the academic discipline on policy makers and political debates surrounding educational policy. Initially that influence was direct and carried by key figures such as Halsey

(1972) especially in relation to the setting up of such experiments as the Educational Priority Areas (see Chapters 1 and 6 by Miriam David and Andrew Pollard). Other debates such as those surrounding child-centred learning and primary education in the Plowden Report (1967) and the development of the comprehensive ideal by the Labour Party were also affected by sociological research particularly the 'political arithmetic tradition' of early research into social class and achievement and the later critical analyses of Basil Bernstein who figures in a number of chapters as a highly significant figure in establishing key sociological debates about the impact of educational structures and processes in the 1970s.

As the Centre for Contemporary Cultural Studies (1980) in *Unpopular Education* has already analysed in some depth, sociological research aided the policy making processes by colluding in its agenda in the post war period. Clearly social democratic principles with their emphasis upon equality of opportunity, liberal education (rather than vocational training) and economic regeneration had shaped not just politicians' priorities but also the terrain of critical debate. Thus sociology of education, as Halpin indicates in Chapter 7, focussed primarily upon secondary education. Certainly sociological analysis of primary education was late in arriving, urged on more by contemporary Conservative interest in restructuring its curriculum and challenging the autonomy of its teaching force than by the development of progressive ideologies and curriculum development in the 1970s. Higher education, as Walford demonstrates in Chapter 10, although attracting early attention from sociologists in the 1960s also failed to sustain the interest of researchers despite the vital role played by higher education institutions in shaping the school system and in affecting individuals' life chances. The sociology of the school never found a partner in a sociology of universities and polytechnics.

It now seems in retrospect that the agenda of sociology of education, whilst critical, also reflected it now seems in retrospect many of the assumptions of those with whom it shared a platform in educational circles. As Roger Dale points out in Chapter 11, sociological theorising was premised upon assumptions about the effectivity of educational reform to promote social change. Despite its traditional hostility to liberalism, much critical sociological research supported the view that education was a social good and that egalitarian principles could still be discussed within the structures of a capitalist economy. What characterised the period leading up to the 1980s was a quest for more effective approaches to achieving that goal. Thus there was a shared consensus around the value of, for example, the autonomy of educators to determine the curriculum whether in primary schools (see Chapter 6 by Pollard) or in teacher education (see Chapter 9 by Furlong) or in universities (see Chapter 10 by Walford). The concept of partnership can also be found reflected in sociological research which encouraged a concept of parental responsibilities and a partnership between parents and schools - at the same time paradoxically as investigating and revealing the unequal effects on children's chances of parental origins (discussed by Miriam David, Chapter 1).

The awareness of limits of educational reform were most clearly expressed, as Halpin demonstrates (Chapter 7) in the sociology of the curriculum and theories of cultural and social reproduction. Nevertheless that analysis, according to Dale, never fully appreciated the role of the state or indeed of much more than the 'politics of education'. Increasingly sociological analysis by the end of the 1970's had concentrated upon cultural rather than economic formations and had begun to focus on the particular circumstances of Conservative political reforms.

The limits of sociological research under the conditions of social democracy are explored in a range of chapters in this collection. Liz Kelly (Chapter 2) for example, takes issue with the failure of mainstream sociological research to investigate the relationship between schooling and sexual identities and to uncover the experiences of gay and lesbian students in the context of discrimination and prejudice. The range of feminist research on issues of sexuality points to need to challenge essentialist accounts which, if implicit before, have become increasingly explicit in the Conservative era.

Arnot (Chapter 3), in contrast, takes to task mainstream sociological research for its failure to recognise the considerable challenge to social democratic principles represented by feminist research. Such research had raised serious questions about the impact of comprehensivisation, co-education, child-centred learning, voluntary curriculum choice etc. The concern with economic and political relations had blinded sociologists in the past and are still blinding them in the present, she argues, to the significance of patriarchal relations within educational policy-making.

What Kelly's chapter on sexuality and Arnot's chapter on feminism have in common is a recognition of the moral dimensions of Conservative politics - a dimension which appears to be neglected in contemporary sociological accounts of the New Right. Such moral dimensions introduce the significance of the family within a market economy and the role which education could be asked to play in emphasising traditional domestic and heterosexual relations as the norm. Miriam David's chapter on parents and the state complements this analyses especially when referring to the continuity of assumptions about gender and parenting, especially the role of the mother. From these feminist perspectives, the introduction of New Right thinking into educational policy making has not represented so much a radical break with past traditions, more of a deepening of an existing vein in educational policy making.

Other absences in sociology of education are identified in this collection. Len Barton & Mike Oliver (Chapter 4) take sociology to task for leaving the whole area of special education in the hands of psychology with its discourses of individualism, 'needs' and special provision either in separate schools or in mainstream schools. They argue that sociologists, other than the outstanding exceptions such as Sally Tomlinson, have failed to recognise the class, race and gender implications of these categorisations and has neglected a major, and politically significant, component of contemporary education reform.

However, even more critical analyses of the traditions of sociology of education are provided by Ahmed Gurnah and Roger Dale. Gurnah in Chapter 5, offers a hard hitting critique of the empiricist and formalist assumptions behind the sociology of 'race' and education. Taking up earlier criticisms of sociology's failure to challenge politicians' discourses surrounding black communities, Gurnah suggests that the weaknesses of sociological research lies in its failure to be relevant to the political struggles of black people. In this respect Gurnah echoes a theme in Roger Dale's concluding chapter when he suggests among other things, that the current low profile of sociology of education may be a result of, on the one hand, its irrelevance to the educational concerns of teachers and students and, on the other, its failure to address the deeper conditions which sustain political ideologies.

All chapters offer some analysis of Conservative educational ideologies and policies. Some chapters, for example those by Tony Edwards, Sharon Gerwitz & Geoff Whitty, John Furlong and Geoffrey Walford focus upon particular initiatives. Each takes a particular stance when trying to account for those initiatives. Thus Edwards et al (Chapter 8) investigate in careful detail the participants, their statements and assumptions, the documentation and the implementation of the City Technology Colleges. They uncover the key figures, expose the intended outcomes and consider the practical effects. In this latter task they offer the insights of preliminary research findings on how the schemes are being implemented and the contradictions contained within the new schools, their curricula and the types of pupil they are attracting. Similarly Pollard (Chapter 6) discusses the impact of external forces on primary education. He examines the issues of teacher ideology and practice and the social outcomes of differentiation processes in schools. He reveals some of the concerns and the ways in which primary teachers have responded to, and are implementing, the National Curriculum and assessment in schools.

Other analyses of the Conservative government reforms, such as those in the sphere of higher education (Walford, Chapter 10) and teacher education (Furlong, Chapter 9) discuss the ideological significance of those policies in contrast with other political ideals. Contrasting values contained within the projects, described by liberalism, conservativism and 'modernisation' emerge from such accounts along with the contradictory ways in which they are put together in particular policies. Further, reading such analyses one begins to see not the success of the New Right in presenting a unified political force, but its failure to act either consistently or coherently. If nothing else the speed with which reforms were put into place within the last decade has militated against a new consensus. Instead we read in these accounts about, amongst other things, the weak response of industry to the city technology college ideal, the reshaping of educational reforms by primary teachers resisting the loss of their autonomy, the fighting back by teacher educators particularly those in control of specialist subjects, the campaigns mounted by higher educational institutions to protect their freedom and extend student access.

New arguments are also put forward about the nature of New Right thinking. The rational technocratic models of teacher education are for example illustrated in John Furlong's analysis (Chapter 9) whilst the commitment to equality of opportunity and biological essentialism of Conservative party thinkers are discussed in Arnot's and Kelly's chapters.

Whilst these analyses into contemporary educational reforms have provided useful insights into the ideological reshaping of education and the conditions of its implementation, they remain, according to Dale, at the level of concept development. His critique of current attempts at policy analysis suggest that far more is needed by way of theory development especially if we are to relate to international developments rather than just to our own parochial concerns - a view with which, we are sure, the other authors in this book would agree. Clearly there is far more work to be done in deepening our understanding of the nature of educational change. These chapters have only begun to indicate the directions in which sociological researchers should go.

For those such as Halpin, the real debates have not yet been addressed. In his discussion (in Chapter 7) of the problems of ensuring that pupils 'stay on' and 'stay in' secondary education, he proposes a number of alternative models (e.g. the international baccalaureate, community education) and suggests a range of sociological projects which could further the development of these models. The key issue of educational entitlement and access also comes through all the chapters, showing very clearly that the future of the discipline is tied closely in with egalitarian principles. However, new research is proposed which would deepen and extend the commitment of the discipline to these principles. The message seems to be that we need to reassess very critically our own assumptions, for example, about the school curriculum and the qualifications provided by post-16 education, higher education and teacher education. At the same time sociologists need to learn to listen to the voices of those who have historically been excluded by the social democratic agenda - gay and lesbian students, black people, working class women, and disabled students. Sociologists are being called upon to start talking to new audiences - especially teachers and schools - and to become relevant not necessarily by abandoning their critical functions but by addressing the real concerns of those in education.

These are difficult and challenging times, and opportunities and encouragement to discuss and debate have never been more necessary. We, as editors, and the authors would not want to claim that this book represents the final answers to issues relating to sociology of education. What we hope it achieves is encouraging dialogue both between sociologists and between sociology and those in the educational sphere at all levels. We also hope that this book encourages the development of further significant work in this field.

References

Bash, L. & Coulby, D. (Eds) (1989) *The Education Reform Act. Competition and Control.* London: Cassell.

Centre for Contemporary Cultural Studies (CCCS) (1980) *Unpopular Education: Schooling and Social Democracy in England since 1944.* London: Hutchinson.

Clarke, K. (1992) Speech to the North of England Conference, January.

Cox, C. & Marks, J. (1982) What has Athens to do with Jerusalem?: Teaching Sociology to Students on Medical, Nursing, Education and Science courses, in C. Cox & J. Marks (Eds) *The Right to Learn: Purpose, Professionalism and Accountability in State Education.* London: Centre for Policy Studies.

Dawson, G. (1981) Unfitting Teachers to Teach: Sociology in the Training of Teachers, in D. Anderson (Ed) *The Pied Pipers of Education.* London: Social Affairs Unit.

Flude, M. & Hammer, M. (Eds) (1990) *The Education Reform Act 1988: its Origins and Implications.* Lewes: Falmer Press.

Gould, J. (1977) *The Attack on Higher Education: Marxist and Radical Penetration.* London: Institute for the Study of Conflict.

Halsey, A.H. (Ed) (1972) *Educational Priority.* Volume 1: EPA Problems and Policies. London: HMSO.

Ozga, J. (1987) Studying Educational Policy through the Lives of Policy Makers: an attempt to close the macro-micro gap, in S. Walker & L. Barton (Eds) *Changing Policies Changing Teachers.* Milton Keynes: Open University Press.

Chapter One

Parents and the State: how has social research informed education reforms?

MIRIAM DAVID

Relations between parents and the state underpin any education system, but what these consist in differs in time and place. The current right-wing education policy agenda has been by discussion of individual parental rights, rather than collective duties, aimed at raising educational standards. The notion of parental choice has informed the education reforms developed by the Right during the 1980s, culminating in the Education Reform Act of 1988, and heralded as a new era for parents as consumers of education. The then Secretary of State, Kenneth Baker, argued in the passage of the bill through Parliament:

> *I would sum up the bill's 169 pages in three words <u>standards, freedom and choice</u> .... We must give the <u>consumers</u> of education a central part in decision-making. That means <u>freeing schools and colleges to deliver the standards that parents and employers want</u> .... (Hansard, 1.12.87, columns 780, 771-2) (my emphases).*

The government has sought to reduce the role of the state in decisions about educational provision, allowing for greater individual parental choice in the process, with the aim of improving educational standards.

This is in direct contradiction to previous state education policies, which sought to raise educational standards by requiring greater parental involvement in the educational process, in the interests of reducing social differences on the basis of parental circumstances of privilege or poverty. Social research on education, over the last 40 years, had demonstrated a clear relationship between state education and parental involvement, which formed the basis of policy developments.

Saran & Trafford have recently argued (1989, p. 240):

> *Since the passing of the 1988 Education Reform Act, the education service is entering a new era largely untainted by past research findings ....*

In this paper, I shall review both the 'past research findings' and the current evidence about parents and education, to speculate on what the impact of the new era might be on these relationships.

'Past research' was framed within a particular set of social and political values to which the current right government does not subscribe. The research on families and education was largely conducted within a particular liberal or 'social-democratic' framework, as developed after the Second World War. Educational policy was part of what has been called the post-war settlement (CCCS, 1980, p. 47) in which social policies were developed as part of the welfare state to sustain economic growth. This came to be seen as a 'bipartisan political consensus', by which both post-war Tory and Labour governments were committed to some form of state social policy to underpin economic policy and growth (Mishra, 1984). Social researchers tried to develop ways of implementing the principle in education in particular, of equality of opportunity, reducing private family privilege and providing education on the basis of academic merit (Banks, 1976).

The Thatcher administrations did not accept the same political values about the necessity of state intervention in social and educational policies in order to sustain economic growth (David, 1986). They argued for the necessity of markets and competition between individuals and private families to create wealth. Brown (1990) has nicely contrasted the two periods in education ideology: the former as the 'wave of meritocracy' and the Thatcher period as the 'wave of parentocracy'. In this paper, I shall review the 'research findings' in both periods to assess the effects of changing the relationship between parents and the state.

Policies on Parents and Education

The Education Reform Act of 1988 (ERA) is the culmination of the Conservatives' change in direction of education policy for the whole education system, not just schools but also higher education (David, 1989). For the purposes of this chapter, I shall review the provisions for schools and the changing role of parents. The ERA transforms the relations between families and the state.

Through the 1944 Education Act, local education authorities (LEAs) were required, by statute, to provide schools in sufficient number to accommodate all the school-children in the locality whose parents wished them to be educated in state schools albeit on the basis of 'age, aptitude and ability'. Parents were able to opt out of the state system and choose private schools for their children or educate them otherwise than at school.

A series of amending legislation gave parental wishes more strength, leading up to the 1980 Education Act (David, 1980). This Conservative legislation built upon Labour's proposals, but made a balance between the LEAs and parents in choice of state school (Stillman & Maychell, 1986), and gave parents more legal powers to appeal against LEA decisions (Stillman, 1986). It also established individual school governing bodies with parent representatives. Under the 1986 Education Act, parents were afforded more 'political' powers on school governing bodies. Parents, under ERA, were to be the major decision-makers rather than the local authorities. Their choices are no longer only to be amongst state schools whether county or voluntary-aided religious schools, but, for some parents, between state and schools run independently of the local authorities.

The Right's aim with these changes was to produce better educational standards, based upon individual parents' demands. First, parents may choose schools in the LEA based upon information supplied about courses, curricula and examination results. Schools are no longer able to limit the numbers of children admitted (as previously specified by the Education Act of 1980), but to provide open enrolment. Secondly, parents of children currently in a school are offered a chance, through the school governing body, on which there are now to be a majority of parent governors, to vote, through a secret ballot, to take the school out of local authority control. The school will then become a 'grant maintained' school, supported by a central rather than local government; but based upon the per capita amount of money the local authority had to spend upon the school. The grant is taken from the local authority's revenues through the community charge and central government financial support to local authorities. Thirdly, parents of secondary school-age children may choose schools financed variously by special business sponsorship and central government, namely the city technology colleges. Fourthly, parents are also able to choose private schools, entirely independent of the local authority, which may offer places to children whose parents do not have the financial means to afford the fees. The assisted places scheme has, from the 1980 Education Act, been considerably widened to cover the majority of traditional independent and public schools (Edwards, Fitz & Whitty, 1989). In other words, the aim of the central government, in this educational policy, has been to move the locus of decision-making about schools from the state, but most especially local government, back to individual parents, or the private family.

Part of the concern of the Tory government has been with the monopoly power of local authorities over decision-making in education. Hence the change to allow parents to get some schools to 'opt out' of local authority control and become grant-maintained schools. Even those schools which remain within the ambit of local authorities are to be less circumscribed by local government controls than hitherto. First they are given more powers to determine how to finance the schools, through the scheme of local financial delegation now known as local management of schools (LMS). Local authorities are required to determine through a centrally prescribed formula, the average, per capita spending on education in their area and to delegate to individual schools such finances as necessary to spend on their own complement of teachers and educational resources.

Thus local authorities are reduced to being more of a *financial conduit* than a decision-maker over the determination of educational resources. This power may also be eroded if proposals to reform the community charge by removing educational expenditure from local to central control are enacted. However, for the moment, they also retain modest powers of inspection or advice. Yet, at the same time, the Education Reform Act also contains the means for maintaining common education standards throughout the state maintained schools through the implementation of the national curriculum.

Despite these apparently contradictory tendencies between the central government specification of a national curriculum and the development of 'parent power' through the detailed choice of different types of school, it seems to be clear that there is no longer to be one system of state educational provision. Rather there is a variety and range of schools provided variously by the LEAs, central government, by business enterprise and sponsorship, as well as through the private sector. By the end of 1988, the scene was set for parents to have a major part, both individually and as school governors, in school decision-making, a significant departure from the system that had pertained for the previous forty years, whereby parents played a minor part in the partnership with LEAs. I turn now to look at that previous system and the ways in which social research influenced how parents were involved in educational provisions.

'Past Research Findings' in the 'Wave of Meritocracy'

The origins of the sociology of education are to be found in the aftermath of the Second World War, reviewing how to implement the 1944 Education Act and its key principle of equality of educational opportunity, or education according to academic merit rather than parental circumstances. Social researchers assessed the conditions and limits under which the principle could develop, including reviewing the effects of educational policies oriented to it. They focused upon the extent to which 'nature' (in terms of intelligence or merit) or 'nature' (in the form of families or education) contributed to the successful educational progress, performance or achievements of school age children whether as individuals or social groups (Banks, 1976). The early sociology of education, in particular as developed by Halsey and Floud in association with others (Martin, 1956;

Anderson 1961) came to be seen as the classic example of sociological research, with its interest in the links between social class, defined as social status, socio-economic parental circumstances or home background, and educational achievement and/or social mobility. This kind of research was conducted for various levels of educational institution: from primary schools, to secondary schools, to access to further and higher education. (Banks, 1976; Burgess, 1985). It was also conducted at various levels of sociological and quantitative sophistication: from official, statistical reports and analyses to more theoretically informed studies of the complexity of social class and education.

The overarching value framework was the assumption that *all* children had the potentiality, given the appropriate and relevant *family* or home, defined as social and economic, circumstances to achieve in accordance with their abilities. To what extent the state should attempt to provide those appropriate conditions to enable all children to participate in and benefit from education became a key research question.

In the formation of the sociology of education there was a clear link between policy makers and social research. This relationship has subsequently been analyzed carefully by a group of social historians at the Centre for Contemporary Studies (1980).

> *In both political and sociological writing, the common move ... has been to start with equality of opportunity and move thence to equality ... arguments about 'equality', appear even in the most utilitarian arguments about economic growth ... there was ... a considerable sleight of hand ... in the tendency in the sociology of education to claim a socialist pedigree ... the 'old' sociology of education belong(s) to a long tradition of English middle class reform and social investigation ... the parallel between the long-standing concern with popular morality and behaviour and the sociologist's is (likewise) very close ... (ibid p. 96;99)*

They also see as central to their analysis:

> *Popular interests have been expressed in relation to the family, and particularly through the crucial figure of the 'parent' ... We want to assert the absolute centrality of patriarchal relations for the family ... The family is not ... a merely dependent institution, with no determinacy of its own. It is not merely transformed by capitalism and by the development of schooling: it, or its salient relations, also contribute to the complex determinations on schooling in absolutely central ways. Indeed, it has systematically shaped the very conception of 'education' itself. (CCCS, 1980, p. 25) (my emphasis)*

In other words, the analysis and understanding of the family in the process of educational policy making itself contributed to the development of education. This analysis of post-war educational developments showed both the limits and conditions under which educational policy was made and developed, especially for working class and subordinated groups. It was an analysis at a critical juncture, presenting both a review and a pessimistic analysis of the limits and possibilities of social democracy.

5

Both official and independent social research investigating the precise relations between families and schools were begun in the 1950s. They covered both primary schools and access to secondary and/or higher education. The cohort studies by Douglas and his research team at the London School of Economics, which were one of the first in this genre, was an analysis of the relationship between families and primary schools, especially in terms of children's early reading performance. One of the studies, entitled *The Home and the School*, (1964) was eventually published about the same time as the officially commissioned report on primary education, which was subsequently entitled *Children and Their Primary Schools*, a report for the Central Advisory Council on Education, chaired by Lady Plowden (1967). Although this latter report was an official investigation of the state of primary education in England and Wales, it both reviewed and commissioned additional social research evidence. Both reports reached very similar conclusions: that children's family and home circumstances had strong and lasting effects on their abilities to benefit from educational provision, with the result that children from social disadvantaged home backgrounds did not perform academically as well as more middle class schoolchildren.

The Plowden report proposed a number of remedies to this situation, drawing on the policies developed from similarly accumulated social (and psychological) research evidence in the United States (Higgins, 1976). Given their presuppositions, the evidence pointed to the possibilities of social change through education. Indeed, the concept of 'educability' was gaining currency in both Britain and the USA, as a term to indicate that the evidence suggested that children's intellectual and academic abilities were not fixed in nature, but capable of change and development, through improvements in home or school circumstances or both.

The policy proposals initially fixed upon were for changes in educational provision, making more and better early childhood education available for children deemed to be in need through their poor home circumstances. For example, following the American lead, the notion of pre-school educational provision for poor and socially disadvantaged children was one of the major suggestions of the Plowden report. The Americans had developed an early childhood education policy entitled Headstart, to provide for young children in the summer before they commenced compulsory schooling, to ensure that such disadvantaged children started their schooling with the same chances as children from better home circumstances.

Similarly, there were proposals to improve the quality of primary schooling in the poor areas of cities, also drawing on American research. The Plowden committee suggested ways of designating areas of cities for additional educational resources, in the form of teachers and teachers aides. Indeed, this policy of creating Educational Priority Areas for the receipt of additional educational resources in schools was quickly followed through, unlike the policy on preschool education which was never fully implemented. Like its American counterpart, it also became one of the first officially sponsored social research projects, involving what became known as 'action' research. The key sociologist of education, A.H. Halsey, an Oxford don, also became the principal social researcher.

The action research projects involved a great range of schemes from developing social indicators of educational disadvantage in London for the particular areas to receive additional resources (Little & Mabey, 1972) to schemes to provide pre-school education, to improving home-school relations. This latter resulted in the development of two notions: one of the education social workers, a person who would visit the parents of identified socially and educationally disadvantaged children in their own homes, to provide them with advice and support over their child rearing activities. The other was that of greater parental involvement in schools. All of these schemes were monitored and evaluated and the results published in a series of official reports in the early 1970s (Halsey, 1972; 1973-6). All pointed the way to attempts to provide greater educational opportunities, through improving school provision and parental involvement in school.

The Plowden report had been very directive about parental involvement in education as the means to increasing children's educational and life chances. However, a number of sociologists of education were critical of its cruder formulations. Bernstein (1970), for example, in a now classic paper argued that "Education cannot compensate for society": and that provision of improved home-school relations or early childhood education would be insufficient to remedy the fundamental differences between the 'culture' of education and that of working class families. This 'policy' critique was drawn from his more theoretical sociological analyses of the developments of different language 'codes' in middle and working class families, making for a dissonance for some families between home and school. However, despite his critique, Bernstein continued to develop his more fundamental research around the issues of the relations between families and schools. In one other seminal paper, drawing on the work of Bourdieu in France, he demonstrated the significance of the role of the mother of very young children in the reproduction of class relations through home as well as school based pedagogies (Bernstein, 1974, Vol 2).

Bernstein's work had two effects. He was a critical influence on changing the course of the sociology of education from one which emphasized the possibilities of social change through interventions in the home and/or school to one which began to emphasize the limitations of social transformation. The sociology of education became more theoretical and analytical. However, his critiques of policy developments were ineffective: policy developments continued to focus on the goal of improving children's life chances especially through parents or school or both.

The notion of parental participation or involvement in schools to improve children's educational performance was also taken up for secondary schools. The concept was modified from that of daily involvement in either classroom activities or parental interest at home to the notion of parental participation in educational decision-making (David,

1987). The concept of the home-school links was less specific for secondary schools. It also required the idea that children's educational chances should not be limited by their home backgrounds, whether economically or educationally disadvantaged. Official reports such as Crowther (1959) and Newsom (1963) had demonstrated the inadequacy of secondary education provision for children's full educational potential. Together with the Robbins report on higher education (1964), they all made the case for improving educational opportunities in secondary, further and higher education, without regard to parental privilege or poor home circumstances. In other words, they, too, demonstrated that there was a greater potential for young people to benefit from education and access to job opportunities than was being realised. They developed variously the notions of 'educability' and the 'untapped pool of ability', regardless of social class and parental socio-economic circumstances.

Policy developments in the 1960s drew upon these social investigations and sociological research into different types of secondary education. Again, American research was also particularly influential. Here the Coleman report (1966), a federal sponsored study, from the Economic Opportunity Act of 1964, provided the most complex, sociological and statistical analysis ever conducted. Coleman, a sociologist of education directed a massive survey of over 500 schools and several thousand teachers and pupils to determine children's educational fates. His research, entitled On Equality of Educational Opportunity, demonstrated, inter alia, the necessity of social (and racial) mixing in education to achieve maximum educational opportunities, rather than socially segregated schools. In the USA this became an argument for racially as well as socially integrated schools and led to major policy developments on educational integration, especially in the northern states where de facto, rather than de jure segregation was still practised (Glazer, 1975; Orfield, 1976).

In Britain, the arguments were taken up on differential social and economic grounds, rather than those of 'race' per se. These became arguments for state comprehensive as opposed to tripartite schemes of secondary education. The 1944 Education Act had allowed for selective secondary schools based on academic ability, ranging from grammar to technical to secondary modern schools. Although the arguments had been couched in terms of parental choice, the research evidence collected during the 1950s and early 1960s showed its limitations. It showed clearly that parental choice was tied to social class chances of children's educational performance in the intelligence tests at age 11, for selection to secondary school. During the 1960s arguments were presented to transform secondary selective education to comprehensive schools, either on the grounds of social class mixing or community based schools improving educational performance. Pedley's (1956) early study of comprehensive schools and Jackson & Marsden's (1964) study of the relationships between social class backgrounds and educational achievement for boys provided critical evidence. Nevertheless, as Marsden (1972) later argued, it was never clear whether the policy change was developed on social, economic or educational grounds. By the early 1970s, however, Benn & Simon (1972) were able to demonstrate through a careful social survey that the policy of secondary school reorganisation to comprehensive education was well advanced.

However, the strong links between social research and policy change, only served to exacerbate a growing political controversy about the relationships between parents and education. Although the concepts of parents and family were never clearly articulated and frequently confused, the 'social democratic' policy, was to reduce class-based, family choice in favour of common educational provision, regardless of family circumstances. In other words, parents' role was to be supportive of the school rather than selective and discriminating between different types of state or private schools. Parental privilege to enable children to have access either to selective state secondary schools was the object of policy concern (Johnson, 1990; Walford, 1990).

At the same time, however, also drawing on American educational research, there was a move to draw parents into the process of educational decision-making (David, 1975). Parental involvement was to be extended from support for their individual child's educational performance in school, through homework and participation in daily activities to participation as representative of the body of school parents on their governing bodies. This shift in the notion of the parental role, from a social to a more 'political' one, was initially to link home and school more carefully and to ensure a more effective democratic, state educational system. It, too, was transformed in the political process (Bacon, 1978; David, 1980).

Throughout this period of transformation of the concepts of family and school, the emphases remained genderless and to an extent blind to social differences on the grounds of race. In fact, the notion of parent within the context of parent participation in early childhood education and primary schools, as well as parent education for such families, relied heavily on the idea of a sexual division of labour in parenting within families. It was mothers who were to be involved in educational provision, either through their regular participation in school based activities, or through learning about parenting with the education social worker or home visitor, or through homework activities (David, 1984; 1986).

At the secondary school level, however, parental involvement was not stated as a gendered activity. But with the shifts in the notions of parental role, it became a clear but tacit assumption that fathers' duties related to school governance and finances. One of the central themes of both sociological research and its attendant policy developments was the specification of mothers' and fathers' responsibilities and rights with respect to both their individual children's educational performance and those of all children in the relevant school context (David, 1988).

Controversies Over Parental Roles:
from meritocracy through participation to parentocracy

The education policy agenda began to change from the beginning of the 1980s, from an emphasis on such parental duties and participation to parental choice. Politicians, educationists and academics in their critiques of the strategy of meritocracy articulated new aims of consumerism and choice. Previously, the views about individual parental rights and wishes represented a relatively minor voice in the political spectrum, even on the right (Knight, 1989, ch. 2).

As stronger policies developed around equality of educational opportunity such as comprehensive education and the expansion of higher education opportunities, the voices of dissent from the right increasingly were expressed. By the late 1960s, these views found more group expression in the, albeit still minority, publication of the Black Papers by a right wing academic pressure group.

The new right-wing arguments revolved around the notion that 'more meant worse': the expansion of educational opportunities inevitably meant a 'decline in academic standards' and a 'growth of mediocrity' rather than a meritocracy. The Black Paperites argued that there should be choice for parents amongst schools and that changes should not be implemented in school organisation or where traditional types of selective schooling had not been proven inadequate.

Nevertheless, the views of these pamphleteers did not greatly influence the development of education policy during the four years of Conservative administration at the beginning of the 1970s. The government remained committed to the principle, and the practice, of equality of educational opportunity as a means of maintaining economic growth. In particular, a White Paper entitled *Education: a framework for expansion* was published in 1972, including the aim to expand opportunities in both nursery schools and higher education (David, 1980).

It was in the next period of Labour administrations (during which there were successive economic crises) that the more right-wing arguments about the need to link education more effectively to the needs of the economy in order to raise standards rather than provide equality of opportunity, began to gain currency.

Expanding educational opportunities without regard to parental circumstances was no longer seen as consonant with economic growth. The Labour government focused on ensuring that parents played a role in the process of restructuring, arguing that there was a clear parallel between state and parental needs. But this did not mean involving parents in the discussions about the question of links between education and work:

> In that context, parental 'interests' were to be represented through the rational organisation, by the state, of the school to work transition, and the matching of the appropriate skills and aptitudes to the needs of the labour

market. Schooling and its social purposes were therefore to be politically
subordinated to the perceived needs of a capitalist economy in the throes of
crisis. A restructuring was required because of the failure of schools to fulfil
the older social democratic equation that investment in education would
produce economic benefits. (CCCS, 1980, p. 220)

In other words, the Labour government began to renege on its
commitment to the principle of equality of educational opportunity and the
policies that it, and previous Labour and Tory administrations, had
pursued.

These policies were seen to have failed to produce economic growth.
The argument that investing in human capital or potential, on the basis of
academic ability, rather than parental background, was questioned. Instead
the government considered ways of developing and improving educational
standards in school, pressured by more right-wing arguments. To this end a
common core curriculum for all state schools was proposed to be taught
throughout primary and secondary schools. However, although this
proposal was not implemented it provided the starting point for
subsequent more right-wing debates (David, 1980).

So, too, did the setting up of a committee of inquiry into the
Government and Management of Schools in 1977. The Taylor committee
eventually proposed the development of a system of representative parent
and teacher school governors along with community representatives. It was
the recommendations of this committee that subsequently formed the basis
of Labour's Education Bill, in the late 1970s which began the process of
transforming the role of parents in education decisions. However, despite
the opportunities to provide a more collective role for parents in the
process of educational decision-making, it was the more individualistic role
that has later been seized upon and elaborated by the Right (Woods, 1988).

During the 1980s, these ideas have gained political and public
credence and been expressed more clearly by a range of right-wing
academics and intellectuals. However, as Dale (1989 ch. 4) has argued there
have been at least five different strands to the conservative educational
philosophy, making it difficult for them to cohere into one particular
strategy. Indeed, Dale argued that the 'distillate' of these five positions –
namely the industrial trainers, the old Tories, the populist, the moral
entrepreneurs and the privatisers – has taken a long time to result in a
specifically Thatcherite educational policy and not one that has essentially
been to provide a 'parents' charter', or a 'parentocracy'.

Part of the difficulty that the right has had in developing a counter
educational philosophy to that of the bipartisan political consensus about
parents has been in proving the latter's success. Despite the development of
a variety and range of educational policies that the right dubbed as
'egalitarianism', whatever sociological evidence has been amassed has
tended still to demonstrate the persistence of the effects of family
backgrounds of privilege or poverty on educational attainment.

Halsey, the main academic chronicler of these effects through both
official analyses (Halsey Report, 1972) and the more detailed sociological

11

analyses (Halsey, Heath & Ridge, 1980) reached relatively pessimistic conclusions about the effects of such policies. Halsey, Heath & Ridge argued, in 1980, that

> ...our retrospect might be held to have demonstrated that expanding a traditional structure of opportunities _guaranteed failure to equalize_. Those who want equality of outcome between classes might then gloomily extrapolate from the past and conclude that this ideal is beyond the reach of public policy. Such an inference would be false. (1980, pp. 216). (my emphasis)

Curiously, they then went on to argue, more optimistically that public policy could still be effective:

> The growth and spread of educational qualifications bears witness to a larger and deeper pool of educability than some policy makers ever envisaged, and the actual history of rising norms of educational attainment discredits both the Black paper pessimism of the political right and the parallel despondency of those who predicted from the political left that working class children were doomed to be incapable of grasping any opportunities apparently offered to them by educational expansion ...
>
> So now, for the first time in our history we stand _on the threshold of a period where a sustained policy of expansion could at last attain what for so long has escaped the intentions of reform_. The fall in the size of the school population will make equality of opportunity easier to achieve, but educational retrenchment will just as surely postpone it .... The least we can say is that the egalitarian potential of expansion has yet to be fully exploited ... Even so, the economy may reasonably be expected to afford higher average material standards of life for children, parents, and teachers than were contemplated by those who framed either the 1902 or the 1944 Education Act. (ibid, pp. 216-219).

These public policy aims, however, were not taken up by the relatively new Conservative administration which was more committed to increasing parental choice as a means to improving educational standards than to afford equal opportunities to vitiate the effects of differential home circumstances.

In fact, the 'guarded optimism' of Halsey and his co-authors was based on the most traditional 'egalitarian' arguments, and on data about the fates and prospects of a sample of schoolboys in the 1930s and 1950s. They did not provide any evidence for the prospects for girls or women; neither did they contemplate the effects of such equalising strategies on the lives of either boys or girls from minority ethnic groups, such as from the Asian or Afro-Caribbean communities. Similar gloomy conclusions had been reached in the United States by social researchers, such as Jencks et al (1973), and followed by Rutter et al (1979) in Britain in the late 1970s.

Indeed, by the end of the 1970s, sociological research in education had tended to shift its focus from social change through educational policies for the family to social reproduction theories, demonstrating the parallels between education, the economy and family life (Bowles & Gintis, 1976).

And more policy oriented research began to develop school effectiveness studies, drawing on Rutter et al's (1979) study, rather than studies concerned with ironing out differences on the basis of family background whether including 'race' or not.

Research Findings in the 'Wave of Parentocracy'

The close relationship which had developed in the 1950s between social researchers and education policy makers began to break down during the 1970s as public policy shifted to the right. Most social researchers, albeit pessimistic, remained committed to some measure of equal opportunities. Hall's (1979) memorable phrase that the "Tories had gained territory without taking power" encapsulated the notion that right wing pressure and economic crises meant that policy aims such as equality of educational opportunity could not be sustained. More important, however, was the evidence that social and economic inequalities persisted between families at all levels of the education system, despite the increasingly sophisticated policy mechanisms suggested by social researchers, whether working officially or independently. Right-wing policy-makers and researchers have seized these arguments to try to develop a new ideology of education, from that of 'meritocracy' to that of 'parentocracy' (Brown, 1990).

A bifurcation of social research developed in the 1980s. The 'old' sociology of education has become more pessimistic about the prospects of social transformation through education and/or the family, except through limited schemes of parental participation. The Right has argued that social development and wealth creation can be achieved only through individual, rather than collective, parental demands and pressure (David, 1989).

However, some social researchers have continued to try to develop and test notions around the principle of equal opportunities. Some of this has focused on issues of gender or race rather than social class. Indeed, there have been some official investigations of these issues, but they have reached relatively limited conclusions about the prospects for social change. In terms of gender and employment, given a sexual division of parental responsibilities the prospects for equal job opportunities remain bleak. In terms of race, changes in education are predicated on conservative rather than more social democratic principles (Rampton, 1981; Swann, 1985).

In general, however, the conclusions of this kind of research are relatively modest. Macbeth (1984, p.185) has neatly summarized the findings:

> What we_can say is that a very large number of studies in different cultures has indicated that parental attitudes have an influence on children's attainment, even if we cannot put an exact value to that influence: there is a relative death of contrary evidence, in-school factors seem to be related to these home factors. At the very least, home seems to influence school

13

performance and it would appear that a strengthening of partnership between home and school could improve the quality of children's learning.

Gone was the commitment to a 'meritocracy' or social mobility based upon educational achievements rather than family fortunes. The commitment had become one about improving the quality of schooling for similar social groups. The possibilities of this have been well demonstrated by Mortimore et al's study of junior schools, (1988) which followed on from Rutter et al's study of Inner London secondary schools (1979). Both demonstrated that the quality of children's learning could be enhanced by forms of schooling, holding social or home circumstances constant. An even more extensive study by Tomlinson & Smith (1989) has shown how particular forms of schooling can have differential effects, taking into account social and racial differences in home circumstances.

However, a series of reviews of the implementation of the Plowden committee's policy proposals, twenty years on, found that the only successful schemes were those involving parents more clearly in educational provision rather than those which attempted to iron out differences in home circumstances through new forms of pedagogy, schooling or curricula (*Oxford Review of Education*, 1988).

These kinds of research findings have led into renewed attempts to find ways of improving children's learning through specific curricula schemes – reading, language and mathematics – as well as what is called a 'whole school approach' (Bastiani, 1989). Taking school curriculum issues back into the home, especially in policies for early childhood education, has been the result of many of these developments (Mertens & Vass, 1990; Bastiani 1987; Macbeth 1989). Innovative schemes of mathematics education or new forms of parent education, developed at LEA or school level, have created a new set of relationships between parents and state schooling, in which more 'education' takes place at home than in school (David, 1984). This may have consequences for parents', especially mothers', other occupations outside the home.

Given the policy changes developed by the Conservatives during the 1980s, social researchers have also become interested in investigating their impact and effects. In particular, there have been studies of the implementation of the changes in policy around parental choice in school, in terms of both accountability and the balance between LEAs and parents. Elliot et al, in the Oxford accountability studies (1981, 1982) found that changes in the law as regards widening parental choice of secondary school did not have much effect on the majority of families. However, they did find that families had different preferences in terms of achievement, what they termed 'product', and happiness at school, or 'process'. In other words, this small sample of parents based at one school, did not necessarily prefer a school to ensure the best academic achievement of their children, but rather a balance with happiness. Hitherto, what parents had wanted in terms of the balance between 'process', 'product' and 'proximity' (or location) of school had not been investigated. The concern had been with the more 'objective' effects of education policy. This study also showed that, on balance, it was fathers who opted more for 'product' and mothers for 'process', although the differences were not significant.

Stillman & Maychell (1986) conducted a large scale study in a range of LEAs on the impact of changes in parental choice, using to some extent the variables identified above. They found, in particular, that the balance had swung slightly more towards parents than LEAs, although at the margins few parents objected to the choice of school allocated them. Similarly, a Scottish study by Adler et al (1989) found that despite greater changes in the law in the direction of stronger parental choice, few parents exercised it strongly and few used the processes of appeal, and the Ombudsman (Bull, 1985). However, such legal changes did affect parents to the extent of being concerned about their 'right' to involvement.

Three sets of studies have focused on how parents have made choices about private schools: one was a study of boys' parents from prestigious public schools (Fox, 1985). A second looked at a range of families making choices over a long period of time (Johnson, 1987). A third looked at the operation of the Assisted Places Scheme (Edwards, Fitz & Whitty, 1989). In all three cases there was a large minority of parents, especially mothers, of ex-public or independent school backgrounds. They had chosen such schools on the grounds that they were likely to produce a better level of educational achievement than state schools. Thus, they were continuing to try to buy privilege at the expense of equal opportunities. However, none of the studies demonstrated that this had happened; merely that this was the explicit intention of parents. In the case of the study of assisted places, forty per cent of the families were lone mother households with extensive educational backgrounds, who had fallen on hard times.

However, studies of state schooling have also tended to have more of a policy focus in terms of improving schooling rather than altering its forms in relation to equal opportunities. Those studies of school governors, especially parent governors (or 'mothers') have shown the limited powers that they have acquired and their lack of 'business' skills in exercising them (Deem, 1989; 1990; Sallis, 1988; Golby & Brigley, 1989; Brehony & Deem, 1990).

The research on policy changes in the 1980s has, on the whole, tended to demonstrate their limited effectiveness. Nevertheless, it has also shown that previous more 'egalitarian' policies have been relatively ineffective, such that inequalities remain between families in different material circumstances, and that parents may indeed be concerned with the quality of schooling only from their own child's perspective.

Conclusions

The 'new era' of educational policy, particularly with respect to families, has as its aim the improvement of educational standards through parental demands. Yet the research evidence for parents being able 'properly' to discriminate between 'good' and 'bad' schools and choose effectively appropriate schools for their children remains limited (Adler, Petch & Tweedie, 1989; Echols, McPherson & Williams, 1990; Johnson, 1990). What does seem clear from the accumulated research evidence over the last 40-50 years or so is that parental interest, rather than private investment, in their children's education, through active involvement in homework, classroom activities or parent-teacher associations, enhances children's educational performance if not achievement. However, if parents still have differential abilities to be actively interested in their children's educational progress, either through other family or employment obligations, or through the kinds of resources available to the schools themselves to sustain such parental interest, then differences between families, on the basis of social and economic circumstances will continue through to the next generation.

The policy of creating a variety of different schools, differentially resourced by central and local government, private businesses or families, independent or religious authorities, will sustain and exacerbate such differences between families. Those families, socially, culturally or economically disadvantaged, will not have access to or the ability to demand better resources and standards in school. The policy of allowing for variety will indeed allow for increasing social and familial differentiation. Parental choice, in other words, allows for the celebration of difference, but difference based upon social, racial and possibly gender inequalities. Thus those families in which the culture matches that of the school – white, middle class families - are in all probability likely again to benefit from the current social changes. Ethnic minority families are likely to be disadvantaged by such developments. Those that wish to opt for minority religious education, such as Islamic separate schools, are also likely to be limited in their freedoms to develop.

The conclusion is clear that bipartisan social democratic policies over equal opportunities did not succeed in reducing differences between children on the basis of their parental circumstances, whether they were fathers or mothers, black or white, let alone working class as opposed to middle class. This was despite the massive amount of social research which attempted to specify the exact relationship between parents and education as a basis for policy developments. It was this relative failure that left the way open for a reversal of policy to allow for the full flowering of parental difference and parental rights – a 'parentocracy'. It has enabled the right to develop policies which build upon the ideas that parents have 'inalienable' rights to choose schools for their children, regardless of the extent to which those privileged families thereby reduce possibilities and the disbursement of resources for poor families, who do not have access to such circumstances (MacBeth et al, 1986).

Moreover, those tendencies in educational policy to modify social and familial differences through a national curriculum are rapidly being vitiated by policy developments to reduce the scope and extent of the national curriculum in favour of more diversity of school provision from state to private resources to cater for different parental demands and desires. By the year 2000, if these policy developments persist, there is unlikely to be a system of state education but rather an array of what may be considered familial schools catering for religious, ethnic minority and social communities. Some children from poor family circumstances may not receive any schooling at all.

REFERENCES

Adler, M., Petch, A. & Tweedie, J. (1989) *Parental Choice and Educational Policy.* Edinburgh: Edinburgh University Press.

Bacon, W. (1987) *Public Accountability and the Schooling System.* London: Harper Row.

Banks, O. (1976) *Sociology of Education.* London: Batsford.

Bastiani, J. (1987) *Parents and Schools,* Vols 1 & 2. Windsor: NFER-Nelson.

Bastiani, J. (1989) *Working with Parents: A Whole School Approach.* Windsor: NFER-Nelson.

Benn, C. & Simon, B. (1972) *Half Way There.* London: Lawrence & Wishart.

Bernstein, B. (1970) Education cannot compensate for society, *New Society,* 26 February, pp. 344-347.

Bernstein, B. (1974-1990) *Class, Codes and Control,* Vols 1-4. London: Routledge & Kegan Paul.

Brehony, K. & Deem, R. (1990) Charging for free education, *Journal of Education Policy,* 5, pp. 333-347.

Brown, P. (1990) The third wave, education & the ideology of parentocracy, *British Journal of Sociology of Education,* 11, pp. 65-87.

Bowles, S. & Gintis (1976) *Schooling in Capitalist America.* London: Routledge & Kegan Paul.

Burgess, R. (1985) *Sociology of Education.* London: Allen & Unwin.

Bull, D. (1985) Monitoring education appeals, local ombudsman lead the way, *Journal of Social Welfare Law,* pp. 184-226.

Centre for Contemporary Cultural Studies, (1980), *Unpopular Education.* London: Hutchinson.

Coleman Report (1966) *Equality of Educational Opportunity.* Washington, D.C.: US Govt. Printing Office.

Cox, C. B. & Dyson, D. (Eds) *Black Papers 1-3.* London: Critical Quarterly Society.

Crowther Report (1959) *Half Our Future.* London: HMSO.

Dale, R. (1989) *The State and Education Policy.* Milton Keynes: Open University Press.

David, M. E. (1975) *School Rule in the USA.* Cambridge. Mass.: Ballinger.

David, M. E. (1980) *The State, the Family and Education.* London: Routledge & Kegan Paul.

David, M. E. (1984) Women, Family and Education, in S. Acker et al (Eds) *World Yearbook of Education,* 1984, Women and Education, pp. 191-202. London: Kogan Page.

David, M. E. (1986) Teaching family matters, *British Journal of Sociology of Education,* 7, pp. 35-37.

David, M. E. (1986) Moral and Maternal: the family in the Right, in R. Levitas (Ed) *The Ideology of the New Right.* Cambridge: Polity Press.

David, M. E. (1988) Home-school relations, in A. Green & S. Ball (Eds) *Inequality and Progress in Comprehensive Education,* pp. 139-158. London: Croom Helm.

David, M. E. (1989) Education, in M. McCarthy (Ed) *The New Politics of Welfare, an agenda for the 1990s,* pp. 154-178. London: Macmillan.

Deem, R. (1989) The new school governing bodies: are gender and race on the agenda? *Gender and Education,* 1, pp. 247-261.

Deem, R. (1990) The Reform of School Governing Bodies: the power of the consumer over the producer?, in M. Flude & M. Hammer (Eds) *The Education Reform Act 1988: its origins and implications.* Basingstoke: Falmer Press.

Douglas, J. W. B. (1964) *The Home and the School.* London: Panther.

Echols, F. McPherson, A. & Willms, J. D. (1990) Parental choice in Scotland, *Journal of Education Policy,* 5, pp. 207-223.

Edwards, A., Fitz, J. & Whitty, G. (1989) *The State and Private Education: an Evaluation of the Assisted Places Scheme.* Basingstoke: Falmer Press.

Elliot, J., Bridges, D., Gibson, R. & Nias, J. (1981) *School Accountability: the SSRC Cambridge Accountability Project.* London: Grant McIntyre.

Elliot, J. (1982) How Do Parents Choose and Judge Secondary Schools?, in R. McCormick (Ed) *Calling Education to Account.* Milton Keynes: Open University Press.

Fox, I. (1985) *Private Schools and Public Issues: The Parents' View.* London: Macmillan.

Glazer, N. (1975) *Affirmative Discrimination.* New York: Basic Books.

Golby, M. & Brigley, S. (1989) *Parents as School Governors.* Tiverton, Devon: Fairway Publications.

Halsey, A. H., Floud, J. & Anderson, J. (Eds) (1961) *Education, Economy and Society.* Glencoe, Illinois: Free Press.

Halsey, A. H., Floud, J. & Martin, J. (1956) *Social Class and Educational Opportunity.* London: Heinemann.

Halsey Reports (1972; 1973-6) *Education Priority,* vols 1-6. London: HMSO.

Halsey, A. H., Heath, A. F. & Ridge, J. M. (1980) *Origins and Destination: Family, Class and Education.* Oxford: Clarendon Press.

Higgins, J. (1976) *The Poverty Business.* Oxford: Basil Blackwell.

Jackson, B. & Marsden, D. (1964) *Social Class and Education.* Harmondsworth: Penguin.

Jencks, C. et al (1973) *Inequality: A Reassessment of Family and Schooling in America.* Harmondsworth: Penguin.

Johnson, D. (1987) *Private Schools and State Schools: Two Systems or One?* Milton Keynes: Open University Press.

Johnson, D. (1990) *Parental Choice in Education.* London: Unwin Hyman.

Knight, C. (1989) *The Making of Tory Conservative Education Policy in Post-war Britain.* Lewes: Falmer Press.

Macbeth, A., Strachan, D. & Macauley, C. (1986) *Parental Choice of School.* University of Glasgow: Department of Education.

Macbeth, A. (1989) *Involving Parents: Effective Parent-Teacher Relations.* London: Heinemann.

Marsden, D. (1972), in Bosanquet, N. & Townsend, P. (Eds) *Labour and Inequality.* London: Fabian Society and GAU.

Matthews, R. & Vass, J. (1990) *Sharing Maths Cultures: IMPACT Inventing Maths for Parents and Children and Teachers.* Basingstoke: Falmer Press.

Mishra, R. (1984) *The Welfare State in Crisis.* Brighton: Harvester Wheatsheaf.

Mortimore, P. & Salmon, P. et al (1988) *School Matters: the junior years.* Wells, Somerset: Open Books.

Newsom Report (1963) *All Our Children.* London: HMSO.

Oxford Review of Education, Volume 13, Number 1 (1987) 'Plowden Twenty Years On', pp. 1-138.

Orfield, G. (1976) *0Racial Desegregation.* New York: Basic Books.

Pedley, R. (1956) *The Comprehensive School.* Harmondsworth: Penguin.

Plowden Report (1967) *Children and their Primary Schools.* London: HMSO.

Rampton Report (1981) *The Education of West Indian Children.* London: HMSO.

Rutter, M. et al (1979) *15,000 Hours.* Wells, Somerset: Open Books.

Sallis, J. (1988) *Schools, Parents and Governors.* London: Routledge.

Saran, R. & Trafford, V. (Eds) (1989) *Research in Education Management and Policy: Retrospect and Prospect.* London: BEMAS.

Sexton, S. (1990) Reward, responsibility and results, the new 3Rs, *Sunday Times,* 21 October, p. 9.

Smith, D. & Tomlinson, S. (1989) *The School Effect.* London: Policy Studies Institute.

Stillman, A. (Ed) (1986) *The Balancing Act of 1980: parents, politics and education.* Windsor: NFER-Nelson.

Stillman, A. & Maychell, K. (1986) *Choosing Schools: Parents, LEAs and the 1980 Education Act.* Windsor: NFER-Nelson.

Swann Report (1985) *Education For All.* London: HMSO, Cmnd 9453.

Walford, G. (1990) *Privatisation and Privilege in Education.* London: Routledge.

West, A., Varlaam, A. & Mortimore, P. (1984) Attitudes to School: a study of the parents of first year pupils, in D. Hargreaves (Ed) *Improving Secondary Schools: Research Studies.* London: ILEA.

West, A. & Varlaam, A. (1991) Choosing a secondary school, parents of junior school children, *Educational Research,* 33, pp. 22-30.

Woods, P. (1988) A strategic view of parent participation, *Journal of Education Policy,* 3, pp. 323-334.

19

Chapter Two

Not in Front of the Children: responding to right wing agendas on sexuality and education

LIZ KELLY

A sex education programme that is sensitive to the issues of gender, sexual orientation and sexual violence is, of course, a potential challenge to the 'traditional family'.

(Lenskyj, 1990, p. 220)

During the 1990 Tory party conference Dame Margaret Fry welcomed Angela Rumbold's [1] keynote address on the family with the words "Thank you for a wonderful speech Angela and thank you most of all for being so normal". The implicit sub-text was 'thank you for being a white, middle class, heterosexual, married woman with children'.

The family, and more directly, sexuality have been the ideological terrains on which conservative discourse has laid claim to the moral high ground throughout the 1980's. Education has been one of the central focuses in this modern day 'crusade'. The absence of contest or resistance in the formal political arena has been marked, and likely to continue if the recently published *The Family Way* (Coote, Harman & Hewitt, 1990) represents the 'alternative' vision of the Labour Party (see Egerton, 1991). The only visible and concerted resistance to right wing challenges to both liberal and radical positions on the family and sexuality have come from the lesbian and gay movements in resisting attempts to suppress discussion of sexuality in schools, and the women's movement in relation to a range of issues from child sexual abuse through to reproductive rights. These social movements have, to greater or lesser extents, understood the necessity of problematising the 'naturalism' that pervades conservative thought in this area.

The failure of mainstream sociologists and educationalists in theory, policy and practice to integrate an understanding of sexuality in their frameworks and the fact that sexuality has been the 'optional extra' in equal opportunities initiatives, resulted in sexuality being a soft target for conservative attack in the media and through legislation.

In this chapter I want to outline briefly recent right wing thought and action, highlight some of the multiplicity of ways in which sexuality is present in education, and the challenge to mainstream sociological perspectives that new research by feminist and lesbian and gay researchers poses. This analysis will, I hope, reveal the dilemmas and possibilities that now face staff and students in schools [2]. My hope is that a more coherent and felt resistance, from school staff, students and parents, will develop to challenge the reactionary lobby which persists in both denying the realities and complexities of daily life and children and young people's right to information and choice.

Private Issues or Public Struggles?

Several recent commentaries on the 'New Right', or in the case of Britain 'Thatcherism' have pointed to competing strands in their political philosophy: an emphasis on individual freedom/economic liberalism alongside an authoritarian populism. The two strands have been viewed by some as contradictory (see, for example, Gamble, 1988), or at least a source of tension, but there is another way of conceptualising the split. The libertarian strand is most obvious in relation to the economic sphere (including public services - 'choice' for the 'consumer'), the authoritarian in social policy relating to the family and sexuality: the two strands could be explored as a reworking of the traditional public/private divide, which was indeed a key feature in 'Victorian values'.

Two examples highlight this apparent paradox. The development of work around AIDS revealed how little is currently known about sexual practice. A pilot for a major study on sexual practice amongst adults was funded by the ESRC, but the personal intervention of Margaret Thatcher vetoed the second stage funding. Her action was justified in terms of the research being an unwarranted invasion of privacy. Yet in the five years prior to this decision many women's magazines carried explicit reader surveys about aspects of sexuality and thousands of readers responded [3]. Government attitudes to basic research reveal a set of public and private distinctions: private enterprise is not required to respect the privacy of the general public.

The increasing numbers of media 'sexperts', coupled with a 'health' model of sexuality are part of an expanding commercial marketing of sexual information and imagery, sex talk and advice and includes manuals, sex therapy, TV and radio phone-ins, telephone advice and chat lines. Young people are increasingly learning about sex through these commercial sources, and probably represent one of the biggest markets. The only governmental response to this creation of a new product and market, following lobbying from a couple of vocal right wing MPs, has been to regulate certain aspects of chat line services. Yet what young people learn through these sources and how it affects their behaviour subsequently could be as threatening to 'traditional family values' as the areas in which government intervention has been swift and uncompromising.

What the last decade has demonstrated is the skill of small groupings within the Conservative party to exploit local controversies, generate enormous media support and have MPs then respond with speedy legislative fixes - a number of these local controversies have been initially located in education and have focused particularly on sexuality and race. Each of these interventions has fed a specific construction of family and nation that lies at the heart of New Right philosophy: their creation of a 'traditional way of life', which they then become defenders of. This spurious unity requires the exclusion, or at the least de-legitimation, of those who represent an alternative set of values: those outside the white 'Persil' family - e.g. single women choosing to have children; lesbians and gays; Black families which seek to maintain some of their own cultural values; those who represent sectional interests (workers, Black people, women, or combinations of all three); those who have a different vision of nation - anti-nuclear/anti-war protesters, socialists or radical teachers. The success of this ideological strategy is evidenced in the increasing acceptance of the view that equal opportunities programmes promote 'minority' interests, when in fact, if successful, they would benefit the majority of the population who are not white, male, heterosexual and able-bodied.

Some innovative and challenging approaches to addressing sexuality in schools emerged during the 1980's, and a more liberal approach to certain kinds of sexual information for young people had been developing over two decades. It was these realities that prompted reactions. At a number of points during the decade sexuality became a public issue, and in the majority of cases schools were held accountable for indoctrinating children and/or usurping parents' rights (see, for example, Tingle, 1986). Each of these incidents included attempts to limit even further the information given about, and attention paid to, sexuality in schools.

The centrality to the Conservative party of challenging progressive positions on sexuality in education was evident in one of their last election posters. The heading read 'Is this Labour's idea of comprehensive education? and underneath were three book covers - Police: out of school'; 'Young, Gay and Proud' and 'The Playbook for Kids about Sex'. At the bottom was the disingenuous slogan 'Take politics out of education: vote Conservative'.

Victoria Gillick's campaign to prevent contraception advice being given to young people under 16 would have placed limitations not just on doctors and clinics, but teachers as well. It would have removed one of the main topics currently addressed in sex education. She, like the right wing pressure group Family and Youth Concern, attributes complex demographic and social changes to the universal provision of sex education, a position that no research on the impact of sex education has supported.

The now infamous Section 28 of the Local Government Act 1989, had similar origins. It was drafted in response to a small local parental reaction, and subsequent large scale media coverage, which focused on certain actions by Haringey council: the purchase of a book *Jenny lives with Eric and Martin* for use by school teachers, and an exhibition called 'Positive Images'. Both were seen as illegitimate attempts to present homosexuality as 'normal'. Some of the reactions at the time were nothing short of hysterical: a press statement from the Tottenham Conservative Party described Haringey's lesbian and gay unit as "a greater threat to family life than Adolf Hitler"! (Cooper, 1989).

Section 28 made it illegal for any local authority to "intentionally promote homosexuality" and to "promote in teaching in any maintained school the acceptability of homosexuality as a pretended family relationship". Whilst no case has yet been taken under this section of the 1989 Act and most legal opinions view it as an extremely poorly drafted piece of legislation, it has nonetheless been a powerful brake on attempts to challenge heterosexism in schools in particular, and society in general. Whilst the passage of such a retrogressive piece of legislation is to be abhorred, the fact that it was felt necessary to take this step is revealing. It demonstrates a recognition of the emergence of a strong opposition to traditional notions of family and sexuality, and implicitly undermines the right wing's essentialist case. Some of the statements made at the time and subsequently suggest such an instability in sexual identity that simply mentioning homosexuality will result in children and young people immediately wanting to practice it. If this standard were applied to all aspects of the school curriculum, what remained would be meagre fare indeed. What has yet to be answered directly is if heterosexuality and the nuclear family are such 'natural' institutions, why is it necessary to legislate against other forms?

Whilst unwilling to forbid all sex education in schools, government actions since 1986 have all focused on limitation and restriction, confirming their commitment to the sub-text of the election poster - take any explicit recognition of sexuality out of schools. There are currently no national standards for sex education in Britain. In fact the 1986 Education Act removed any responsibility for providing sex education, leaving the decision to school governors. The Act states that:

where sex education is given...it [should be] given in such a manner as to
have due regard to the moral considerations and the value of family life.
[Further there is] no place in any school, in any circumstances for teaching

which advocates homosexual behaviour which presents it as 'normal' (from Melia, 1989)

The 1988 Education Reform Act made provision for the new national curriculum, which further marginalises both sex and health education, The guidance from the DES suggests that the 'facts' in relation to these areas be explored in science classes and "opportunities for considering broader emotional and ethical dimensions...may arise in other subject areas" (quoted in Melia, 1989). The National Curriculum Council issued guidance in 1990 on how sex education can be a cross curricular theme within health education. Whilst concerned teachers and commentators have pointed to the many ways in which these restrictive guidelines can be interpreted, the predominant response is likely to be a retreat from more challenging positions. The fact that there may well be little, if any time, within a much more tightly controlled curriculum places limitations on what can be achieved even where there is a commitment to addressing sexuality in schools.

At the same time as issuing these restrictive guidelines the government has financed costly health education campaigns on AIDS for use in schools and recognised the need for programmes which educate children about sexual abuse. The result of these processes is a contradictory position which attempts to balance appeasing on the one hand powerful lobbyists within the party who want sex education to be the sole preserve of parents and on the other the concerns of parents, young people and health educators about specific issues. However, since both AIDS and child sexual abuse require addressing complex issues about intimacy and sexual practice, isolating them from a coherent sex education programme means that the specific programmes are likely to be ineffective, and may result in heightened anxiety and confusion.

During the 1980's we have not witnessed a coherent and consistent development of government policy, but rather an authoritarian interventionist strategy where the targets are seen to have an alternative vision of sexuality and family and a laissez-faire tolerance where conventional heterosexuality is used as a resource for business and profit.

What's Sociology Got To Do With It?

What sociology and social research offers, in contrast to other disciplines, is a way of approaching and attempting to understand individual behaviour within social and historical contexts. Whilst within sociology there are a range of competing theoretical perspectives, what unites them is a recognition that individual experience and behaviour takes place within the confines and possibilities of particular historical and cultural settings. We ought, therefore, to find a rich resource within sociology which would enable alternatives to the essentialism underlying Conservative policy.

Unfortunately, in relation to sexuality, mainstream sociology - with a few notable exceptions - has had remarkable little to say. Sexuality as a feature of social divisions/inequality is still rarely discussed. For example, in Anthony Giddens' *Social Theory and Modern Sociology* (1987) there is no index reference to sexuality, even in relation to Foucault. Ken Plummer's observation in 1975 that to research, let alone deconstruct, the sexual is deemed irrelevant at best, and dangerous and meddling at worst has resonances in the 1990's. Sociology too, has yet to fully divest itself of distinctions between public and private.

Until that distinction is broken down, it is unlikely that mainstream sociological research will offer an alternative to the prevailing common sense view of sexuality, which is reworked in many right wing ideologies which refer to the 'natural family' (see for example, the 'Who Cares?' pamphlet from the Policy Studies Institute). In this essentialist model, sexuality is natural, drive based; both uncontrollable and requiring control. Control occurs both through individual restraint and responsibility and public morality. Within this perspective 'sex' is defined as heterosexual penetration and preferably confined to marriage (see Scruton, 1986 for the most sophisticated exposition).

The challenges to schools and to mainstream sociology and this renewed focus on essentialism have come from three main areas: feminist theory and research; historical and contemporary studies by lesbian and gay academics and the emergence of new theoretical frameworks drawing on Foucault and psychoanalysis (not mutually exclusive perspectives). Within this diversity of approaches there is a unifying interest in exploring and exposing the social construction of sexuality: that individuals learn about and become sexual within the confines and possibilities afforded by the particular historical culture into which they are born.

In this chapter it is impossible to do justice the range and complexity of feminist thought, but two basic concepts which underlie contemporary feminism are 'the personal is political' and the importance of sex and gender as fundamental organizing principles of social life. Successive waves of feminists have problematised naturalistic conceptions of sexuality in general, and of male sexuality and heterosexuality in particular. Whilst there are a range of feminist perspectives on sexuality, the gendered hierarchy within essentialist conceptualisations of sexuality, and the blurring for women of sexuality with reproduction, has been exposed and criticised. The historic and contemporary use of the sexual as a form of power over women by men, exemplified in the crimes of rape and sexual abuse has also been uncovered. Another central focus has been the enforcement of heterosexuality for women and the invisibility and pathologising of lesbianism (see Rich 1983). Catharine MacKinnon (1989) illustrates the fundamental questions feminists have raised:

> *What sex is - how it comes to be attached and attributed to what it is, embodied and practised as it is, contextualized in the ways it is, signifying and referring to what it does - is taken as a baseline, a given, except in explanations of what happened when it is thought to have gone wrong... Sexuality, in feminist light, is not a discrete sphere of interaction or feeling or sensation or behaviour in which pre-existing social divisions may or may not*

> *be played out. It is a pervasive dimension of social life, one that permeates the*
> *whole, a dimension along which gender occurs and through which gender is*
> *socially constituted; it is a dimension along which other social divisions, like*
> *race and class, partly play themselves out.* (p. 129-130)

Black feminists have demonstrated the complex ways in which culture and race are also connected to variations in belief and practice with regard to both sexuality and gender. For example, the white western construction of African-Carribean women's sexuality is neither the same as that of African-Carribean men's nor of other groups of women. It is a remaining legacy of slavery that African-Carribean and white women's sexuality are often defined and represented in opposition to one another, and that African-Carribean men are viewed as sexual predators, especially in relation to white women (Hill-Collins 1990, hooks 1989).

Differences between African-Carribean, Asian, Mediterranean and Latin American cultural heritages in relation to sexuality are frequently denied, trivialized and/or negatively valued through arrogant notions of freedom and 'civilized' behaviour which inform most western perspectives (see also Carby, 1987). This so-called freedom rapidly comes under question when we observe the denial of sexuality for children and young people, young people (and adults) with disabilities and the elderly which is also a feature of western societies.

Lesbian and gay social theorists/researchers have investigated the historical shift from homosexuality as a form of behaviour to that of a category of person. Both Jeffrey Weeks (1981) and Sheila Jeffreys (1985; 1990) document the shift to medical and sexological explanations and definitions which pathologised gay men and lesbians. This view of homosexuality as a 'sickness' has strong legacies today and has had profound influences on generations of men and women. The liberal response to this construction was to view homosexuality as an unfortunate, but unalterable state, and to propose a benign tolerance. Both perspectives continue to inform public debate and policy.

Foucault's work (1978) echoes themes from both these alternative frameworks. He takes power as a central theme and suggests that sexuality is best understood as a potential that develops in relation to varying combinations of social definition, regulation, organization and categorization. In his view human beings make sense of their behaviour and that of others through discourses: socially produced forms of knowledge which define and organize experience and which always embody power. His work on the history of sexuality has focused on the emergence of new discourses in the nineteenth century, primarily those of medicine and psychiatry, which classified behaviour as 'normal' and 'deviant': both contain within them elements of control and regulation, which can operate through legal as well as therapeutic contexts.

Whilst outside of the scope of this essay, mapping how and understanding why sexuality in the late twentieth century is both visible yet invisible, spoken about yet silenced, designated as private yet pervasively public is an important task for sociological enquiry. So to is integrating sexuality into mainstream sociological perspectives.

An Uncomfortable Presence

Whatever conservative ideologues might say, schools are places where sex talk, sexual behaviour, sexual relationships, sexual abuse and harassment, sexual identity, sexual divisions and sexual politics are threaded throughout the wharp and wheft of interactions between students, staff and students and staff. This reality exists alongside the cautious inclusion or the deliberate exclusion of sexuality in the formal taught curriculum.

The content of many subjects and courses are imbued with the sexual. Most reading schemes and written work given to young children draw on assumptions and conventions about 'the family'. Traditional models of appearance and femininity are constitutive of content in secretarial, business, catering and hairdressing courses. The fundamental issue being how women can use, whilst also attempting to control, sexuality in their work. The same issues, although in a different form, are evident in the implicit messages given to young women (and the few young men) who choose to study 'non-traditional courses': the manual trades and science based courses such as engineering and physics for young women, and child-care and nursing courses for young men.

These uncomfortable presences are reinforced by accompanying absences. Whilst the nationality, class and gender of important thinkers, writers, individuals are seen as relevant information, the fact that they did or may have had lesbian or gay relationships is seldom noted. Subtle forms of censorship exist which, for example, redefine the passionate friendships of literary and political women with each other as an emptiness, a lack. At the same time writing by men which depicts coercive heterosexuality (for example, the novels of Thomas Hardy and D.H. Lawrence) are usually taught uncritically, reinforcing the 'normalcy' of this kind of behaviour. Even history teaching which seeks to explore daily life (also unpopular with the present government) seldom asks questions related to the sexual: were same sex relationships evident during this period?; were contraception and abortion practiced and what were the laws/rules relating to them?; what were the formal laws/rules about marriage and sex and who did and did not keep to these rules?

In most writing on education, and in most schools, there is a studied silence around these issues, broken occasionally by 'special' sessions on sex education or personal safety. This official silence makes routine and normal, not to be remarked upon, the everyday expressions of sexuality within schools (Holly, 1989; Wood, 1984). It is feminist, lesbian and gay researchers who have highlighted these contradictions and their implications for educational policy.

Sexuality, Education and Equal Opportunities:
the challenge of feminist research in the 1980s

Within the sociology of education as in schools it has become commonplace to discuss how schooling reproduces class relations, and increasing attention has been paid to how it reproduces race and gender relations. However, apart from recent work by feminists and lesbian and gay researchers, there has been relatively little exploration of how the formal and hidden curriculum reproduce dominant forms of sexuality. Few writers and researchers have moved into the crucially important area, highlighted by the Burnage report [4], of how forms of dominance and subordination interact in reinforcing or cross-cutting ways. Reflecting on what we know about sexuality and how this is or is not reflected in educational policy and practice presents an opportunity to examine one nexus of social inequalities. The complexities in this area would be highlighted if we examined in detail how sexuality, in formal and informal ways, is present or absent in the variety of schools children and young people in Britain attend: single and mixed sex; state comprehensive; private and denominational; predominantly white or Black and multi-racial; and special schools.

The feminist approaches to sexuality referred to above have prompted new, innovative research in this hitherto neglected area of the sociology of education. These studies, published throughout the 1980's, highlight the ways in which images, language, concepts and ways we come to know about the sexual all connect to power.

Whilst there is ongoing debate as to whether babies are born with sexuality or it is acquired solely through acculturation, nonetheless most social theorists recognise the importance of childhood as a period which includes an increasing awareness of the body and its possibilities. Most adults can recall curiosity about their own bodies and those of other children, and ritualised games which enable some form of shared exploration. It is an open question as to whether these explorations should be labelled sexual, although they are commonly referred to 'sex play'. In an ongoing project on the prevalence of child sexual abuse [5], many more young people (the sample is one thousand two hundred and forty four 16-21 year olds) told us they had played 'doctors and nurses' than answered questions about 'sexual experiences with other children before they were 12'. This raises complex issues, which we currently cannot answer, such as at what point does information and/or experience become 'sexual'? The fact that a number of the young people defined their experiences of "sex play' as either forced or pressured raises further questions about accepting these forms of behaviour as 'normal and natural'. The fact that something happens frequently, is not sufficient reason to regard it as either 'natural' or harmless. If more educational researchers problematised sexuality in their work we might begin to develop more complex understandings of 'sex play'.

It is again feminist practice and research which has increased awareness about the numbers of children who experience intrusive sexuality from peers and adults (see, for example, Kelly 1988; MacLeod & Saraga 1988). Without a language with which to name, and information with which to understand, these experiences, children have very limited ways of either making sense of, or communicating about them. Adult constructions of childhood innocence have the unintended consequence of making children more vulnerable to abuse, and less able to find support to stop it. Reports from teachers and nursery workers represent one of the largest categories of child abuse referrals to social services, but as we will see later the government response to these issues has been inadequate.

Most adults in the West remember adolescence as the period in which sexuality became an important feature of their lives. It is predominantly during this period that young people become sexually active with each other, although for a considerable proportion intrusive encounters with adults have already, and may continue, to occur.

A number of surveys suggest that young people are sexually active at an earlier age, many before the legal age of consent. For example, 30% of the young people in our current project (see note 5) had had heterosexual intercourse before they were 16, percentages being somewhat higher for boys than girls. Over a quarter of the young women stated that they were pressurised or forced in their first experience. Further evidence of sexual activity before the age of consent can be found in the numbers of young women having abortions or children before they are 16 years old.

Research on dating relationships, primarily undertaken in the USA, reveals gender differences in experience and levels of coercion and even violence. Young men demand higher levels of intimacy sooner, and expect young women to place limits on their expectations (see Kelly, 1988). Angela Hamblin's (1983) survey of 200 readers of Spare Rib revealed similar patterns of pressure and coercion in Britain, and drew attention to the increasing use of pornography to legitimise sexual activity and forms of sexual practice. In our survey (Kelly, 1991) over three quarters of the young men and women reported having seen a pornographic video or magazine, with young men markedly higher in relation to both any and frequent viewing. Following up the titles we recorded, the Metropolitan Police Obscene Publications Squad confirmed that a sizeable minority of these young people had seen 'hard core', and illegal material. We see this data as significant in a number of ways, the most important being that more of young people's sexual knowledge comes from coercive experience and/or pornography than from education either at home or in school.

During the 1980's feminist research also documented the ways in which sexuality was a critical feature of both young and adolescent girls and women teachers' experience of schooling. Valerie Walkerdine (1987, p. 167), for example, describes interactions between two four-year-old boys and their nursery teacher to demonstrate how use of the sexual in language can undermine, or at the very least challenge, the power inherent in adult/child, teacher/pupil relations by repositioning them as male/female interactions in which the adult female teacher is 'woman-as-sex-object'. The teacher in this instance chose not to challenge the boys, interpreting their behaviour as 'normal and natural' for their age. Other researchers have noted the extent to which the sexual is present in routine interactions, and how these verbal exchanges both confirm and construct gender differences (see for example Kutner & Brogan, 1974; Spender 1980).

Sexualised language used by boys (and some girls) in secondary schools objectifies and humiliates girls. A central concern of the young women interviewed by Sue Lees (1986) was sexual reputation "[girls are] blamed for exciting sex and for rejecting it" (p. 180). The power of the term 'slag' is such that girls react by denying their involvement in sexual relationships, rather than contesting the term. One of the most important insights of Lees' work, which is confirmed by Jacqui Halson's research (1989) is that the label 'slag' is often used as an attempt to police, or at least express contempt for, girls who act independently. Being labelled a 'slag' can mark a young woman as a legitimate target for further abuse and harassment.

The extent and pervasiveness of sexual harassment in schools has been documented by Pat Mahony (1985) and Carol Jones (1985). Jacqui Halson (1989) has extended this knowledge describing girls' experiences of 'being got', which includes being chased, grabbed, groped, pinned down, assaulted. It is not only peer interactions which are affected by these sexualised definitions of young women. At least one researcher (Middleton, 1987) has suggested that teachers define, and therefore treat, as 'academic' girls who are not seen/known to be sexually active.

Mirroring these studies of young women's experiences are a few studies which problematise young mens' behaviour (Willis, 1977; Wood, 1984). They confirm that the use of sexist slang, sex talk and sex practice are attempts by boys and young men to assert male power and control over girls and young women. Tricia Szirom's (1988) study involving Australian 15- and 16-year olds revealed that the only aspect of sex education boys see as relevant to them concerns their own heterosexual satisfaction, everything else is girls' concern and responsibility.

The fact that young women suffer negative consequences from being seen to be taking control in the area of sexuality has enormous implications for sex education and social policy. A range of studies have pointed to the gap between providing young people with contraceptive advice and their acting on this knowledge. Only a few of these researchers have recognised the critical role which gender relations might play in both preventing young women obtaining contraception and/or enforcing its use by male sexual partners (see for example Hayes, 1987). A feminist research team exploring the responses of young women to AIDS education have made the issues of power and control central to their study. Holland et al (1990b) argue that:

> using or not using a condom is not a simple, practical question about dealing rationally with risk, it is the outcome of negotiation between potentially

unequal partners. Sexual encounters are sites of struggle between exercise and acceptance of male power and male definitions of sexuality, and of women's ambivalence and resistance. (p. 5)

Another area of critical concern for young women in schools is menstruation. The cultural injunction on them to hide this biological process results in the expenditure of an immense amount of time and energy. The failure in many schools to ensure easy access to sanitary wear and toilet facilities (the frequent complaint being that the machines are always empty and toilets locked for considerable 'periods' during the day) compound the problems, as do the ways in which boys and young men use the issue to humiliate and embarrass (see Prendegast, 1989; Laws 1990).

We currently know very little about the experiences of young lesbians and gays in school except through exploratory studies like those of London Gay Teenage Group, and anecdotal evidence from teachers. Lorraine Trenchard & Hugh Warren (1987) surveyed 416 young people (two thirds male, predominantly white and almost half working class), all whom had faced hostility and abuse because of their sexuality. Sixty percent said that homosexuality or lesbianism was never mentioned by any of their teachers, the vast majority of cases where it had been mentioned was in a negative or unhelpful way. Only one in forty recalled it being mentioned in sex education lessons. A very different picture than that suggested by recent right wing propaganda. Moreover, this failure to address the needs and experiences of lesbian and gay pupils had serious consequences: a strong sense of isolation; verbal abuse and teasing; for some being beaten up in school. One in five of these young people had attempted suicide.

Young people were constantly exposed to uninformed and derogatory images of homosexuality and lesbianism through the media, playground talk and anti-homosexual/anti-lesbian jokes. (Trenchard & Warren, 1987, p. 226)

It is this reality of having to hide, pretend, be dishonest or face taunts, hostility and worse that is never addressed by right wing lobbyists - their remarks are couched in terms of concern for children and young people, yet they display remarkably little when those young people are lesbian or gay.

Canadian research cited by Lenskyj (1990) reported that: over a third of young lesbian and gay students had gone on heterosexual dates in an attempt to conceal their sexual identity; these young people knew more about heterosexual sex than lesbian and gay sexuality; and that the only images available to them were of 'effeminate' gay men and 'macho' lesbians. Such evidence from Britain and Canada shows that the resulting confusion, anxiety and alienation affected these young peoples' academic performance.

The depth of homophobia amongst some young people, particularly young men, was brought home to us in our current study (see note 5) through volunteered responses to a question about sexual identity. The hostility and violence in some of the young men's responses was matched only by their responses to a question about policy in relation to child abusers. Some of the spontaneous comments about lesbians and gays we recorded included: 'shoot them all'; 'put them in the gas ovens'; 'makes me sick to even think about it!'

So long as sexuality is not regarded as a basic equal opportunities issue, the only or dominant form of sexuality which is affirmed in schools is a macho male heterosexuality. The majority of students are not only excluded in the process, but are potential targets for abuse from those boys, young and adult men who choose to use this potential source of power over others.

Tackling Sexuality in Schools: dilemmas and new strategies

Despite the restrictions imposed by government policy and the failure of mainstream sociology to address sexuality, exciting and innovative strategies have emerged during the 1980's. Unsurprisingly, it is feminist and lesbian/gay teachers who have devised and instigated these courageous initiatives.

The most influential perspectives on educational policy and practice continue to draw on theories of child development, which encompass models of psycho-sexual development. Implicit or explicit in the majority, if not all, of these frameworks is an essentialist notion of sexuality as an innate, biologically determined, form of human behaviour, which develops through 'natural' and universal processes, particularly during childhood and adolescence. The other major influence has been the liberal view that sexuality belongs in the private sphere, where individuals are free to pursue their own interests. An additional issue influencing the willingness and ability of educationalists to tackle sexuality in schools is the fact that varying rules governing its expression are constitutive of most religious doctrine and cultural belief systems.

Whilst the many contradictions in the public/private division have been a target of feminist critique, it is the combination of this definition of the sexual and biologically defined frameworks which have determined the way sexuality has been handled in schools. Where it has been addressed through sex education, the information given has been about biological functioning, seldom have the range and diversity of children and young people's concerns and experiences been reflected. The account by Terri Marsh & Kerena Marchant (*The Times Educational Supplement*, 21 September 1990) of the framework they used in developing the new BBC programme Sex Education is revealing in what it includes and excludes. Whilst espousing an ethic of equality and recognising that sex has been portrayed as a male dominant occupation the standard fare of heterosexual intercourse and childbirth remains: no mention is made of homosexuality, sexual abuse receives a passing reference and disabled children are referred to in the teachers' programme. Clearly many of the issues which children and young people raised - the example they give is masturbation - are those which the teachers notes point to as potentially "unacceptable to members of [particular] faiths". The implicit message in the traditional 'plumbing and prevention' approach is that it is girl's knowledge and activity which is both the problem and target (see Lenskyj, 1990).

Whilst there are no easy answers to the complexities teachers face when raising the issue of sexuality in schools, continuing to represent sexuality as something which only exists and occurs outside of the institution schools will fail to reflect children's and young people's experience and concerns. It is precisely this recognition, that social issues are present in our daily lives and experiences, which is part of a feminist perspective. Raising questions about the pervasive use of sexuality as a form of 'power over' has revealed profoundly disturbing aspects of 'normal' heterosexuality and family life, in which women and children are the all too frequent victims. This disturbing knowledge has supported critiques of how and why heterosexuality is the dominant and privileged form of sexuality in Britain, and most other western countries (see for example MacKinnon, 1989, Rich 1983).

Not only are issues about sexuality connected to all other areas of social in equality, but as a specific area of concern there is a strong argument that failing to address it directly within educational policy and practice undermines attempts at promoting equal opportunities. The failure to challenge the power relations underpining heterosexism, and the male dominance within it, mean that girls are undermined by what Holly (1989, p. 3) has called "a predatory heterosexual environment"; young lesbians and gay men may withdraw from education and institutions in which their existence is denied and/or where they face hostility and harassment (Scott, 1989); children who are being sexual abused may withdraw and 'cut off' in order to cope, and thus loose out educationally (Kelly, 1988); children and young people who are seropositive or have AIDS may be denied access to education, as may young women who choose to continue a pregnancy whilst still in full-time education.

Isobel Allen's (1987) study of sex education revealed that 95% of students and their parents wanted schools to provide sex education as part of the curriculum. Her analysis of the content of most current sex education confirms that the focus remains almost exclusively on reproduction and disease; on sex (heterosexual) not sexuality. The gap between the experiential world of children and young people and what sex education offers remains a yawning one. There are, however, a number of other models that could be the basis for new forms of practice.

Several primary school teachers have developed for a creative approach involving a sealed box in the classroom into which pupils can anonymously place questions they are concerned about. Whilst not confined to 'sex education' many of the questions relate to this area. Once a week/fortnight the question box is opened and issues discussed. In this way the teacher responds directly to the concerns her pupils raise, and is neither dependent on a school policy nor a commercially produced sex education programme.

Whilst there are examples throughout the country of individual teachers and schools developing innovative sex education programmes for secondary schools, the most instructive example is that of Sweden. Philip Meredith (1989) documents the intense and extensive consultation process which was undertaken in order to develop a national curriculum involving teachers, pupils, parents and interested organisations. The resulting programme is both an attempt to give accurate information and engage in a dialogue with children and young people. There is explicit recognition that sexuality is an area about which there is can be no simple consensus position, no one community of values which can underpin all the issues that need to be tackled. The Goldman's (1982) cross-cultural study of children's sexual thinking demonstrated the positive impact of a nationally agreed curriculum. Swedish children both knew more and were more comfortable with the issues than any of the other groups of children. The most misinformed group of children and young people were from the USA, where decisions about sex education are made in each school and where sex education has been targeted by the right wing for attack. The USA also has the highest rate of teenage pregnancy of any western country.

A DES circular (41 88, July 1988) offered guidance to schools about how to respond to concerns about sexual abuse. It provided for the appointment of designated teachers with a limited child protection brief, some suggestions about enabling teachers to recognise behaviour that might indicate a child had/was being abused; suggestions that governors discuss how to include sex education programmes in the curriculum; and some provision for training of teachers (although this falls far short of the provisions made in relation to social work). Teachers and nursery workers are not seen as core participants in the much vaunted 'multidisciplinary' approach, despite the fact that they are responsible for many referrals of children. Nor is the role that teaching staff could play in long-term support for children and young people who have been sexually abused recognised. There are suggestions that the DES will issue guidelines about reporting, possibly making it mandatory, in 1991. It seems unlikely that any debate and discussion about the implications of this move for teachers and pupils will take place. Lenskyj (1990) points to an unintended consequence of mandatory reporting in Australia: an increased unwillingness of teachers to broach the issue, in order to avoid moral dilemmas.

A different model of response is recommended by a number of feminists, at least two of whom have been involved in developing policy in schools (Kitzinger, 1989; Jones, 1989; O'Hara, 1988). They argue for a whole school policy, which begins not from ideas about how adults can tell which children are being abused, but from creating the conditions in which children choose to tell adults about the abuse they are experiencing. Some of the questions which such whole school policies must address are:

How are forms of harassment and bullying which occur in school dealt with?

Does policy on this and other related areas cover teacher/pupil relationships?

Do children think that they will be listened to, believed, taken seriously?

What images of the male/female body are visible in textbooks, posters, artwork and graffiti?

How is menstruation dealt with?

What information and resources are available about sexual abuse? Are they accessible?

What policy exists to cover when a child tells about sexual abuse?

What role should a teacher who a child chooses to tell play in subsequent events

Does the policy address issues around race, culture, disability and sexuality?

What policy exists to cover situations where teachers have suspicions?

Teachers who have attempted to develop these more integrated approaches have encountered much resistance. Not only do most teachers and heads not see the connections between behaviour in school and sexual abuse, but aspects of the policy require making staff more accountable for their interactions with pupils.

Since very few schools have even begun discussing, let alone implementing, whole school policies, their effectiveness cannot be evaluated. There is no doubt, however, that feminist teachers who attempt to put these principles into practice as individuals are much more often approached by young women wanting to tell about abuse (see Jones, 1989). There is critical work which needs to be done in order to extend whole school policies to include the forms of physical and sexual aggression noted earlier in young women's relationships with their peers. The current case in Landaff High School in Wales where large numbers of staff have gone on strike in protest at the unwillingness of school management to expel three boys who sexually assaulted a female pupil (*Guardian*, 14 March 1991) is a clear example of the consequences of failing to address these issues in policy.

Isobel Gil first published her reflections on being a white lesbian teacher in boys' secondary school in 1986. That piece and the responses to it informed an attempt to develop another whole school policy which addressed heterosexism in the context of formal ILEA support for anti-sexist policies. The document was reproduced in a later article (Gil, 1989), and covers the following areas: definitions of sexism and heterosexism; the impact of sexism; sexual harassment in school; sexual harassment of lesbians and gays in schools; and the harassment of individuals who do not conform to gender stereotypes. Teachers are encouraged to use different resources in their teaching; to enable students to recognise bias and prejudice themselves; to reflect upon how language and assumptions can reinforce stereotypes; to offer different models of masculinity to boys and young men; to find ways of involving all parents, especially those who are lesbian and gay, in putting the policy into effect. In 'trying not just to survive' Isobel Gil, like all lesbian and gay teachers who choose not to hide, faced hostility from some students and staff and lack of support from heterosexual colleagues who were formally sympathetic to the policy.

> 'Miss is a lesbian' is written on my door. 'So what' I write beneath. I go on existing, I go on teaching my lessons. Maybe on some days the atmosphere is soft enough, I have enough energy to take an insult into a conversation, to 'talk it through' with a student, to re-interpret physically threatening behaviour as a quest for information.

Until more schools and educational policy makers are willing to tackle sexuality as an equal opportunities issue, as an issue which is as much about interactions in school as it is about life beyond it, then individual teachers will carry impossible burdens of knowledge about individual pupils and responsibility for change. Each of the teachers whose work has been mentioned in this section has taken personal and professional risks in order to raise contentious issues; risks which are increasing rather than decreasing.

Conclusion

The reassertion of centralised control and an increasingly desperate appeal to the 'natural' family by the current government and right wing lobby groups is a reaction to the success of radical social research and activism in challenging the prevailing orthodoxy. Schools are sites of struggles over inequality, struggles which occur between teachers, teachers and pupils, teachers and parents, and parents and pupils. In each group there are differences within as well as challenges from without.

In facing the contentious issues sexuality raises we must be wary of stereotyping, for example seeing all Asian parents as traditionalists, if not fundamentalists. Many of the most powerful voices of reaction are white, middle class parents. Nor are all right wing thinkers and politicians thoroughly reactionary: several Tory women MPs have consistently voted against restricting women's access to abortion. They, like many others, are resisting (some of) the attempts by the New Right to move these issues back into the private sphere (Levitas, 1986). Understanding that it is the influence of a relatively small, but extremely powerful grouping within the right that has been able to orchestrate media and legislative responses in relation to this area might offer different strategies for challenge and change (see also Radford, 1991). Developing an alternative vision means that sexuality has to be seen as central to equal opportunities, a critical factor in determining the educational experiences of all young people, but young women and young lesbians and gays in particular. Integrated whole school policies, which include but are not limited to sex education, offer the most promising alternative.

One key to resisting recent attempts at censoring what children and young people may know about is exposing the specious 'naturalism' of right wing ideology. Each time it is raised, just what this so called 'natural' family and 'normal' sexuality consists of must be highlighted: supporting 'traditional values' means supporting, rather than challenging, the existence of child sexual abuse, domestic violence, rape, sexual assault and sexual harassment. We need approaches to sexuality in education that enable children and young people to question, rather than accept, these realities.

Notes

[1] Angela Rumbold was Secretary of State for Education at this time.

[2] Whilst 'education' includes schools, further and higher education, in this chapter I concentrate on schools, partly because the new research and strategies have emerged in schools, and partly because government policies have been directed at this sector. That said, however, many of the issues raised are equally relevant to other education institutions, especially the presence of sexuality and sexual harassment in interactions between men and women and the treatment of sexuality in the taught curriculum.

[3] Welcome have subsequently funded the study, yet another irony of the public/private distinction.

[4] *Murder in the Playground: The Burnage Report* (MacDonald, 1989) documents an enquiry into the killing of an Asian boy by white fellow students. It highlights the danger of policies which target only one form of inequality, in this case race, to the exclusion of other divisions, particularly those of class and gender.

[5] This project is an exploratory study of the prevalence of sexual abuse funded by the ESRC, conducted by Liz Kelly, Linda Regan and Sheila Burton. One thousand two hundred and forty four 16-21 year olds from seven further education colleges in England, Scotland and Wales completed a detailed self-report questionnaire. The final report was submitted in May 1991.

REFERENCES

Allen, Isobel (1987) *Education in Sex and Personal Relationships*. London: Policy Studies Institute.

Carby, Hazel (1987) Black Feminism and the Boundaries of Sisterhood, in M. Arnot & G. Weiner (Eds) *Gender and the Politics of Schooling*. London: Hutchinson.

Cooper, Davina, (1989) Positive Images in Haringey: A Struggle for Identity, in C. Jones & P. Mahony (Eds) *Learning Our Lines: sexuality and social control in education*. London: Women's Press.

Coote, Anna, Harman, Harriet, & Hewitt, Patricia (1990) *The Family Way: A New Approach to Policy-making*, Social Policy Paper No. 1. Institute for Public Policy Research.

Department of Education and Science (1988) Circular 541/88. London: HMSO.

Egerton, Jane (1991) The family ways: Labour's policy on the family, *Trouble and Strife*, 20, pp. 2-6.

Foucault, Michel (1978) *The History of Sexuality, 1: An Introduction*. New York: Pantheon.

Gamble, Andrew (1988) *The Free Economy and the Strong State*. London: Macmillan.

Giddens, Anthony (1987) *Social Theory and the Strong State*. Cambridge: Polity Press.

Gil, Isobel (1989) Trying Not Just to Survive: a lesbian teacher in a boys' school, in L. Holly (Ed) *Girls and Sexuality: teaching and learning*. Milton Keynes: Open University Press.

Goldman, Ronald & Juliette (1982) *Childrens' Sexual Thinking*. London: Routledge.

Halson, Jaqui (1989) The Sexual Harassment of Young Women, in L. Holly (Ed) *Girls and Sexuality: teaching and learning*. Milton Keynes: Open University Press.

Hamblin, Angela (1983) Is Feminist Heterosexuality Possible?, in Sue Cartledge & Joanna Ryan (Eds) *Sex and Love: New Thoughts on Old Contradictions*. London: Women's Press.

Hayes, Cheryl (1987) *Risking the Future: Adolescent Sexuality, Pregnancy and Childbearing*. Washington DC: National Academy Press.

Collins, Patricia Hill (1990) *Black Feminist Thought*. London: Unwin.

hooks, bell (1989) *Talking Back - Talking Feminist, Talking Black*. London: Sheba.

Holland, Janet, Ramazanoglu, Caroline & Scott, Sue (1990a) From panic stations to power relations: sociological perspectives and problems, *Sociology*, 24, pp. 499-518.

Holland, Janet, Ramazanoglu, Caroline, Scott, Sue, Sharpe, Sue & Thompson, Rachel (1990b) *Don't Die of Ignorance - I Nearly Died of Embarrassment: condoms in context*. London: Tufnell Press.

Holly, Lesley (Ed) (1989) *Girls and Sexuality: teaching and learning*. Milton Keynes: Open University Press.

Jeffreys, Sheila (1985) *The Spinster and her Enemies: feminism and sexuality, 1880-1930* London: Pandora Press.

Jeffreys, Sheila (1990) *Anti-climax*. London: Women's Press.

Jones, Carol (1985) Sexual tyranny: male violence in a mixed secondary school, in G. Weiner (Ed) *Just a Bunch of Girls*. Milton Keynes: Open University Press.

Jones, Carol (1989) Asking the Wrong Questions: schools' responses to the sexual abuse of children, in C. Jones & P. Mahony (Eds) *Learning our Lines: sexuality and social control in education*. London: Women's Press.

Kelly, Liz (1988) *Surviving Sexual Violence*. Cambridge: Polity Press.

Kelly, Liz (1991) Abuse in the making?: exploring the connections between pornography and sexual violence, paper for Edinburgh International Science Festival, March.

Kitzinger, Jenny (1989) Child sexual abuse and the role of the teacher, in L. Holly (Ed) *Girls and Sexuality: teaching and learning*. Milton Keynes: Open University Press.

Kutner, Nancy & Brogan, Donna (1974) An investigation of sex-related slang vocabulary and sex role orientation among male and female college students, *Journal of Marriage and the Family*, 36, pp. 474-484.

Laws, Sophie (1990) *Issues of Blood: the sexual politics of menstruation* London: Macmillan.

Lees, Sue (1986) *Losing Out: sexuality and adolescent girls.* London: Hutchinson.

Lenskyj, Helen (1990) Beyond plumbing and prevention: feminist approaches to sex education, *Gender and Education*, 2, pp. 217-230.

Levitas, Ruth (1986) *The Ideology of the New Right.* Cambridge: Polity Press.

MacDonald. Ian (1989) *Murder in the Playground: the Burnage Report.* Lonsight: Burnage High School.

MacKinnon, Catharine (1989) *Towards a Feminist Theory of the State.* Boston: Harvard University Press.

MacLeod, Mary & Saraga, Esther (1988) Challenging the orthodoxy: towards a feminist theory and practice, in *Feminist Review* Special Issue 'Family Secrets: Child Sexual Abuse Today', 28, pp. 16-55.

Mahony, Pat (1985) *Schools for the Boys? Co-education Reassessed.* London: Hutchinson.

Marsh, Terri & Marchant, Karena (1990) Sexual healing, *The Times Educational Supplement* 21 September, p. 3.

McRobbie, Angela & Nava, Mica (Eds) (1984) *Gender and Generation.* London: Macmillan.

Melia, Julie (1989) Sex education in schools: keeping to the norm, in C. Jones & P. Mahony (Eds) *Learning our Lines: sexuality and social control in education.* London: Women's Press.

Meredith, Philip (1989) *Sex Education: political issues in Britain and Europe.* London: Routledge.

Middleton, Sue (1987) Streaming and the Politics of Female Sexuality: case studies in the schooling of girls, in G. Weiner & M. Arnot (Eds) *Gender under Scrutiny.* London: Hutchinson.

O'Hara, Maureen (1988) Developing a feminist school policy on child sexual abuse, *Feminist Review*, 28, pp. 158-162.

Plummer, Ken (1975) *Sexual Stigma: an interactionist account.* London: Routledge.

Prendegast, Shirley (1989) Girls' experience of menstruation at school, in L. Holly (Ed) *Girls and Sexuality: teaching and learning.* Milton Keynes: Open University Press.

Radford, Jill (1991) Immaculate conceptions: the 'virgin birth' controversy, *Trouble and Strife*, 21, pp. 18-23.

Rich, Adrienne (1983) *Compulsory Heterosexuality and Lesbian Existence.* London: Only Women Press.

Scott, Pip (1989) Challenging Heterosexism in the Curriculum: roles for teachers, governors and parents, in C. Jones & P. Mahony (Eds) *Learning our Lines: sexuality and social control in education.* London: Women's Press.

Scruton, Roger (1986) *Sexual Desire.* London: Weidenfeld & Nicholson.

Spender, Dale (1980) *Man-made Language*. London: Writers and Readers.

Szirom, Patricia (1988) *Teaching Gender? Sex Education and Sexual Stereotypes.* London: Allen & Unwin.

Tingle, Rachel (1986) *How Public Funds are used to Promote Homosexuality Among Children and Young People.* London: Pickwick.

Trenchard, Lorraine (Ed) (1984) *Talking About Young Lesbians.* London: Gay Teenage Group.

Trenchard, Lorraine & Warren, Hugh (1984) *Something to Tell You.* London: Gay Teenage Group.

Walkerdine, Valerie (1987) Sex Power and Pedagogy, in M. Arnot & G. Weiner (Eds) *Gender and the Politics of Schooling.* London: Hutchinson.

Weeks, Jeffrey (1981) *Sex, Politics and Society: the regulation of sexuality since 1800.* London: Longman.

Weiner, Gaby & Arnot, Madeleine (Eds)(1989) *Gender Under Scrutiny: new inquiries in education.* London: Hutchinson.

Willis, Paul (1977) *Learning to Labour: how working-class kids get working-class jobs.* Farnborough: Saxon House.

Wood, Julian (1984) Groping Towards Sexism: boys' sex talk, in A. McRobbie & M. Nava (Eds) *Gender and Generation.* London: Macmillan.

Chapter Three

Feminism, Education and the New Right

MADELEINE ARNOT

The purpose of this chapter is to consider the Conservative educational reforms of the 1980's from a feminist perspective and to analyse the significance of New Right ideology for women in the United Kingdom. Recent socialist feminist writings suggest that existing understandings of the New Right have paid inadequate attention to "the patriarchal basis of the state and society" (Eisenstein, 1987). Gender relations have, yet again, been marginalised in the conceptualisations of contemporary politics. According to Ten Tusscher (1986),

> *...the debate around the New Right has become moribund - stuck in a treadmill of male-defined analyses offering male answers to male questions on what has become the dominant force in contemporary western politics. This gender bias has led to a partial explanation of the New Right - on the left, one couched in economic and class terms - which fails to explain (and indeed lacks the analytical tools to be able to explain) the moral/traditional/familial aspects of the present administration's ideology and politics (p. 67).*

This chapter therefore aims to take such feminist critiques into the sociological analysis of contemporary educational reforms. I hope to extend, if not to challenge, current understandings about the nature of the Conservative educational restructuring and its underpinnings in neo-liberal and neo-conservative political philosophies. Of particular interest will be the tensions between Conservative approaches to the family and to women, tensions expressed in the contradictions between on the one hand a 'moral crusade' in support of the patriarchal family and, on the other, the principles of a free market society. Such ambivalences can be found within the new educational reforms, and are likely to have differential impact on women from different social origins.

The starting point for my analysis will be a broadly defined 'sociology of women's education' (MacDonald, 1980). Although some feminist research fits easily within the conventional boundaries of 'sociology', other feminist analyses or projects have nevertheless contributed to sociological debates from outside the academic discipline. Patriarchal relations within higher education have positioned women as a minority of the academic profession and a majority of those in lower status academic related posts. Feminist educational research therefore has been generated in the various niches women academics have managed to find for themselves not just in sociology or education departments but also in, for example, curriculum studies, adult education and extra mural studies. Black female sociologists, with a few exceptions, have been excluded from the academic profession and can be found working as education advisers, local authority personnel and in black feminist collectives. It is essential therefore that such feminist authors are not further excluded from the academic arena.

Research on women's educational experiences began to emerge in the United Kingdom in the early 1970's in the context of increasing disillusion with the social democratic principles underlying education and social policy. The principles of universalism and collectivism had not, it seemed, delivered the promised equality of opportunity to women.

After a slow start at the margins of the sociological world where issues of social class dominated, ironically the majority of British sociological research projects and texts on female educational experiences were published well after the 1979 election, when the Mrs Thatcher led the Conservative party to victory. The next ten years were to witness a phenomenal growth of interest in feminist educational analyses at a time, paradoxically when the 'pursuit of equality' was increasingly challenged by central government initiatives.

Yet the shift in political discourse and the reality of the new educational era promoted by the Conservative Government rarely drew the attention of feminist academics and teachers. Sometimes it appeared as if the educational processes feminist researchers identified, and indeed the research agenda itself, existed within a political vacuum, so devoid was the gender research of any mention of the political and economic climate of the period. On the whole the foci of feminist research, as I shall show, were the discourses and internal structures of a liberal democratic state shaped by the ideologies of welfarism. There seemed to be little preparation therefore for the attack on 'egalitarianism', allegedly brought to an abrupt end (or so claimed the then Secretary for State, Mr Kenneth Baker) by the successful passage of the 1988 Education Reform Act. It is only in the last year that we can see the emergence of a more sustained feminist response to the educational programme of the New Right.

One way to explain this delay in analysing the significance of the New Right's educational policy for women is to consider the particular relationship which feminist education theory has had to educational policy-making. The relationship between theory and practice, I would argue, is different in the context of gender and education than that which holds for sociological analyses of class or 'race' . Like those committed to 'race' and to some extent class equality, feminist academics and sociologists have attempted to engage with broader political liberation movements. However where the issue of gender differs is that women teachers, the keenest audience for such feminist educational research, are the majority of the teaching profession. Many of the reference points for feminist educationalists therefore are to be found not just in the sociological domain but in female teachers' campaigns and initiatives. Thus feminists may have waited to see the impact of the latest round of contemporary reforms on women teachers before responding publicly to these reforms.

The first section of this paper will focus on this relationship between the growth of feminist sociology of education and educational policy making - in particular social democratic educational policy. In the second section of the paper I will consider the growing number of feminist critiques of the Education Reform Act 1988 which offer 'alternative' accounts of the New Right from that currently available in the sociology of education. These feminist critiques can be placed in the broader context of socialist feminist analyses of the New Right and its impact upon women. I conclude the chapter by suggesting new agendas for sociological research on gender and education.

Modern Feminism and the Critique
of Social Democratic Education Policy

Feminist analyses of education, in much the same way as the sociology of family and school (see Chapter 1 by Miriam David) can only be understood as an integral part of the political constellations of the post-war period. The coincidence of social democratic reforms and the women's liberation movement of the 1960's generated major contradictions and a new agenda for women. The results of such conflict were the development of a sustained critique of the purposes and shape of social policy and practice as well as an ambivalence towards the role of the state in promoting female rights. Such feminist criticism was further strengthened by its interaction with anti-racist and socialist analyses of state action in this period.

The aims of the post-war settlement were to promote not merely economic growth and ideally full employment, but also to try to ensure that all benefited in some way from that prosperity. Promises were made to use schooling to encourage the full development of an individual's abilities and talents and to ensure genuine equality of opportunity (Finch, 1984). The education system was therefore to be used as a major vehicle for social engineering. On the one hand, the welfare state could try to meet individual needs, particularly those of the social disadvantaged and, on the other, it could try to alleviate various social problems within the existing social and economic framework. The objective was not the transformation of social inequalities or power relations within society, it was essentially about the redistribution of resources within it.

With such an agenda, it was not surprising that doubts were consistently and frequently expressed about the strength of political commitment of politicians, and particularly of educational policy makers, to promote social equality. The version of social equality being used emphasized equality of access rather than equality of outcome - a much weaker version therefore than some would wish. In the liberal democratic state, open access would ensure that those with merit would succeed in a competitive environment, whilst compensatory programmes might help others to overcome the effects of their disadvantaged social origins (Arnot, 1991).

Contained within the 1944 Education Act, with its promise of education for all, were the possibilities of women's liberation from their domestic destinies even if little was done actively to ensure that this goal was fulfilled (Burton & Weiner, 1990). Ironically it was precisely the ensuing expansion of education which "hurtled a generation (of women) beyond the confines of their mothers' world into the male sphere of public affairs and work", only to result in their discovering that no provisions had been made to care for their children (Rowbotham, 1986, p. 85). The liberalism which framed social policy remained firmly committed to the division between public and private, domestic spheres. Also traditional and unequal gender relations within the family were to be supported rather than challenged by the provisions of the welfare state (Pascall, 1986; Williams, 1989).

It is not surprising therefore to find current re-evaluations of social democracy in the post-war period highly critical of the stance adopted by central government on women's issues. In her wonderfully entitled book, *Only Halfway to Paradise*, Elizabeth Wilson (1980), a leading socialist feminist argues that between 1945 and the late 1960's, women's oppression was not only invisible but women had been silenced by the ideology of equality of opportunity. Thus,

> *Feminism had an underground or Sleeping Beauty existence in a society which claimed to have wiped out that oppression. The assertion that women had 'equality in difference' and then that women had choice, repressed but did not resolve the conflicts surrounding the position of women. (p. 187)*

By the late 1960's such tensions between women's position in the home and in the labour force were to surface and explode in the second wave of the women's liberation movement which found expression in a variety of spheres. As Rowbotham (1986) comments, the project became one of extending the definitions of political or economic democracy to,

> *...include domestic inequality, identity, control over sexuality, challenge to cultural representation, community control over state welfare and more equal access to public resources'. (p. 86)*

Rowbotham's retrospective analysis of the 1960's shows how the women's movement drew upon the insights of the American new left and the civil rights, black power, and student movements. The idea that the 'personal is political' drove the concept of democracy deep into the personal relations of everyday life, especially in relation to sexuality and morality, and the concept of equal rights was exchanged for a demand for 'equality of power'.

Feminist struggles within education were part of this movement and the range of perspectives found within feminist educational thinking and practice have much in common with the political philosophies which shaped the women's movement since the 1960's (Eisenstein, 1984). Indeed in recent years it has become common practice to identify the various tendencies of liberal feminism, radical, socialist and black feminism in educational analysis (Middleton, 1987; Acker 1987; Arnot & Weiner, 1987). Lesbian feminism, more developed in the United States, has had a twilight existence in the context of British educational work (see recent contributions in Jones & Mahony, 1989), especially since sexuality has been such a studiously avoided aspect of school life (c.f. Chapter 2, Kelly).

Yet despite such similarities, there are also key differences between feminist educational work and that which pertains to mainstream feminist political or sociological theory. The material location of academics and teachers as employees of the state education system has also had an impact on the evolution of feminist educational thought. Teachers and academics were partly responsible for the framing of the post-war settlement and for its maintenance. The selection and organisation of school curricula were a case in point, left as they were predominantly in the hands of a relatively autonomous education profession rather than central government.

It is not surprising therefore to find that the principles of social democracy, not merely those of the women's movement, informed feminist educational theory and practice. Even when, by the 1980's, feminist and sociological analysis became more sophisticated, attempting to identify diverse female needs within education and to remove the more subtle obstacles to individual advancement, one can still find a strong commitment to the tenets of individualism, teacher autonomy and the use education as the means of social reform (e.g. Acker & Warren Piper, 1984; Thompson, 1983; Whyte, 1986).

Yet the support which educational policy makers in the post war period gave to the division between public and private spheres, between family and employment was always likely to cause major difficulties for feminist educational research. Early analyses of the official ideology for girls' education contained within, for example, the Crowther (1959), Newsom (1963) and Plowden (1967) reports often assumed a homogeneity of female interests particularly in relation to their domesticity (Wolpe, 1976), and revealed the androcentric bias in their concept of vocationalism, meritocracy and access to higher education. The CCCS (1981) confirmed that not only was there no evidence of 'discomfort' about gender issues in these reports but the 'political arithmetic' of social democracy had failed even to 'count in' women. Similarly, Wickham (1987) showed how state training policy, particularly in relation to skilled occupations, had been designed by men and for men.

Such government approaches to women's education and training set an agenda for the development of female educational studies. The initial concern quite naturally was to make women's education visible to policy-makers and to analyse, especially in the first instance, ways in which female pupils and students might be prevented from developing their full potential and from participating in the full range of educational and training opportunities (e.g. Bryne, 1978; Delamont, 1980).

Increasingly however feminist critiques of social democracy bit deeper and deeper, challenging the liberal philosophy at the heart of educational policy and the specific sets of relations constructed within the liberal democratic state and its institutional arrangements. This more radical thrust to analyses of gender and education in the late 1970's and early 1980's, can be summarised in terms of four themes:

The Reproduction of Public and Private Spheres

As Pascall (1986, p. 103) notes,

> *educational institutions stand at the junction of private and public worlds, mediating between the family and paid employment...There is thus an ambiguity at the heart of girls' education.*

Evidence for the continued existence of the low status of female occupations, the ghettoization of female workers into a narrow range of jobs and training routes, the persistence of women's low paid, part-time employment and lack of promotion prospects (Holland, 1981) was taken as an implicit, if not explicit, starting point for those concerned with contemporary forms of gender differentiation in education. Research focussed therefore on discrimination in curriculum provision, option choice mechanisms, the ideological content of school texts and the channelling of female and male pupils into particular curricular and, hence, occupational routes (e.g. Deem, 1980; Whyld, 1983).

The fact that 'schooling faces two ways' (CCCS, 1981) was also of key importance to feminists, particularly after the so-called domestic labour debate of the 1960's and 1970's highlighted the relationship between capitalism and the family. That women's political and economic destinies were so closely tied in with their position in the domestic sphere and its patriarchal relations was evident from the historical shaping of the schoolgirls' curriculum (see for example Dyhouse, 1978; Purvis, 1987). Feminist sociologists revealed the continuity of that tradition and identified the ways in which the contemporary school curriculum continued to reproduce 'female domestic ideology' within and across class boundaries.

Patterns of gender differentiation and hierarchy found in school provision were interpreted as key to the continuing 'reproduction' of patriarchal relations in the family and employment (e.g. Wolpe, 1977); MacDonald, 1980). Women were being prepared, albeit often indirectly for a range of low status economic positions within the dual labour market, for unpaid domestic labour and for membership of a reserve army of labour. Ideologically girls of different social classes were being subjected (often in different and somewhat contradictory ways) to an education which was as oppressive as it was exploitative.

By the 1980's, this analysis was both criticised and developed by black feminist researchers. Carby (1982), Bryan et al (1985), Phoenix (1987) and Amos & Parmar (1987) amongst others, focussed attention on the ideological impact of imperialism and of institutional racism - seen particularly in the racial segregation of the labour market and the historical shaping of the structure and culture of black families. They drew attention to the need to integrate into the analysis of private and public spheres the impact of racial, not just class and gendered discourses and divisions.

The illusions both of the neutrality of school knowledge and of schools' ability to deliver equality of opportunity to different groups of girls through a liberal education were seriously challenged by such research. Female education in a different way from that of male education was repeatedly shown to lend support to a patriarchal and racially and class divided society. According to Whitty (1985), such research succeeded in contesting the view that class relations were of primary and indeed sole importance in shaping educational provision. Further it 'helped to make the cruder forms of neo-Marxist theory inadequate to an understanding of contemporary social relations' (p. 55).

Gender Relations and the Organisation of Schooling

Whilst the official ideology of female education and curriculum policy was challenged by such research, feminist sociological analyses of the organisational features of schooling raised serious doubts about the coeducational and comprehensive principles which had shaped educational planning since the 1960's. Feminists had been alerted to the dangers of co-education by R.R. Dale's (1969; 1971; 1974) assessment of the value of single sex and mixed schools. His findings focussed on the academic advantages for boys of co-education and only identified social advantages for girls in the creation of a 'healthy' heterosexual environment in which both sexes played different but complementary roles. Further the HMI (DES, 1975) report on curriculum differentiation in primary education and in the tripartite system of secondary schools suggested that gender differences were being promoted, if not as a positive goal, then as a matter of convention. Research evidence on the curriculum and organisation of the newly introduced mixed comprehensive schools also revealed that such gender patterning was being reinforced rather than challenged (Arnot, 1983).

In the late 1970's and early 1980's, numerous small scale research projects on girls' experiences, taken together, constituted a substantial critique of school organisation within comprehensive secondary schools. Although research on gender interaction in classrooms, teaching styles, modes of assessment and teachers' expectations rarely referred to educational policy as such, it could be said to represent a form of policy evaluation (for overviews of this research see Deem, 1980; Weiner & Arnot, 1987a). It challenged the principle of universalism and asked if indeed girls were receiving the same education as boys. It challenged the principle of comprehensivisation in documenting the continued inequalities between male and female education.

Increasingly too gender relations in education were being subjected to more sustained and detailed inquiry. The diversity of gender cultures found in schools was demonstrated in studies of, for example, different types of primary schools (Clarricoates, 1978), private and state secondary schools (Connell et al, 1982), and the experiences of different ethnic groups (e.g. Brah & Minhas, 1985). Sociological and feminist research on gender in school offered fascinating insights into the hidden organisation of educational experiences; for example, at the age of four, male pupils were locked in sexual power struggles with female teachers, having already learned to use the language of sexual abuse (Walkerdine, 1987); within secondary classrooms, male and female pupils of different ethnic groups were united in experiencing hostile racist confrontations with teachers (Wright, 1987); in different subjects male and female students were active participants in the 'feminisation' or 'masculinisation' of both their own identities and educational knowledge (Kelly, 1985).

In light of such evidence, Middleton (1990) argues that the principles of liberal education, with its stress on the rationally autonomous individual, appear to have benefited male pupils more than female pupils, despite the successful performance of some girls in formal school leaving certificates at 16. It was precisely in the spaces created by concepts of such as freedom of choice, teacher autonomy and child centred education that sexism was repeatedly found unchallenged and often thought 'natural' (Arnot, 1991). Feminist research had begun to challenge many dearly held assumptions. For example, it challenged the view that progressive child-centred education would extend girls' development in their early years and that coeducation would make comprehensive secondary schools beneficial to girls. Similarly teachers' policy of 'non- intervention' in gendered practices and relations (documented in classrooms in infant schools, secondary and further education by, for example, Walkerdine, 1987, and Stanworth, 1983) were also being held in question by such feminist analysis.

The effect of social democratic reforms on girls' education had been shown to be uneven. On the one hand, many girls particularly from the middle classes had benefited academically from the opportunities provided by the introduction of comprehensive schools, the raising of the school leaving age and the expansion of tertiary education. On the other hand, traditional female course choices and the low proportion of working class and black female students achieving the necessary qualifications for entry to further and higher education, raised serious doubts about the long term effects of girls' school experiences on their self esteem, their ambitions and their prospects. The whole organisation of schooling (from staffing patterns to classroom interaction) had been rendered deeply problematic.

Gender and the Concept of Power

Theories of power in the sociology of education are located at the centre of critiques of social democratic education policy. The relations between capital and labour provided the guiding theme for radical critiques of liberal education in the late 1970's (Bowles & Gintis, 1978; Bourdieu & Passeron, 1977; Apple, 1982; Giroux, 1983). Following on the work of Willis (1977), sociologists have also sought to identify class struggles not just over education but within it - struggles which were often based in the various forms of cultural resistance of working class, especially male youth. The Centre for Contemporary Cultural Studies (1981) has used such theoretical frameworks to develop a critique of social democracy and the educational policies it generated in the post-war period.

Socialist feminist research has participated in these theoretical debates and policy analyses especially by offering ethnographic studies of working class and black girls' particular responses to schooling (e.g. Anyon, 1983; Griffin, 1985). This research challenged Willis' analysis - his celebration and romanticisation of white working class male culture despite its explicit racism and sexism (McRobbie, 1978, 1980). The social relations of schooling, and in particular the 'correspondence principle' have now been shown to be gendered relations (Valli, 1986).

Perhaps the most critical analyses of power relations in schooling has been the analysis of sexual relations. Here the dominance of heterosexuality has been found for example in the school curriculum, especially topics dealing directly with personal relations, and in the treatment of lesbian and gay pupils and staff (see Chapter 2 by Liz Kelly). Research on gender dynamics in schools suggests that male dominance has considerable impact on girls. The language of sexual abuse, physical harassment and the male colonisation of the space of the school (Mahony, 1985; Jones & Mahony, 1989) shape girls' negotiation of the academic ethos of the school as well as their confidence in their own abilities. Their experiences at school affect their entry not just into the labour market, but also into the marriage and sexual markets (Griffin, 1985).

The identification of these sets of social relations and of female pupils' and teachers' struggles within education revealed the hegemonic role of state schools in sustaining patriarchal as well as race and class structures. By the 1980's such research, although diverse and even at times contradictory, had demonstrated that at the very least no simple concept of equality of opportunity, especially one based upon freedom of choice, could be effective as means of transforming this web of power relations within schooling.

Gender Politics and the 'Partnership'

Feminist analysis of educational policy making has drawn on the direct experience of teachers and academics working within a range of contexts. (Whyte et al, 1985). Teachers, advisers, researchers and lecturers have written about their experiences of setting up equal opportunities/sex equality policies and initiatives. Their analyses have focussed, for example, on the strengths and weaknesses of 'bottom up' or the 'top down' approaches to promoting educational reform, on the difficulties of deciding between strategies of coercion versus consent and on the marginalisation of women's concerns.

Other collective projects such as those of action research and teacher research attempted to break down the hierarchies between academics and researchers and between teachers and taught, in the name of social justice (cf Weiner, 1989b; Weiner & Arnot, 1987). The lessons learnt through such projects revealed the possibilities and limits of democratic educational reform within the existing social structure.

Pluralism, a guiding thread within liberal democracy has also been challenged by feminist research and practice. From a feminist perspective the process involved in educational policy-making is seen as less the result of democratic and consensual politics and more the result of the exercise of male power. It is not surprising therefore if so much concern has been expressed about the extent of female representation in, participation in, and implementation of, educational decisions. Increasingly feminist researchers have revealed the ways in which knowledge, whether contained in educational policy documents or in the school curriculum, has been shaped by (white) men, and often in male interests.

Feminist research has also focussed attention on the experiences of female teachers as the majority of the teaching profession. The relations between teachers and the state within social democracy has been shown to have been affected by the feminization of the teaching profession. Further the debate about teacher professionalism, the proletarianisation of teachers is now no longer possible without some recognition of the politics of gender (e.g. Lawn & Grace, 1987; Acker, 1989). Promoting change therefore within the alleged 'partnership' between central and local government and teachers in the post war period has therefore been shown to be circumscribed by patriarchal relations in education.

Feminist Critiques of the New Right and Educational Reform

Despite the consistent growth throughout the 1980's of feminist research, any initial unity seemed to have been lost by the end of the decade. In the context of the sociology of gender, Connell (1987) argued that:,

It is difficult to think of any other field of the social sciences where work as penetrating and original has been going on. Yet as the social theory of gender has blossomed, the difference between lines of thought have become more distinct, the conceptual and political distances greater. Current theories of gender are not converging. Rather they present incompatible accounts of the issued by marking off separate parts of the field. (p. 38)

The existence of different feminist approaches might appear challenging, suggesting that the time was ripe for a sustained theoretical debate on gender. For feminists, however, the disarray and fragmentation and 'miserable welter of conflict' in the women's movement was deeply depressing, particularly in relation to the emergence of Thatcherism (Loach, 1987).

Such divisions had begun to reveal themselves in feminist and sociological research on women's education, and amongst feminist teachers. Increasingly radical 'egalitarian' approaches had drawn apart from liberal perspectives with the former more closely associated with the politics of municipal socialism and women's campaigns for sex equality, rather than mainstream equal rights initiatives promoted by central government agencies - for example the Women into Science and Engineering Year organised by the Women's National Commission and the EOC (see Weiner & Arnot 1987; Arnot 1991).

There was also conflict within the 'egalitarian' movement between radical and socialist feminism on the one hand, and between increasingly sectarian groups within the Left, on the other. This made it difficult in effect to identify the communality of women's experiences across the divisions of class, race, sexuality and disability - and therefore even more difficult to frame a unified political constituency. Implicit in many of discussions on gender was the assumption that there were 'hierarchies of oppression'. 'Identity politics' or what Parmar (1989) called the 'politics of difference' limited the ability of feminists to frame a coherent political strategy. In the educational world, feminist analyses, whether radical or liberal, were increasingly being identified as white, middle class and heterosexual in orientation (e.g. Carby, 1982; Brah, 1988; Phoenix, 1987; Connell, 1987).

Ideological disarray in feminist educational thought therefore cannot be solely attributed to Conservative government policy especially since the initial impact of Thatcherism was felt more in the context of economic and family policy - rather than in education policy (Pascall, 1986; Williams, 1989). The recession and cuts in local government budgets had affected women, particularly their post-school opportunities (Deem, 1981; David, 1983a & b). However, schools had still retained a reasonable level of autonomy over the curriculum and local authorities still had sufficient finance to invest, if the political will was there, in equality initiatives. If anything the early 1980's was a time of relative excitement and possibility for those committed to sex equality. Local government, particularly in Labour controlled metropolitan authorities, as well as teacher unions were being used as a means of fighting sex and race discrimination but also as sites of political opposition to the Conservative Government (Arnot, 1991).

Even though such egalitarian approaches and campaigning were unlikely to have any major impact on the state education system as a whole (Dale & Foster, 1986), it would be naive to imagine that they would have no political impact. Such developments were to be regarded, along with comparable projects in the area of 'race', as subversive by a central government influenced by the radical right (Klein, 1989; Davies et al, 1990).

Patriarchal structures, especially heterosexual monogamous marriage as the stable institutional form, had been threatened by the egalitarianism and the libertarianism in the women's movement. Feminist campaigns for increasing state intervention especially into family life and personal liberty had threatened the distinctions between public and private worlds sustained by a liberal democratic state. Patriarchy not just the capitalist economy was already in crisis (ten Tusscher, 1986; Eisenstein, 1987).

It was not surprising therefore if feminist demands for equality were seen by members of the New Right as 'ideological extravagances' and as part of the 'forces in contemporary society which are deeply inimical' to the family (Centre for Policy Studies, quoted in Campbell, 1987, p. 170). Demands for sex equality were blamed especially for the rise in the divorce rate and single parenthood.

In retrospect, it seems extraordinary how little concern was shown in feminist education writing about the build up of this Conservative opposition. However two factors might explain such seeming lack of interest. Firstly, the legacy of social democracy as the main target of sociology of education proved hard to break in all aspects of the discipline. Secondly in contrast with Reagan's government in the United States which supported an aggressive Moral Right political movement (Dworkin, 1983), the first Thatcher Government made few explicit 'anti-feminist' statements. It did not directly attack the women's movement, repeal the anti-discrimination legislation or shut down the Equal Opportunities Commission or Commission for Racial Equality as some expected it would (David, 1983a). Initially Thatcher's government remained 'officially neutral' on issues such as abortion, divorce and homosexual rights (Segal, 1983).

David (1983a & b, 1985), Segal (1983) revealed the more subtle forms of anti-feminism used by the Thatcher's government in its first period of office. The initial implications of Thatcherism could apparently be found in family ideology and policy which emphasised 'Victorian values' , in particular the bourgeois family form of the male wage earner and the dependent wife and mother. The much quoted outburst of Patrick Jenkin in 1979 (later to be Social Services Minister), that "If the Good Lord had intended us to have equal rights to go out to work, he wouldn't have created men and women" (quoted in Gardiner, 1983, p. 195), was put a little more delicately but no less conservatively by an Institute of Economic Affairs report (1986) when it commented: "men will expect to specialise in market work and women will expect to specialise in household work" (quoted in Williams, 1989, p. 120).

The assumption underlying the notion that a 'woman's place is in the home' was that biological and natural instincts determined both the sexual division of labour within the family and the separation between the private and public spheres. The family for Roger Scruton, a leading neo-conservative educationalist, was therefore a 'natural form' :

> the family...is a small social unit which shares with civil society the singular quality of being non-contractual, of arising (both for the children and the parents) not out of choice but out of natural necessity. (quoted in Williams, 1989, p. 119).

It is generally recognised that the family occupied a privileged place in New Right ideology. However, the sheer range of functions the family should perform within contemporary society revealed more about the attempts of the Conservative party to hold together various tendencies within its own organisation, than any deep understanding about the actual shifts in contemporary family life (David, 1983a; Campbell 1987). On the one hand, the family was responsible for the 'defence of the individual against socialism and excessive state power'; on the other hand, it was the basis of private property and the location of the consumer responsible for the management of his/her financial affairs. Then again, the family was the 'centre of affections', 'the transmitter of traditions' and the necessary condition of authority. Such functions transcended all allegiances of class, indeed of history itself (Campbell, 1987).

In the context of this vision of family life, the concept of parenthood, actively promoted by the Black Papers (quoted in CCCS, 1981) in their discussion of education reform, became the symbol of not just the economic values of consumerism. Parenthood represented, for neo-conservatives such as Scruton, the political and moral values of hierarchy, authority and loyalty (Williams, 1989).

Because of this role as guardian of social stability within an aggressively competitive economy, family life, it seemed, had to be supported by the state. Paradoxically, "the family had to be maximised in order to minimise the state". By rehabilitating the family, arguably the government could break down the 'scrounger welfare state' and through a 'moral crusade' counter the effects of permissiveness that grew out of the 1960's (Campbell, 1987, p. 166).

Such family ideology, incoherent as it seems, has been interpreted by feminists as a significant attack on women's position in the employment sector and in the family. This was hardly surprising given that cuts in state welfare provision made it more likely that women would be left to cater for young children, the aged, the mentally ill and the unemployed members of the household. If this dismantling of the welfare state assumed rather than asserted the need for women to remain at home, educational policies focussing around the values of a patriarchal family life were given the responsibility of actively promoting traditional sexual divisions. Early statements by Conservative politicians suggested that all children would be encouraged to receive an education in moral values and in parental responsibilities (David, 1983a & b) - thus girls would be prepared for their role as wives, mothers and carers and boys would learn the role of head of household and main wage earner.

Fears were expressed that this rekindled interest in moral education was the thin edge of the wedge. It represented the first attempts "to rescind equal opportunities policies...and to replace them with specific policies which promote sex difference" (David, 1983b). Added to other attacks on women's rights particularly in terms of sexuality and employment, this educational approach was interpreted as an effort to restore patriarchal values.

According to ten Tusscher (1986), the New Right's concern to link monetarism and moralism therefore was an attempt to tackle the dual crises of the capitalist economy and patriarchy and reunite their interests.

> *Thus Thatcherism and the New Right managed to occupy the vacuum created by the breakdown of social democracy combined with the opening stemming from the perceived threat to patriarchy. This determined the nature of the New Right. It embraced the twin goals of restoring class forces in favour of capital and of restoring gender relations in favour of men. (ten Tusscher, 1986, p. 76)*

Yet the patriarchal ideology of the New Right, when applied to policy, was not unproblematic. It generated considerable contradictions, especially in relation to women (Gardiner, 1983; Segal, 1983; Campbell, 1987; Wilson, 1987) and was also not that effective. On the one hand, the impact of the women's movement in the country - even if disorganised, had changed public opinion sufficiently to be able to curtail the extent to which the New Right could promote traditional values, particularly surrounding women's domesticity. Segal (1983) argues that the Conservative government was held back by the "continual vigour and success of feminism in mobilising support for women's rights and equality". Changes in women's employment since the Second World War had encouraged middle class career women, some of whom could be found as female Conservative party members fighting against any simple equation between women and motherhood, excessive moralising, restrictions of sexual freedom or even cut backs on child benefits (Campbell, 1987).

In the event despite harsh social policies, women did not go back en masse to their homes, instead they continued to carry the dual burden of being wives and workers (Wilson, 1987). The early educational initiatives were also less than successful. Curricular reforms encouraging traditional parenting roles were hard to implement within a decentralised system. Education for parenthood and sex education were unlikely vehicles for such a 'moral crusade' since these courses were not mandatory. As Wolpe (1987, p. 45) observed:

> *The implications of a third term of Thatcherism in the field of sex education are not straight forward...Moral values are seen to have declined and there are moves to combat this...What is not clear is whether the way to combat*

this will be through the provision of sex education, given the opposition to its inclusion in the school curriculum in some quarters.

Ironically new legislation had made sex education the responsibility of school governing bodies who could choose to remove such a controversial topic. Courses on family living were also likely to be optional and have the low status ascribed to non-examined subjects. Far more significant to this programme of moral 'clean up' was the legislation against 'promoting homosexuality' through section 28 (see Liz Kelly, Chapter 2), although here again the impact on schools nationally was not likely to be great since so few local authorities had developed policies on sexuality.

Rethinking Women's Rights

If the 'moral crusade' was not easily promoted, the ambiguities in the Conservative party about women's position were also not easily resolved. It has become increasingly clear from recent feminist analyses that despite its emphasis upon traditional family structures, the Conservative Government still wished to be seen as committed at least in rhetoric to a version of equality of opportunity and equal rights. Conservative women themselves sustained notions of themselves as equal to men 'in the sight of God' (Campbell, 1987). Neo-liberals in particular encouraged the notion of individual liberty, particularly economic freedom in the market place and political freedom from coercion and excessive state control. Hayek and Friedman, often quoted as leading theorists of monetarism, saw such freedom being provided by an autonomous and private family unit (equated with women's role) and being found within the public sphere (equated with male activity). The assumption of such gender differences led feminist critics to conclude that logically 'the promise of liberty can only apply to men'. Individualism, property ownership, consumerism were men-only concepts (Segal, 1983, p. 119) even if as Ferdinand Mount, right-wing author of *The Subversive Family* (1982) argued "women's rights to equality are unassailable because women are human beings" (quoted in Williams, 1989, p. 119).

The solution to this contradiction could not necessarily be found by expelling women from the market place especially since capital still required female waged labour. Instead the notion of competitive individualism could be selectively applied to men and women who had no family responsibilities (David, 1983) or alternatively to women who had already fulfilled one of their roles, as home makers, and could now play a role as paid workers. Indeed as Mrs Thatcher herself argued in 1982,

It is of course true that women of our generation are often still comparatively young by the time our children are grown up and therefore we have an opportunity further to develop our own talents...For many that experience can enhance their lives and enlarge their interests. (quoted in Wilson, 1987, p. 295)

55

Such statements from Mrs Thatcher represent for Wilson (1987) an insight into the ways in which the Conservative government sought to represent itself as 'the modern party' -

the party that welcomes and harnesses change and is committed to an attack on the 'old fashioned' dogmas of trades unions and an assortment of blinkered ideologues - Fabians, Marxists, feminists and the like - whose time is past and who have got fatally out of step with the world we live in. (Wilson, 1987, p. 205)

Such 'modernising tendencies' within Conservative party policy were also to find somewhat confused expression within the various education reforms of the 1980's. Cuts in state funds (particularly in adult education, in subjects such as the arts and humanities, in discretionary grants for further education) threatened the educational and training opportunities for women (Deem, 1981). Also the failure to fund pre-school education or reduce it even further in some localities would restrict considerably the chances of married women to fulfil that 'second role' as paid workers in anything other than part time and low paid employment. The DES under Thatcher's Government also continued its largely indifferent stance to issues of sex equality , even though the HMI were able to offer explicit but not very strong support to those concerned about female educational experiences and achievement (Acker, 1986; Orr, 1985). Political complacency and inadequate support for gender issues in education seemed to be the main criticisms made by feminists when analysing central government policy in the 1980's (Arnot, 1987).

Strangely enough the concept of equal rights in Conservative Party thinking emerged most obviously in relation to the so-called 'new vocationalism' which attempted to restructure and 'modernise' the economy through direct state intervention. Initially critics argued that "the new vocationalism signals the abandonment of equal opportunity as a central reference point of educational strategy" (Finn, 1985, quoted in Weiner, 1989b). However, this analysis took little to no account of the possibilities within the Conservative educational programme of 'modernising' gender relations and the female work force.

The Manpower Services Commission (now known as the Training Agency) in contrast with the DES appeared to take more interest in equal opportunities issues. Although it largely ignored the extent of gender differentiation in its youth training schemes and as a result, had dismally failed to break down sexual divisions (Fawcett Society, 1985; Wickham, 1987), the attempt to ensure that all Technical and Vocational Educational Initiatives (TVEI) in secondary schools tackled equal opportunities between the sexes could be interpreted as a significant attempt to 'reshape' gender relations in education.

The promotion of equal opportunities within such vocational initiatives, according to Weiner (1989a) had economic as well as political benefits, especially in relation to the needs of the capitalist economy for a 'free (that is unsegmented) labour market' and 'a flexible work force, undifferentiated by sex'. In other words,

> *liberal/progressive ideas concerning freedom for girls and women to move upwards in educational and occupational hierarchies have become synonymous with 'liberal', 'laissez faire' ideas about labour market freedom. (Weiner, 1989, p. 121)*

Ironically the funding criteria which made it compulsory that all TVEI projects promote equal opportunities came to represent one of their most progressive aspects, even though help and support from the MSC/Training Agency was thin on the ground. A full evaluation of the strategies adopted by TVEI to promote equal opportunities was even commissioned and published (Bridgwood & Betteridge, 1989). In practice, the experience gained by schools suggested that equal opportunities could not be based on principles of individualism and free choice. Increasingly schools were developing their own form of a common compulsory curriculum: they were also pushed into challenging (although slowly at first) the gendered nature of school knowledge, the naming of subjects and the occupational associations of particular courses (Millman & Weiner, 1987).

This experience, together with a long history of calls from the Left and from feminists such as Byrne (1985) for a common curriculum to tackle social inequality perhaps prepared the ground for a muted response to the introduction of the National Curriculum. But also, ideological disunity and the lack of consistent committed political support (Loach, 1987) and perhaps an over-emphasis on personal politics (Rowbotham, 1986) could have weakened feminist campaigns. In the event, despite years of academic research and policy development in schools and colleges, feminist opposition to the Education Reform Act was neither public nor organised. When responses to the Education Reform Bill (GERBIL) were collected, the voices of women were not heard (Haviland 1989). Apart from within those organisations in which women had struggled successfully (e.g. NUT, NATE), feminist educational concerns ironically were represented by the Equal Opportunities Commission (already becoming increasingly partisan in its appointments).

The absence of a coherent feminist response either by sociologists or by women's education groups and networks may perhaps also be explained by the confusion over the likely effects of the legislation. The impact of a combination of centralised control of the curriculum and a blatant lack of concern with the form of pedagogy (other than formal assessment) was not immediately obvious. Early commentators (Kant, 1987; Myers, 1989; Arnot, 1989a) interpreted the legislation as yet another instance of 'missed opportunities' to tackle sex discrimination in education rather than a case of virulent anti-feminism. Having said that, clearly feminists were aware that the list of subjects to be included in the National Curriculum, based on a traditionally 'male' grammar school curriculum, provided early evidence of an androcentric structure. Whilst girls could benefit from the compulsory science and technology, many of them were likely to choose the least intensive or more traditionally 'feminine' options within these subjects; girls' schools were also threatened by lack of sufficient resources especially for technology.

National curriculum planning could theoretically challenge male biases in subject content. Yet as evidence emerged of the low level of female representation on subject working groups, the lack of reference to gender research, no consultation with women's groups and derisory reporting on the issue by the National Curriculum Council (Arnot, 1989; Davies et al, 1990; Weiner, 1990), it became clear that masculinist and racial biases within most subjects were not going to be challenged officially. Indeed working groups have not, to date, taken a major stand on promoting anti-sexist or anti-racist curricula content - arguably subject content and pedagogy has regressed to outmoded styles, reasserting male centred forms of knowledge (Burton & Weiner, 1990).

The ideological significance of the National Curriculum in terms of gender therefore is somewhat unclear. If this centralised control of the curriculum represented a victory of the neo-conservatives, then why were precisely those courses closest to parental education (i.e. child care and domestic science) demoted to the margins of the curriculum? The downgrading of these 'female' domestic courses could be seen either as fortuitous for girls, releasing them from domestic ideologies or alternatively as a signal of the Conservative government's lack of concern for the subjects in which girls achieve. Certainly it is not clear that family values have shaped the selection of subjects nor indeed that subject working groups were actively encouraged to find ways of valuing family life, in anything like the same way as they were pressured to celebrate English history and nationhood (Jenkinson, 1990). Apart from failing to refer to anti-sexist or anti-racist education, the National Curriculum supposedly leaves schools with the duty to choose their own pedagogy, and to find ways of 'promoting equal opportunities' .

Such ideological tensions within the government concerning equal opportunities can also be glimpsed in the approach adopted by the National Curriculum Council. Equal opportunities, for example, was listed as only one of two cross curriculum dimensions for schools to develop as part of the whole curriculum. At the same time, its chief executive Duncan Graham indicated that gender was too 'delicate' an issue to merit a task group, and therefore the production of specific non-statutory guidance for schools. This approach, coupled with the fact that there was no official commitment to monitor sex bias in assessment, to train governors in sex discrimination legislation nor to encourage the teaching profession to improve its expectations of female pupils or reassess teaching styles was unlikely to win support from those committed to sex equality.

In effect centralised intervention appears to have reinforced male control of education policy making and to have delegated the issue of sex equality to teachers to implement (Arnot, 1989b). Whilst at first glance this may seem beneficial, the evidence provided by sociological research on teachers' attitudes to gender difference suggest that although there is likely to be considerable rhetoric about the importance of equal opportunities policies, in practice little will be put into effect. In other words, the rump of teacher autonomy still allowed within the new educational system may well serve to marginalise gender issues and to sustain continued discriminatory behaviour.

Conclusions

The effects of the Education Reform Act on women have yet to be evaluated. Current sociological understandings of the policy intentions and expected outcomes of the Education Reform Act and the National Curriculum have tended to ignore the significance of the gender dimension, preferring to focus predominantly on the relationship between schooling, the state, ideology and the economy (e.g. Whitty, 1990; Ball, 1990). These accounts sit well within the tradition of the British Left who have failed to "understand the nature of the New Right through their gender blind analysis" (ten Tusscher, 1986). They have failed to consider whether the New Right in the United Kingdom had any similarity with the emergence of the New Right in the United States. This latter movement, as Andrea Dworkin (1978) found in her influential study was a "social and political movement controlled almost totally by men and as such it was fundamentally anti-feminist in stance".

The gender analysis offered here demonstrates, I hope, that the context for the emergence and success of the New Right was not just a 'crisis in capitalism'. Feminism, along with anti-racism, had thrown liberalism itself into crisis. As Eisenstein (1987) put it, in the context of the United States'

> *Feminism has uncovered the truth that capitalist patriarchal society cannot deliver on its liberal promises of equality or even equal rights without destabilising itself. (p. 239)*

This challenge was particularly true in education where feminist educationalists and researchers were shattering the illusions of the social democratic project. Many of the fundamental beliefs in equality of opportunity, universalism, coeducation, comprehensivisation and progressive teaching styles had been challenged by gender research. Further, the more that power relations in education were being exposed, the greater the demands for gender, class and race equality and the more outspoken the calls for increased state intervention to limit liberal so-called 'freedoms' and to help restructure domestic relations in the name of social equality (Arnot, 1991).

Thatcherism, if it existed at all as a coherent political philosophy, was not synonymous with the moral right nor indeed with pure neo-liberalism. It attempted to respond to the interests of capital and patriarchy and also the threat to British nationhood. However, as far as women were concerned, since Thatcherism reasserted a form of competitive individualism and attempted to reinforce sexual divisions within and between public/private domains, it did not represent, as Hall (1988) argued, a significant break from social democratic thought.

In the event, the strength of the women's movement in shaping public opinion over the last two decades restricted the options available to the New Right to respond to such crises. Despite the attempt at a 'moral crusade', there has not been a concerted ideological attack on wage earning women per se. Instead we find an assault on the working classes in an apparent attempt to raise productivity, increase profits and weaken collective organisation, especially trades unions. As Wilson (1987) has shown, the range of strategies adopted by the Conservative government in the 1980's had the effect instead of incorporating women into the labour force but under the worst possible terms - by reducing their protection, raising unemployment rates and failing to establish childcare provision, thus adding to their domestic burdens.

The new vocationalism and modernising influences in education arguably promised women more opportunities to extend their occupational horizons. The National Curriculum at least in its early formulations would make available to girls traditionally male subjects and professional scientific and technological careers. The effects of such reforms however are most likely to be felt by middle class women whose opportunities could be enhanced through consumer choice in education and increased concern about access and training.

Working class women and black and ethnic minority women, in contrast, are likely to find their opportunities even further reduced and their rights to choose their own work patterns restricted by Conservative economic and family policies. It is not difficult to predict that there will be a widening class gap between women. Miles & Middleton (1990, p. 201) for example, observe that, "the Education Reform Act will not be neutral in its effects on different classes and ethnic groups...". Thus,

> We have seen...that this openly inegalitarian government is not averse to equal opportunities measures insofar as these may enlarge the pool of talent from which employers may draw. But highly paid and prestigious jobs are, by definition, within such an order, relatively scarce so that the achievement of parity between the sexes will still leave the inequalities between women (as well as those between men) unimpaired.

The key issue for sociologists should therefore be an investigation of the processes involved in the attentuation of class relations in the context of gender and race. Such analyses would need to draw upon the insights which gender research brings to bear on social democracy, on the nature of the public-private division, on the impact of school organisation and gender dynamics within schools. Research into such themes will also no doubt take into account the new era of centralised control which extends even further male power over educational policy making over a predominantly female teaching force; open enrolment and opting out which raises yet again the question of parental choice of single sex or coeducational schools, particularly in relation to separate schools; and local management of schools which will highlight the priorities of educational managers and affect the development of equality policies. Sociological research which takes account of gender, race and class will provide valuable insights into whether full 'entitlement' is either possible or being achieved by such educational reform.

As far as women's position within the family is concerned, the impact of educational reforms is somewhat different. It is difficult to argue that the attempt to use education to regenerate patriarchal values and thus counter the excesses of the egalitarian movements of the 1970's. has been effectively orchestrated. Instead we find an attempt through centralised control of the curriculum to reassert outmoded educational formats against increasing professional resistance. It seems though that feminist research particularly on the effects of school organisation and patriarchal relations within the educational system have had little to no impact on the architects of the new education system. The forms of control over gender relations within schooling has been left largely intact for the 1990's, embedded however within a new more rigidly classified structure of school knowledge. How this new 'gender code' (MacDonald, 1980) will shape the masculinising and feminising process of schooling in the next generation of children is another important topic for sociological investigation.

Let us hope that Segal (1983, p. 214) was right when she argued that

Thatcherism...has not successfully crushed a feminist consciousness which is aware of the oppression of women's lives as vulnerable and exploited workers and as hopelessly overburdened housewives, mothers and daughters.

Feminist research still has a valuable role to play maintaining that consciousness within the sociology of education, but equally important is the integration of that perspective into mainstream sociological theorising and evaluation of these educational reforms.

REFERENCES

Acker, S. (1987) Feminist theory and the study of gender and education, *International Review of Education*, 33, pp. 419-435.

Acker, S. (Ed)(1989) *Teachers, Gender and Careers*. Lewes: Falmer Press.

Acker, S. & Warren Piper, D.W. (Eds)(1984) *Is Higher Education Fair to Women?* London: SRHE-Nelson.

Amos, V. & Parmar, P. (1987) Resistance and Responses to the Experiences of Black Girls in Britain, in M. Arnot & G. Weiner (Eds) *Gender and the Politics of Schooling*. London: Hutchinson.

Anyon, J. (1983) Intersections of Gender and Class: accommodation and resistance by working class and affluent females to contradictory sex-role ideologies, in S. Walker & L. Barton (Eds) *Gender, Class and Education*. Lewes: Falmer Press.

Apple, M. (1982) *Education and Power*. London: Routledge.

Arnot, M. (1983) A Cloud over Coeducation: an analysis of the forms of transmission of class and gender relations, in S. Walker & L. Barton (Eds) *Gender, Class and Education*. Lewes: Falmer Press.

Arnot, M. (1987) Lip Service or Radical Reform? Central government responses to sex equality issues, in M. Arnot & G. Weiner (Eds) *Gender and the Politics of Schooling*. London: Hutchinson.

Arnot, M. (1989b) Consultation or legitimation? Race and gender politics and the making of the National Curriculum, *Critical Social Policy*, Issue 27, pp. 20-38.

Arnot, M. (1991) Equality and democracy: a decade of struggle over education, *British Journal of Sociology of Education*, 12, pp. 447-466.

Arnot, M. & Weiner, G. (Eds)(1987) *Gender and the Politics of Schooling*. London: Hutchinson.

Ball, S. (1990) *Politics and Policy Making in Education*. London: Routledge.

Bowles, S. & Gintis, H. (1978) *Schooling in Capitalist America*. London: Routledge.

Bourdieu, P & Passeron, J.C. (1977) *Reproduction in Education, Society and Culture*. London: Sage.

Brah, A. (1988) Extended review, *British Journal of Sociology of Education*, 9, pp. 115-120.

Brah, A. & Minhas, R. (1985) Structural Racism or Cultural Difference: schooling for Asian girls, in Weiner, G. (Ed) *Just a Bunch of Girls*. Milton Keynes: Open University Press.

Bridgwood, A. & Betteridge, J. (1989) *Equal Opportunities for Boys and Girls with TVEI*. Windsor: NFER Training Agency.

Bryan, B., Dadzie, S. & Scafe, S. (1985) *The Heart of the Race: black women's lives in Britain*. London: Virago.

Burton, L. & Weiner, G. (1990) Social justice and the National Curriculum, *Research Papers in Education*, 5, pp. 203-227.

Byrne, E. (1978) *Women in Education*. London: Tavistock.

Byrne, E. (1985) Equality or Equity? A European view, in M. Arnot (Ed) *Race and Gender: equal opportunities policies in education*. Oxford: Pergamon Press.

Campbell, B. (1987) *The Iron Ladies*. London: Virago.

Carby, H. (1982) Schooling in Babylon, in CCCS (Eds) *The Empire Strikes Back*. London: Hutchinson.

Centre for Contemporary Cultural Studies (CCCS)(1981) *Unpopular Education: schooling for social democracy in England since 1944*. London: Hutchinson.

Clarricoates, K. (1978) Dinosaurs in the classroom: the hidden curriculum in primary schools, *Women's Studies International Quarterly*, 1, pp. 353-364.

Connell, R.W. (1987) *Gender and Power*. Sydney: Allen & Unwin.

Connell, R.W., Ashenden, D.J., Kessler, S. & Dowsett, G.W. (1982) *Making the Difference: schools, families and social division*. London: Allen & Unwin.

Crowther Report (1959) 15-18 (Central Advisory Council for Education). London: HMSO.

Dale, R.R. (1969, 1971 & 1974) *Mixed or Single Sex School*, Vols I - III London: Routledge.

Dale, J. & Foster, P. (1986) *Feminists and State Welfare*. London: Routledge.

David, M. (1983a) Teaching and preaching sexual morality: the New Right's anti-feminism in Britain and the USA, *Journal of Education*, 166, pp. 63-76.

David, M. (1983b) Sex, Education and Social Policy: new moral economy?, in S. Walker & L. Barton (Eds) *Gender, Class and Education*. Lewes: Falmer Press.

David, M. (1985) Motherhood and social policy - a matter of education, *Critical Social Policy*, 12, Spring, pp. 28-43.

Davies, A.M., Holland, J. & Minhas, R. (1990) *Equal Opportunities in the New Era*. Hillcole Group, Paper 2.

Deem, R. (Ed) (1980) *Schooling for Women's Work*. London: Routledge.

Deem, R. (1981) State policy and ideology in the education of women 1944-1980, *British Journal of Sociology of Education*, 2, pp. 131-144.

Deem, R. (1989) The New School Governing Bodies - are gender and race on the agenda, *Gender and Education*, 1, pp. 247-260.

Delamont, S. (1980) *Sex Roles and the School*. London: Methuen.

DES (1975) *Curricular Differences for Boys and Girls*, Education Survey, 21. London: HMSO.

Dyhouse, C. (1978) Towards a feminine, curriculum for English school girls: the demands of ideology 1870-1963, *Women's Studies International Quarterly*, 1, pp. 291-311.

Dworkin, A. (1983) *Right Wing Women*. London: Women's Press.

Eisenstein, H. (1984) *Contemporary Feminist Thought*. London: Counterpoint Unwin.

Eisenstein, Z. (1987) Liberalism, Feminism and the Reagan State: the neoconservative assault on sexual equality, in R. Miliband, L. Panitch & J. Saville (Eds) *Socialist Register*. London: Merlin Press.

Fawcett Society and the National joint Committee of Working Women's Organisations (1985) *The Class of 84*. London: Fawcett Society.

Finch, J. (1984) *Education and Social Policy*. London: Longman.

Gardiner, J. (1983) Women, Recession and the Tories, in S. Hall & M. Jacques (Eds) *The Politics of Thatcherism*. London: Lawrence & Wishart.

Giroux, H. (1983) *Theory and Resistance in Education: a pedagogy of opposition*. London: Heinemann.

Griffin, C. (1985) *Typical Girls?* London: Routledge.

Haviland, J. (1988) *Take Care Mr. Baker!* London: Fourth Estate.

Holland, J. (1981) *Work and Women*, Bedford Way Papers 6. University of London Institute of Education.

Jenkinson, F. (1990) Multicultural Education and the National Curriculum, unpublished M.Phil dissertation, University of Cambridge.

Jones, C. & Mahony, P. (Eds)(1989) *Learning Our Lines: sexuality and social control in education*. London: Women's Press.

Kant, L. (1987) National Curriculum: nationally equal, *NUT Education Review*, 1 (2), Autumn.

Kelly, A. (1985) The construction of masculine science, *British Journal of Sociology of Education*, 6, pp. 133-154.

Klein, G. (1989) New Right - New ERA, *NUT Education Review*, 3 (2), pp. 14-8.

Lawn. M. & Grace. G. (Eds)(1987) *Teachers: the culture and politics of work*. Lewes: Falmer Press.

Loach, L. (1987) Can feminism survive a third term? *Feminist Review*, 27, pp. 27-36.

MacDonald, M. (1980) Socio-cultural reproduction and women's education, in R. Deem (Ed) *Schooling for Women's Work*. London: Routledge.

Mahony, P. (1985) *Schools for the Boys: coeducation reassessed*. London: Hutchinson.

McRobbie, A. (1978) Working class girls and the culture of femininity, in Centre for Contemporary Cultural Studies Women's Studies Group, *Women Take Issue*. London: Hutchinson.

McRobbie, A. (1980) Setting accounts with subculture: a feminist critique, *Screen Education*, 34, pp. 37-49.

Middleton, S. (1987) The Sociology of Women's Education, in M. Arnot & G. Weiner (Eds) *Gender and the Politics of Schooling*. London: Hutchinson.

Middleton, S. (1990) Women, Equality and Equity in Liberal Educational Policies, 1945-1988, in S. Middleton, J. Codd & A. Jones (Eds) *New Zealand Education Policy Today*. Wellington, New Zealand: Allen & Unwin.

Miles, S. & Middleton, C. (1990) Girls, Education in the Balance, in M. Flude & M. Hammer (Eds) *The Education Reform Act 1988: origins and implications*. Lewes: Falmer Press.

Millman, V. & Weiner, G. (1987) Engineering Equal Opportunities: the case of TVEI, in D. Gleeson (Ed) *A Critical Appraisal of TVEI*. London: Routledge.

Myers, K. (1989) High heels in the market place, *Education*, 16 June.

Newsom Report (1963) *Half Our Future*. Central Advisory Council for Education. London: HMSO.

Parmar, P (1989) Other kinds of dreams, *Feminist Review*, 31, pp. 55-65.

Pascall, G. (1986) *Social Policy: a feminist analysis*. London: Tavistock.

Phoenix, A. (1987) Theories of gender and black families, in G. Weiner & M. Arnot, (Eds) *Gender Under Scrutiny*. London: Hutchinson.

Purvis, J. (1987) Social Class, Education and the Ideals of Femininity in the Nineteenth Century, in M. Arnot & G. Weiner (Eds) *Gender and the Politics of Schooling*. London: Hutchinson.

Rowbotham, S. (1986) Feminism and Democracy, in D. Held & C. Pollitt (Eds) *New Forms of Democracy*. London: Sage.

Segal, L. (1983) The Heat in the Kitchen, in S. Hall & P. Jacques. (Eds) *The Politics of Thatcherism*. London: Lawrence & Wishart.

Stanworth, M. (1981) *Gender and Schooling: a study of sexual divisions*. London: Hutchinson.

ten Tusscher, T. (1986) Patriarchy, Capitalism and the New Right, in J. Evans et al (Eds) *Feminism and Political Theory*. London: Sage.

Thompson, I (1983) *Learning Liberation: women's responses to men's education*. London: Croom Helm.

Walkerdine, V. (1987) Sex, Power and Pedagogy, in M. Arnot & G. Weiner (Eds) *Gender and the Politics of Schooling*. London: Hutchinson.

Weiner, G (1989a) Feminism, equal opportunities and vocationalism: the changing context, in H. Burchell & V. Millman (Eds) *Changing Perspectives on Gender*. Milton Keynes: Open University Press.

Weiner, G. (1989b) Professional self-knowledge versus social justice: a critical analysis of the teacher - research movement, *British Educational Research Journal*, 15, pp. 41-53.

Weiner, G. (1990) The future for social justice in the 1990s, *NUT Education Review*, 4, pp. 56-59.

Weiner, G. & Arnot, M. (Eds)(1987b) Teachers and Gender Politics, in M. Arnot & G. Weiner (Eds) *Gender and the Politics of Schooling*. London: Hutchinson.

Whitty, G. (1985) *Sociology and School Knowledge*. London: Methuen.

Whitty, G. (1990) The New Right and the National Curriculum: state control or market forces, in M. Flude & M. Hammer (Eds) *The Education Reform Act 1988: its origins and implications*. Lewes: Falmer Press.

Whyld, J. (Ed)(1983) *Sexism in the Secondary Curriculum*. London: Harper & Row.

Whyte, J. (1986) *Girls into Science and Technology*. London: Routledge.

Whyte, J. et al (Eds) (1985) *Girl Friendly Schooling*. London: Methuen.

Wickham, A (1987) *Women and Training*. Milton Keynes: Open University Press.

Williams, F. (1989) *Social Policy: a critical introduction*. Cambridge: Polity Press.

Willis, P. (1977) *Learning to Labour*. Farnborough: Saxon House.

Wilson, E. (1980) *Only Halfway to Paradise*. London: Tavistock.

Wilson, E. (1987) Thatcherism and Women: after seven years, in R. Miliband, L. Panitch & J. Saville (Eds) *Socialist Register*. London: Merlin Press.

Wolpe, A.M. (1976) The Official Ideology of Education for Girls, in M. Flude & J. Ahier (Eds) *Educability, Schools and Ideology*. London: Croom Helm.

Wolpe, A.M. (1977) Education and the sexual division of labour, in A. Kuhn & A.M. Wolpe (Eds) *Feminism and Materialism: women and modes of production*. London: Routledge.

Wolpe, A.M. (1987) Sex in schools: back to the future, *Feminist Review*, 27, Autumn, pp. 37-48.

Wright, C. (1987) The Relations between Teacher and Afro-Caribbean Pupils: observing multiracial classrooms, in G. Weiner & M. Arnot (Eds) *Gender Under Scrutiny*. London: Hutchinson.

Valli, L. (1987) *Becoming Clerical Workers*. London: Routledge.

Chapter Four

Special Needs:
personal trouble or public issue?

LEN BARTON & MIKE OLIVER

With the introduction of the Education Reform Act the question of special needs has become a more urgent and serious topic in Britain. One reason for this is due to the issue of entitlement and the National Curriculum. This legal right now covers all pupils. The extent to which it is being implemented, therefore, raises questions of equity and social justice. The impact of the publishing of results, Open Enrolment and the Local Management of schools will also be significant in relation to the allocation of monies, support services, statementing and the role of LEAs in special needs provision.

This chapter is concerned with providing an overview of the main characteristics and developments of sociological approaches to the issue of special needs. The analysis is set within the context of the centrality of equal opportunities and social justice. Key aspects of the Warnock Report and the 1981 Education Act are identified and discussed. Aspects of the Educational Reform Act (1988) and their possible implications for pupil entitlement and integration are also explored. Finally, a series of topics for further sociological research are outlined.

Sociology of Education

Sociological analysis of education has been characterised by the application of different perspectives to a range of topics. These have covered both structural and interactional features of the educational system (Barton & Meighan, 1978; Barton & Walker, 1978; Karabel & Halsey, 1977; Robinson, 1981; Reid, 1978).

Research, fundamentally influenced by structural functionalism, was particularly influential in the initial development of the discipline (Floud et al, 1956; Glass, 1954; Banks, 1955). This work was restricted to a specific set of concerns, including the issue of achievement and social mobility. Investigations examined input-output measures and the findings supported the view that there was a serious wastage of working-class ability (Jackson & Marsden, 1962; Jackson, 1964; Douglas, 1964).

The interest in the social determinants of educability led to the highlighting of a depressing picture of the extent and stubbornness of inequalities. These were in terms of access, duration and outcomes of educational opportunity and experience. Such inequalities were depicted as both unjust and the expression of an inefficient system of provision.

More recent work, critical of many of the presuppositions and explanations of earlier analyses, whilst confirming the centrality of inequality as a socially divisive issue, identified, for example, the complex ways in which race and gender factors compounded social divisions (Arnot, 1981; Davies, 1984; Weiner, 1986; Carrington, 1986). This form of analyses encouraged a greater interest in the politics of social reproduction and equal opportunities. Anti-sexism and anti-racism became crucial issues of concern. New research topics, questions and explanations began to be established (Williams, 1986; David, 1986; Gillborn, 1988; Demaine, 1989).

However, whilst such analyses focussed on the situation of working class girls and minority groups, hardly any consideration was given to the question of disabled people or special educational needs. A number of reasons can be identified for this omission. By focussing on the task of demonstrating the nature and extent of inequalities of selection by 'brightness' or 'ability', sociologists of education have given little consideration to the relationship between the ordinary and special school system. This is particularly in relation to the transfer of pupils from one system to another on the basis of 'special need' (Tomlinson, 1982). Also, studies concerned with deviancy have tended to focus on the more 'exotic' forms of pupil life and behaviour, thereby failing to consider deviancy in terms of those who have been identified as having 'special needs' (Quicke, 1986). The dominance of medicine was also significant in powerfully characterising the notion of 'special needs' in terms of illness or individual pathology (Bart, 1984). Finally children in special school settings were assumed to be politically insignificant and thus not a powerful force, in terms of enhancing the more general interest in the sorts of comprehensive changes that sociologists were advocating. Historically therefore, the nature and functions of the special educational system, has been an essentially invisible entity as far as sociological analysis is concerned.

Medical and psychological perspectives have been extremely powerful in shaping the definitions, policies and practices of special education. Stigmatising labels have been applied to those individuals deemed in need of such provision. Thus, *children are viewed as possessing a handicap, a learning difficulty, an emotional disturbance. (Dessent, 1988, p. 5)*

This form of exclusive discourse has legitimated qualitative distinctions between 'special' and 'normal' as well as contributed to the belief in the necessity of experts. Their task has been to identify and treat such individuals. The priorities and values of these approaches have also given legitimation to the establishment of segregated settings (Wolfensberger, 1975; Ryan & Thomas, 1980; Scull, 1982).

Both the grounds for, and the difficulties of, providing a sociological analysis can, therefore, be summarised in the following way. First, special education has been dominated by a form of reductionism which gives a privileged status to individualistic explanations. Within-the-child factors are emphasised, encouraging 'special needs' to be viewed as a personal trouble and not a public issue (Mills, 1970). This has had the effect of de-politicizing the issues involved. Secondly, given the restrictive nature of this viewpoint, attempts to introduce complex questions of class, gender and race into the analysis, will be seen as unnecessary and unhelpful. This will be particularly so, where the 'special' quality of such provision is justified on the grounds that all children are treated equally. Lastly, the strong tradition that professionals involved with 'special needs' are caring, patient and loving, make it difficult to raise questions, for example, about low-expectations, patronising and over-protective practices and stigmatising labels. However, sociologists are concerned with the ways in which society deals with 'deviant' groups or individuals. Where discrimination and oppression exists then the interest will be on how this occurs and under what conditions (Fulcher, 1989).

Developing Interests

Within Britain, therefore, sociological analysis of special education is a relatively new development. An important basis for such work is that an understanding of the plight of marginalised groups gives us some crucial insights into the nature of society. Part of the growing sociological interest has been in identifying and critiquing such individualistic and deficit views of disability (Barton & Tomlinson, 1981, 1984; Barton, 1988). This has involved examining the ways in which legislation, policy and practice contributed to the legitimation of key assumptions and categories. Analysis has focussed on the centrality of power, control and vested interests, with the intent to generate a more adequate understanding and explanation of the complex issues involved (Barton & Smith, 1989; Tomlinson, 1982, 1985 & 1988).

New questions and topics for examination have been generated including, for example, the social construction of categories; the ways in which definitions are shaped by economic and political factors; the role of professional groups in the development and legitimation of disablist practices; the relationship between 'normal' and special schooling; the role of ideology and the ways in which disabled people make sense of their world. Historical and comparative material has also been an important feature of the application of the sociological imagination to this field of study (Scull, 1982; Ford et al, 1982; Barton & Tomlinson, 1984; Fulcher, 1989; Barton, 1989).

One of the most important and influential contributions to a sociology of special education has been made by Tomlinson. Strongly influenced by Weberian ideas, she is particularly interested in the issue of the vested interests of professionals. Analysis is made of professional ideologies and practices in relation to how they both define and implement definitions of 'need'. Labels are seen as social constructions and therefore as problematic. The nature of 'special provision' is seen as a social process in which questions of context and relations are crucial.

Critical of those justifications for professional involvement based on claims of benevolent humanitarianism, Tomlinson maintains that the issue of power and control must be seen as essential features of a critical analysis. Using historical material and insights from research, including a three year study of her own of children moving into a particular form of special education (1981), she argues, that individuals placed within such provision are mainly the unwanted, objectionable and difficult pupils. They are largely from lower socio-economic backgrounds and black children are over-represented among them. These individuals are of low-status, relatively powerless and vulnerable. Indeed she argues that:

...to be categorised out of 'normal' education represents the ultimate in non-achievement in terms of ordinary educational goals. (1982, p. 6)

This procedure has served an important social function, that of enabling the mainstream system to run more smoothly and be more effective.

A key feature of her analysis is the distinction drawn between normative and non-normative categories. In the former, there is some agreement between professionals and lay-people about those categories which are "...defined as a medical sphere of competence " (p. 65). These include the blind, epileptic and speech defects. However, Tomlinson contends that:

On the other hand the categories of feeble-minded, educationally sub-normal, maladjusted and disruptive are not, and never will be, normative categories. (1982, p. 65)

This provides the basis for dispute between interested parties over the nature of such categories. The power-struggles involved in the construction of categories are seen as significant in this analysis. These often have little, if anything, to do with the personal qualities of the children concerned.

Tomlinson believes that part of a sociological approach is to encourage new ways of thinking about the issues. In special education this means moving away from clinical definitions and establishing a different agenda. This involves raising key questions such as:

In whose interests did special education actually develop? Do the social origins lie more in the interests of ordinary education?...

How is the system of administration of special education linked to the use of professional expertise? And are the vested interests of expanding groups of professionals and practitioners served by the discovery of more and more children with 'special needs'?

Are some types of special schooling more a form of control for particular groups of children? (Tomlinson, 1982, pp. 18-19)

It also means establishing relationships between the processes and politics of interaction and the structural conditions of society. By this means Tomlinson maintains, it is possible to see the discourse of special needs as a form of 'ideological rationalisation' in which the crucial political and economic needs being served by the increased provision of special education are hidden (Tomlinson, 1985)

Tomlinson's work has made an original contribution to the development of a sociological approach to special education, providing a vital stimulus to many of the debates within the literature.

Another particularly significant development has been the more recent contributions made by disabled sociologists to the establishment of a political and social theory of disability. These analysts share a number of basic ideas with Tomlinson, including, a critical approach to questions of professional involvement, social control and the negative features of segregated provision. However, in contrast, they also offer a much stronger commitment to a class analysis and to the centrality of politics in this process. They are critical of 'personal-tragedy' models of disability. For them, the difficulties of participating in society are not due to personnel limitations, but arise from the prejudices, discriminatory policies and practices and social restrictions of an unadaptive society. Disability is a fundamentally political, social issue, which is a form of oppression. Through the process of social engagement, particularly those of an institutional and professional nature, disabled people are encouraged to view themselves as helpless and dependent. Oliver (1990) expresses this position in the following manner:

All disabled people experience disability, as social restrictions, whether these restrictions occur as a consequence of inaccessible built environments, questionable notions of intelligence and social competence, the inability of the general public to use sign language, the lack of reading material in braille, or hostile public attitudes to people with non-visible disabilities. (p. xiv)

Disabled people within such conditions and relationships are often treated in a patronising and dehumanising manner. Although age, race, gender and class will have an impact on the nature and degree of these experiences, people's perceptions are a common source of distress and offence in the everyday encounters of disabled people.

Advocating the social nature of oppression implies that disabled people are viewed as inferior to other people because they are disabled and Abberley (1987) also notes:

It is also to argue that these disadvantages are dialectically related to an ideology or group of ideologies which justify and perpetuate this situation. Beyond that it is to make the claim that such disadvantages and their supporting ideologies are neither natural nor inevitable. Finally, it involves the identification of some beneficiary of this state of affairs. (p. 7)

Recognising the importance and exploring the origins of differences in the lives of disabled people compared to the rest of the community, are thus fundamental elements in a social theory of disability. Capitalism is seen as significant in this process through the prominence it gives to work and the distinction it encourages between productive and non-productive people. This legitimates a form of social relations in which disabled people are viewed in terms of what they cannot do. The problem is thus individualised.

Spurious forms of empathy, in which the desire to be 'normal' is emphasised, are challenged and viewed as counter-productive to the best interests of disabled people. The lack of a coherent and rigourous understanding of the social and political nature of disability is evident in these positions. The role of the disability movement as a vehicle for change and mutual support is depicted as central to the struggle against disablist policies and practices. Thus, the voice of disabled people needs to be heard if they are to realise a greater control over their own lives, including the services they need and how they are delivered. This inevitably involves a political process in which questions of choice, power and change are central to the agenda.

Disabled sociologists have been instrumental in providing a stimulus to ensuring that 'disability' is seen as a serious topic of investigation. They have brought a fresh vigour, vitality and urgency to the analyses (Abberley, 1987 & 1989; Oliver, 1985, 1989 & 1990; Barnes, 1990).

The Past Legacy

Before considering some of the current developments and their possible impact on special needs, we will briefly examine two past influences. These will provide a context for understanding the present. The Warnock Report on the Enquiry into the Education of Handicapped Children and Young People (DES, 1978) and the 1981 Education Act, are viewed by many commentators as landmarks in the history of special education.

The Warnock Report provided a challenge to orthodox models based on the identification of defects. The Report emphasised the importance of context, resources and proposed a service model based on delivering the goods. It introduced:

71

...a new conceptual framework within which special educational provision should be made. This entails a continuum of special educational need rather than discrete categories of handicap. It embraces children with significant learning difficulties as well as those with disabilities of mind or body.
(Warnock Report, 1978 p. 327)

The notion of 'special educational need' applied to more than the 2% of children within special schools. According to Warnock, it related to approximately 20% of all children at school. One in five school children would, from this perspective, have special needs at sometime in their school career.

The Committee sought to focus positive attention, not on defects, but on what a child needs if they are going to benefit from education. A clear commitment to the principle that the purpose and goals of education are the same for all children is stated in the opening pages of the Report. Education is "...a good, and a specifically human goal, to which all human beings are entitled" (p. 6). This is not a question of charity, but a matter of right in order that their real potential be developed to the full.

Several criticisms have been made about different aspects of the Warnock Report. Lewis & Vulliamy (1981) are critical of the significance given to psychological presuppositions and categories, of the emphasis on administrative systems and the creation of an elaborate bureaucracy staffed by more 'experts'. They believe the Committee largely neglected the issue of social factors in the creation of learning difficulties. Kirp (1983), in a comparison of British and United States special education, maintains that the Warnock Committee was dominated by professional groups. This is compared unfavourably with the United States in which the rights of consumers are viewed as essential. This led, in the British case, to the importance of benign professional discretion in discussions relating to children or parents. Finally, Fulcher (1989) is critical of the limited consideration given to curriculum issues. This reflected a conservative and politically expedient view of integration and questions which Fulcher believes should inform discussions about integration were not raised. This included the question 'why do children fail in school?'.

However, the definition of special educational needs which Warnock advocated was seen by many professionals and parents as a major advancement in terms of removing deficit views of the child. For Pumfrey & Mittler (1990) the concept has been powerful as a tool for consciousness-raising and uniting pressure groups in their demands for greater resources. Several questions have been raised over the value of the concept and how it means different things to different people. Also, the word 'special' has certain connotations relating to difference in a negative sense. It is a divisive word, one which has been said to separate and segregate pupils from pupils. An individual identified as being outside of the range of acceptability is thus defined as special. The notion of 'need' is also problematic in that, for example, the tacit meaning implies being needy, thus, helpless, powerless and to be controlled (Freeman & Gray,

1989). Also, the use of this term 'need', tends to obfuscate the question of power-relations between professionals and clients, and, importantly, the disagreements between professionals over what constitutes the 'needs' of a particular child (Baldwin, 1986).

Mary Warnock (1982), in a re-evaluation of the concept 'special needs' several years after the publication of The Warnock Report, acknowledges some of the precarious assumptions underpining the Committee's position, and yet, still maintains that:

> I still see that there was a kind of simplicity in the concept which made it attractive; and it was useful, insofar as it at least departed from the medical model based on diagnosis of defects, and turned attention to a service model, based on delivering the goods. And it might have worn better, this smart little number, if it hadn't been for the recession. (p. 57)

Whilst it is important to see reference being made to economic factors and their influence on the implementation of policy, the weakness in the position of Warnock is the apparent inability to recognise the structural conditions of schooling and the ways in which the concept, expressed within such conditions, could be used to serve interests other than those of the individual.

Carrier (1990) in an analysis of research findings in the United States and the United Kingdom, is interested in the ways in which pupil performance is understood, how pupils are identified in terms of that understanding and what external forces influence these practices. He maintains that the notions of educational success and pupil failure have been largely taken for granted within the school system and that there has been no demand to articulate them. Within special education such practices are given much greater significance, in that models of difference are essential to the functioning of those institutions. Pupils are defined as bright or failures within a social process and cultural understandings have, in the United States, influenced the ways 'retarded' people have been viewed. They have been seen as menaces needing control; unfortunate people needing services and members of an under-priviledged minority. By identifying the significance of cultural factors in the social construction of categories, Carrier (1990) maintains that, in relation to professionals, we cannot:

> ...assume that they understand what those pupils do in terms of unproblematic objective assessments, so we cannot assume that those dealings will unproblematically reflect pupil's abilities and disabilities. (p. 215)

This raises, therefore, the relevance of social factors in this process and the power of significant others to define the nature of people's abilities and behaviour. External forces play their part in shaping the nature of these interactions and outcomes. For Carrier, these include the rise of industrial capitalism, the growth of egalitarianism and individualistic beliefs and the spread of mass compulsory schooling. They have contributed to the development and maintenance of special education and to its primary function of legitimating the distinction between the 'special' and 'normal' child.

A system of education based on selection and competition gives priority to particular conceptions of 'ability' and 'disability'. Hargreaves (1982) captures some of the basic factors involved in his discussion of the nature of secondary education, in which he argues, that:

The more profound and disturbing message is that the very concept of ability becomes closely tied to the intellectual - cognitive domain. 'Intelligence' becomes defined as the ability to master cognitive - intellectual aspects of school subjects. Pupils who experience difficulty in so doing are labelled with the euphemism of the 'less able' or even the overly insulting epithet of 'the thickies'. (p. 60)

Ability labels under such a system are seen as 'generalized judgements' and Hargreaves continues:

The 'less able' understand that they lack the very quality on which the school sets most store; a sense of failure tends to permeate the whole personality leaving a residue of powerlessness and helplessness. (p. 63)

Thus decisions about people's needs and abilities involve value-judgements and power-relations. The notion of 'special educational needs' has been applied to increasing numbers of pupils, many of whom are not statemented, and thus, it serves the purpose of controlling difficult, objectionable and problem pupils. These pupils are deemed unable to meet the standards by which the system measures success. However, by emphasising the pupils' failure, the fundamental issue of the system's failure to meet the needs of all pupils is masked.

In a school system dominated by selection, competition and academic success, the notion of 'special educational needs' can be viewed as a euphemism for pupil failure at an individual level. To analysts like Dyson (1990) this is unacceptable and there needs top be the development of a 'system-level' change model, in which the system must change in order to accept the difference of pupils.

The 1981 Education Act

For some people this was heralded as a major breakthrough with regard to significant developments relating to the issues of integration, parent rights and special educational needs. One of the difficulties in terms of the implementation of the 1981 Act relates to the existing baseline of provision and practice. Local Education Authorities (LEAs), schools and other service providers start from established traditions when new legislation is introduced (Croll & Moses, 1989). Existing patterns of provision within and across authorities all played an important role in mediating the impact of new legislation. This resulted in a wide divergence of practice as Croll & Moses (1989) also note:

Because of this variation in provision before the Act, and the different interpretations which can be put on parts of the legislation, the changes accomplished have themselves varied. (p. 26)

Patterns of existing social inequalities have their impact on the extent to which vulnerable groups have protection under legislation. Locality and its effects on the socio-economic standing of individuals are crucial factors with regard to this issue.

A further difficulty concerning the 1981 Act was that it came on the statute-books at a time of contracting resources and pupil numbers (Croll & Moses, 1989). Thus, much of the Act can be viewed as illusory in practical terms, not being a resource-led piece of legislation, it lacked the support of political will on the part of Government.

The 1981 legislation introduced the statementing procedures for LEAs and parents. The LEAs varied in terms of their exact interpretation of the legal requirements on them and the ways in which they met such requirements. The outcome was that children who had the protection of a statement in one authority may well not have had it in a different authority. In a recent research project into the topic of 'Making an Educational Statement' the researchers argue that several criticisms can be made about current practice, For example:

The full procedures involved in the statementing process, as defined by legislation, are not followed. The amount of discrepancy varies from Psychologist to Psychologist and from authority to authority. (p. 47)

It often seems that Statementing is viewed as a tedious administrative chore, rather than a considered part of a decision-making process or a way of safeguarding parents' and children's rights. (Malek & Kerslake, 1989, p. 47)

This aspect of the legislation has been severely criticised for the extensive and unwieldy bureaucracy it required.

In a survey entitled *Caught in the Act* (Rogers, 1986) the findings revealed that half of all LEAs failed to give parents adequate information on the assessment and statutory procedures; only a third told parents they had a right to be fully consulted and to receive all relevant information; most failed to provide details about sources of support and advice and almost half did not give information on appeal arrangements. The recent DES sponsored national survey conducted by Goacher et al (1988) indicated clear LEA differences in policies about the role of parents in the statutory process. The extent to which some parents understood the process is worrying, particularly as a significant finding of the research was that:

...it is clear that in most authorities it is still true that a Statement can be equated largely with a decision to make a special school placement. (p. 55)

This is a reminder of the gap which often occurs between legislation, policy and its effective implementation in the lives of those it is allegedly serving. It is also an example of the authority of professional judgements in relation to decisions over access to opportunities and resources.

Educational Reform Act and Integration

We are in the midst of an extensive restructuring of educational provision and practice. Centralised control is being accomplished through the articulation of a new vision over what schools must achieve and how that success and effectiveness is to be defined and monitored. A new set of values are being advocated. Central to this approach is a belief in the importance of competition and consumer choice. In a powerful analysis of the growing differentiations within school provision, Ball (1990) maintains that:

> *Taken together this emerging stratification of schools not only rests upon a competition between schools, it also creates the basis for a large-scale return to competition for places between pupils. The competitive self-interest of families is underlined and the logic of Thatcherist individualism is ramified in the education system. The education market will tend to weaken social bonds (the social engineering project of comprehensive education is anathema to conservative thinking) and encourage strategies of exclusion and social closure; that is the generation of boundaries of positional hierarchy. (p. 93)*

An effective market must involve a range of products for consumers to choose from. This necessitates an increased diversity of school provision (Ranson, 1990). Within this climate pupils with special educational needs are not viewed as politically significant and questions of social justice and equity become marginalised. Thus the possibility of establishing a comprehensive integration policy becomes more difficult. Indeed, the whole question of integration may well become an increasingly contentious issue.

In this world of enterprise culture a new management language is being applied to schools which includes such key concepts as: efficiency, cost-effectiveness, targets, performance indicators, competencies and appraisal. In this highly pressurised world, the task is to market or sell yourself. This will intensify competition throughout the system and with the introduction of LMS, Open Enrolment and Opting Out, serious questions need to be asked about the vulnerability of particular groups in this process. The divisive aspects of a market-led system could give greater legitimation to the demands for segregation.

It is important to discuss these issues within the context of education for all and the pursuit of a system of schooling in which the dignity of *all* pupils is realised and protected. Thus the introduction of the legal *entitlement* of all pupils to a broad and balanced curriculum is something to be cherished and defended. The National Curriculum Council's (NCC) recent document *A Curriculum for All* (1989) places the issue of 'special educational needs' within an equal opportunities dimension. Now whilst the NCC document is couched in such terms as:

The schemes of work should reflect whole-school approaches to teaching and learning. (p. 5)

NCC trusts that every effort will be made to keep exceptional arrangements to a minimum. (p. 9)

NCC does not expect the demands of the National Curriculum to lead to a rise in the numbers of pupils assessed for statements under the 1981 Education Act.... (p. 11)

No ordinary schools should be tempted to use the statementing procedures as a pretext for transferring certain pupils to special schools or units merely because they are not expected to perform well on national assessments at 7,11,14 or 16. (p. 11) (our emphasis)

It is important to recognise that these are only 'guidelines to follow' (p. 13). The extent to which schools will actually take up the advice of the NCC has still to be determined. However, several developments give grounds for anxiety. House of Commons debates highlight the dilemma facing the Conservative Party over what to do with special needs in the changing educational context. Parental worries are evident in the increase in letters to MPs dealing with this issue. We have reports of major increases in referrals of children for statements in order to claim funds or excuse any 'failure' of school results (Croall, 1991; Pyke, 1990; Lee, 1990a).

Supporting evidence is derived from Educational Psychologists who have reported being under pressure from colleagues in their LEAs to produce reports in particular ways. These emanate from LEAs inability to provide for such needs in the current stringent economic climate (Hofkins, 1990; Berliner, 1990). These increases have resulted in a backlog of unfinished statements. Many pupils who have statements are not being given their annual review and some children are being given home tuition when they could be in school (Croall, 1991).

Very worrying are the increasing reports of cuts in support services and the number of mainly male pupils from poor socio-economic backgrounds with emotional and behavioural difficulties who are being excluded from school (O'Connor, 1991; TES Editorial, 1991; and BBC, 3 May 1991). Equal opportunities is a dimension with no NCC non-statutory guidance given to schools on this matter. It is unlikely therefore that schools will give priority to this task. A significant factor giving support to this form of interpretation is, according to Lee (1990a), to be located in the fundamental tensions between the 1981 and 1988 Educational Reform Act. He argues that:

The former, with its emphasis on the individual needs of children, is effectively overruled by the 1988 Act with its focus on the rights of self-determination for schools, including total control over the budget and how it is spent. (p. 28)

Thus the impact of LMS, the publication of results and open enrolment will be crucial with regard to how schools, and particular heads and governors, respond to the NCC advice.

The discourse relating to special educational needs tends to both individualize and homogenize social differences and experiences. Yet recent research shows how essential it is to examine special needs in relation to class, gender, race and age. In a survey of findings derived from questionnaires returned by head teachers in 206 special schools and units for pupils with emotional and behavioural difficulties in England and Wales, Cooper and his colleagues (1991) examined the extent to which pupils from various ethnic backgrounds are represented in these schools. They were also interested in the level of ethnic minorities representations among the teaching staff of these institutions. They found that Afro-Caribbeans and white European boys were over-represented in the sample and teachers from all ethnic minority groups were severely under-represented. The significance of class, race and gender is evident they maintain, in that specific types of pupils from particular backgrounds were more likely to be labelled 'maladjusted' and 'disruptive' (Cooper et al, 1991).

This perspective becomes even more significant if one agrees with the future prognosis of Howard and Lloyd-Smith (1990) who contend that:

> ...it will be the disruptive and disaffected groups that will increase most rapidly and cheap unit provision in disused parts of existing education buildings expand accordingly. Attempts may be made to justify poor provision for the disruptive and disaffected on the moral ground that they are responsible for their behaviour and their consequent educational failure. (p. 35)

Both the continuance and legitimation of 'social, institutional and professional labelling and categorisation' will be strengthened through such developments.

In his discussion of school effectiveness and the impact of the 1988 Education Reform Act on schools, Reynolds (1989) claims that:

> The Education Act 1988 increased the probability of schools competing against each other for children through its provisions allowing popular schools to increase in numbers through open-enrolment. Such competition will again intensify the pressure on schools to concentrate on those pupils who can deliver examination result passes that will make the schools attractive in the eyes of the parents .... Many have voiced fears that proposals to allow state schools to **opt-out** of local education authority control will lead to a neglect of lower ability or special educational needs children because of an opted-out school's likely concentration on other parts of the ability range. (p. 41)

Nor are the divisive outcomes of open enrolment and opting out the only ones to be concerned about. Under LMS local education authorities will devolve expenditure to the school level and the role of heads and governors will become crucial with regard to setting priorities for the allocation of such monies (Russell, 1990). Thus, the extent to which, for example, structural changes to school buildings will take precedence over staffing issues, is one which gives grounds for concern. Other aspects of provision raise similar worries. In a survey of 48 LEAs the question of the delegation of monies to schools over the next three years was examined. One key issue relates to 'discretionary spending'. On, for example, such services as educational welfare, psychology, library and in-service training. The future will see the delegation of costs of such services to schools, allowing them to 'buy in' such support. However as Lee (1990b) maintains:

> One problem with giving schools such an option to 'buy in', of course, is that they may choose not to. Instead of costly specialist support they may choose to increase their general level of staffing. (p. 18)

This is not unrelated to the contentious issue of LEA formulas for school funding and, for example, the way in which some LEAs have decided to use the 'number of pupils at a school authorised to receive free school meals, excluding sixth formers' (Avon, 1989, p. 38) as the indicator of special needs. The House of Commons Selected Committee on Education, Science and Arts (1990) is clearly aware of the dangers resulting from those LMS formulae adopted by LEAs which are too restrictive. They will, according to the Committee, damage progress towards integration. With the very real possibility of the development of a new hierarchy of schools driven by market pressures, children with special educational needs:

> ...may well become concentrated in those schools which have difficulties recruiting other pupils. (Whitty & Menter, 1991)

In these circumstances, particularly in the inner cities, these children will increasingly constitute an educational underclass who will experience a qualitatively inferior form of educational provision and opportunity. No wonder one analyst had described the present 'policy' relating to such pupils as catastrophic (Welton, 1989).

It is essential, therefore, to view integration as complex and multi-faceted and not simply a matter of changing the place to which children are sent. Warnock (1978) distinguished between functional, locational and social integration and subsequent studies (Hegarty et al, 1981) argued that integration was not a new form of provision but a "process geared to meeting a wider range of pupil needs". The ILEA (Fish Report) (1985) took this further and affirmed a commitment to the process of integration and spelled out in considerable detail the consequences of this view of integration for the whole education system and not just those limited parts that integration has previously been thought to reach.

One of the difficulties is that integration as a process has taken on, to paraphrase Cohen (1985), 'the language of rhetoric'. It has become re-ified and become an end in itself and not a means to an end. Sociological analysis needs to raise serious questions about integration. For example, if integration is a means to an end, what is that end and how might it be achieved? How can integration be achieved in an unequal society? What are the consequences of integrating children into an education system which reflects and reinforces those inequalities? What part will a fragmented school system play in realising or inhibiting integration policies?

Integration is a political and educational process. From our perspective, integration is underpined by a philosophy which we call the politics of personal identity. Through a growing collective identity, this demands, (and has the confidence to demand) that difference must not be merely tolerated and accepted but positively valued and celebrated. Further, in making these demands, it is not just a matter of providing a legal framework but backing that framework with moral fervour and political will to ensure its implementation. Translating such moral commitment into political rights is part of the struggle for empowerment. Schools must become welcoming environments for children with special needs with no questioning of their right to be there. Organisational changes are part of an acceptance and understanding that the purpose of schools is to educate all children, not merely those who meet an increasingly narrowing band of selection criteria (ILEA, 1985).

The legacy of the past provides us with some powerful reminders of the difficulties to be faced in the struggle for integration. Historically, education has been seriously under-resourced. This has had an impact on the system of provision in terms of. for example, environmental barriers to integration. HMI Reports have consistently identified the unsuitability of many school buildings. In a Report (DES, 1989a) on services for primary aged pupils with special needs in 43 mainstream schools in 11 LEAs, several criticisms are offered. Many classrooms had insufficient space to accommodate pupils who needed personal aids and equipment. The quality of the acoustics in most classrooms was viewed as poor. In some schools there was a lack of suitably adapted toilets and changing facilities (p. 7). An HMI Report (DES, 1989b), which included the issue of integration in secondary provision, contained similar findings with the added discriminatory factor of the effect on pupil's choice of curricular options in year four and five. The question of curriculum access is vital in that writers like Fulcher (1989) maintain that the discourse surrounding integration is political, emphasising disability, and is thus concerned with discipline and control. By raising curriculum issues, the question becomes one of the extent to which schools exclude pupils from this basic entitlement? The disabling impact of patronising and over-protective staff, are also significant factors requiring attention.

Previously we argued for the necessity of placing the question of special educational needs within an equal opportunities policy. Within the developing school provision this will be a very difficult task. Nevertheless, in the struggle for greater social justice for all pupils the development of whole-school policies will be essential. Issues relating to the curriculum, organisation and interpersonal relations of school life will need to be seriously addressed. Prejudice, discrimination and oppression must be understood and challenged. Conflicting objectives and priorities will need to be worked through and an effective means of monitoring such policies will be absolutely necessary. The role of the head teacher and governors will be significant in this process.

Conclusion

We believe that sociological research in this particular area is both important and urgent. However, it is essential that those involved in such work take seriously Becker's fundamental question - 'Whose side are you on?' The book in which he posed the question was called *Outsiders* (1963). This is an apt term in relation to the subjects of such research, in that they constitute the vulnerable, marginalised and discriminated groups within society. It is necessary, therefore, for researchers not only to clarify their value-positions, but also, examine the extent to which involvement in the research process, including the outcomes, can be *enabling*. Questions of social justice, equity, power and control will be perennial concerns in this field of human enquiry. Part of the sociological task will be to contribute to the establishment and maintenance of special needs as a key equal opportunities issue. This is necessary because it will provide a basis for the identification of those features of the existing society, policy and practice that are unacceptable, offensive and need to be challenged and changed. Also, through this approach any attempts to redirect resources in order to provide opportunities for the most marginalised, disadvantaged and discriminated people in society cannot pretend to be apolitical. It also provides stimulus for the crucial task of establishing connections between other discriminated groups in order that attempts can be made to engage in common struggles (Roaf & Bines, 1989; Rieser & Mason, 1990). This inevitably necessitates a socio-political perspective which challenges individualised and social pathology explanations. However, there are difficulties in taking this position in that equal opportunities policies at both LEA and school levels are overwhelmingly concerned with issues of race and gender. In many instances disability is merely a bolt-on tokenistic gesture (Leach, 1989). Also the possibility of the incorporation of equal opportunities concerns within the dominant hegemony of new right ideas, is one to be constantly aware of and to struggle against (see Arnot, Chapter 3).

One of the dangers of living in a period of extensive educational and social change is that it tends to anaesthetise the mind with regard to the importance of the past. In a discussion of teacher evaluation Grace (1978) advocates the necessity of a historically located inquiry because:

> ...it has the advantage of sensitising us to the principles and procedures which have been dominant in the past so that we are alert to the mode of their reproduction, reconstitution or change. It has the advantage also of concretely exemplifying and making visible the relations between educational structures and processes and wider structures of power, economy and control in particular periods of social change. (p. 4)

The importance of such an approach is essential in relation to the issues we have outlined in this chapter. What historical analysis does exist seriously neglects questions of ideology and politics in the accounts offered (Pritchard, 1963; Cole, 1990). The discourse of special needs has encouraged an individualised perspective. By examining the relationship between special schools, school provision generally and the socio-economic order, we can begin to unpack complex relationships and contradictory factors. Also, we can explore the extent to which such discourse and practices have served social, political and ideological factors in particular historical periods. Whilst policy analysis which focuses on specific practical issues can be viewed as attractive and cost-effective, it is important to recognise the complex and contentious notion of policy. Thus as Grace (1990) also argues, conflicts and struggles are endemic to the policy-making process and historical studies raise questions about the power-relations which influence the nature of education policy. This is particularly applicable to special needs provision.

Disability is a social construct and sociological research needs to address the development of a social theory of disability in which issues of power, oppression and politics are carefully worked through. Documenting and evaluating the institutional form of discriminatory practices and disablist images will be necessary if the cycle of dependency creating pressures are to be challenged and changed. We have no serious ethnography in education of special needs policy and practice. An urgent research task is to carefully explore, in given social contexts, how disablist ideas get constituted and re-constituted through the minutiae of daily interactions. The role of professionals in this process will be crucial. How disabled people make sense of their world and struggle within oppressive conditions and social relations needs to be seriously examined. The divisive impact of a market-led system makes this research task absolutely essential. The question of labelling and its effects on both the labelled and the labeller is a significant one. Removing a label does not mean that the values and expectations associated with it become moribund. Professionals are adept at creating new labels. The notion of the 'Level-One Child' is a classic example. How identities are constructed therefore is a topic which future research needs to address. Given the over-representation of black pupils in certain forms of special provision such work will also involve confronting the issue of racism and racial stereotyping (Coard, 1971; ILEA, 1985). The politics of difference is thus an urgent task for sociological enquiry.

In the beginning of this chapter we raised the crucial issues of the publishing of test results, the local management of schools and the contentious question of LEA formulae funding. These provide significant topics and opportunities for sociological research, and in particular, the effects of these developments within school. A number of serious questions arise which need to be explored. For example, how far will these factors lead to an increase in ghettoized or segregated forms of provision within the inner cities? Will the pupil make-up of such provision be overly representative of children and young people from particular socio-economic and racial backgrounds? To what extent will the distribution of resources be shaped by subject-specific concerns to the neglect, or reduction, of support services for special educational needs? Within a period of such extensive and rapid change how far will teachers be able and/or willing to express a strong commitment to questions of entitlement and the rights of disabled pupils? What role will statementing play and what will be its impact on integration? Finally, how far do the social relations and practices within school legitimate particular power relations, which result in the marginalisation of pupils who are seen as different?

The aforementioned topics are not exhaustive of the areas of investigation sociologists can undertake. In the struggle for change, we must not underestimate the demanding issues which have to be engaged with. The process will be difficult but absolutely necessary if special needs provision and practice is not to lead to the creation of an underclass.

Acknowledgements

We are grateful to Madeleine Arnot and Jenny Corbett for their helpful comments on earlier drafts of this chapter.

REFERENCES

Abberley, P. (1987) The concept oppression and the social theory of disability, in *Disability, Handicap and Society*, 2, pp. 5-19.

Abberley, P. (1989) Disabled people, normality and social work, in L. Barton (Ed) *Disability and Dependency*. Lewes: Falmer Press.

Arnot, M. (1981) Culture and Political Economy: dual perspectives in the sociology of women's education, in B. Davies (Ed) *Educational Analysis*, 3, pp. 97-116.

Avon, County of (1989) *Local Management of Schools: A Consultative Paper*.

BBC (1991) *Children with Special Needs - in Danger of Neglect?*, Public Eye Programme, BBC 2, 3 May.

Baldwin, S. (1986) Problem with needs - where theory meet practice, *Disability, Handicap and Society*, 1, pp. 139-146.

Ball, S. (1990) *Politics and Policy Making in Education and Explorations in Policy Sociology*. London: Routledge.

Banks, O. (1955) *Parity and Prestige in English Secondary Education*. London: Routledge.

Barnes, C. (1990) *Cabbage Syndrome*. Lewes: Falmer Press.

Bart, D. (1986) The Differential Diagnosis of Special Education: Managing Social Pathology as Individual Disability, in L. Barton & S. Tomlinson (Eds) *Special Education and Social Interests*. Beckenham: Croom Helm.

Barton, L. (Ed) (1989) *Integration: myth or reality?* Lewes: Falmer Press.

Barton, L. (Ed) (1988) *The Politics of Special Educational Needs*. Lewes: Falmer Press.

Barton, L. & Meighan, R. (Eds) (1978) *Sociological Interpretations of Schooling and Classrooms: a reappraisal*. Driffield: Nafferton Books.

Barton, L. & Smith, M. (1989) Equality, Rights and Primary Education, in C. Roaf & H. Bines (Eds) *Needs, Rights and Opportunities*. Lewes: Falmer Press.

Barton, L. & Tomlinson, S. (Eds) (1984) *Special Education and Social Interests*. Beckenham: Croom Helm.

Barton, L. & Tomlinson, S. (Eds) (1981) *Special Education: Policy, Practices and Social Issues*. London: Harper & Row.

Barton, L. & Walker, S. (1978) Sociology of education at the crossroads, *Educational Review*, 30, pp. 269-284.

Becker, H. (1963) *Outsiders: studies in the sociology of deviance*. New York: The Free Press.

Berliner, W. (1990) Handicapped pupils: the scandal of the lies parents are told, *Observer*, p. 52, 4 February.

Carrier, J. (1990) Special Education and the Explanation of Pupil Performance, *Disability, Handicap and Society*, 5, pp. 211-226.

Carrington, B. (1986) Social mobility, ethnicity and sport, *British Journal of Sociology of Education*, 7, pp. 3-18.

Coard, B. (1971) *How the West Indian Child is Made Educationally Subnormal in the British School System: the scandal of the black child in schools in Britain*. London: Beacon Press.

Cohen, S. (1985) *Visions of Social Control*. Cambridge: Polity Press.

Cole, T. (1990) *Apart or A Part? In Integration and the Growth of British Special Education*. Milton Keynes: Open University Press.

Cooper, P., Upton, G. & Smith, C. (1991) Ethnic minority and gender distribution among staff and pupils with emotional and behavioural difficulties, *British Journal of Sociology of Education*, 12, pp. 77-94.

Croall, J. (1991) Special needs, muddled deeds, *Education Guardian*, p. 25, 26 March.

Croll, P. & Moses, D. (1989) Policy and Practice in Special Education: the Implementation of the 1981 Education Act in England and Wales, in R. Brown & M. Chazan (Eds) *Learning Difficulties and Emotional Problems in Children and Adults*. Calgary: Deseling.

David, M. (1986) Teaching family matters, *British Journal of Sociology of Education*, 7, pp. 35-58.

Davies L. (1984) *Pupil Power: Deviance and Gender in School*. Lewes: Falmer Press.

Demaine, J. (1989) Race, categorisation and educational achievement, *British Journal of Sociology of Education*, 10, pp. 195-214.

DES (1978) *Special Educational Needs* (The Warnock Report). London: HMSO.

DES (1989a) Report by HM Inspectors. *Provision for Primary Aged Pupils with Statements of Special Educational Needs in Mainstream Schools*. Middlesex: DES.

DES (1989b) Report by HM Inspectors. *Educating Physically Disabled Pupils*. Middlesex: DES.

Dessent, T. (1988) *Making Ordinary Schools Special*. Lewes: Falmer Press.

Douglas, J.W.B. (1964) *The Home and The School*. London: Panther.

Dyson, A. (1990) Special educational needs and the concept of change, *Oxford Review of Education*, 16, pp. 55-66.

Editorial (1991) Excluding a stitch in time, *The Times Educational Supplement*, p. 13, 3 May.

Floud, J., Halsey, A.H. & Martin, F.M. (1956) *Social Class and Educational Opportunity*. London: Heinemann.

Ford, J., Mongon, D. & Whelan, M. (1982) *Special Education and Social Control: Invisible Disasters*. London: Routledge.

Freeman, A. & Gray, H. (1989) *Organising Special Educational Needs: A Critical Approach*. London: Paul Chapman.

Fulcher, G. (1989) *Disabling Policies? A Comparative Approach to Education Policy and Disability*. Lewes: Falmer Press.

Gillborn, D. (1988) Ethnicity and educational opportunity: case studies of West Indian male-white teacher relationships, *British Journal of Sociology of Education*, 9, pp. 371-386.

Glass, D.V. (1954) *Social Mobility in Britain*. London: Routledge & Kegan Paul.

Goacher, B., Evans, J., Welton, J. & Wedell, K. (1988) *Policy and Provision for Special Educational Needs: Implementing the 1981 Education Act*. London: Cassell.

Grace, G. (1978) *Teachers, Ideology and Control: a Study in Urban Education*. London: Routledge & Kegan Paul.

Grace, G. (1990) Labour and Education: The Crisis and Settlements of Education Policy, in M. Holland & J. Boston. (Eds) *The Fourth Labour Government*. Auckland, New Zealand: Oxford University Press.

Hargreaves, D. (1982) *Challenge to the Comprehensive School*. London: Routledge & Kegan Paul.

Hegarty, S., Pocklington, K. & Lucas, D. (1981) *Educating Pupils with Special Needs in the Ordinary School*. Windsor: NFER-Nelson.

Hofkins, D. (1990) Pressed to alter rights on special needs, *The Times Educational Supplement*, 26 October.

House of Commons Select Committee on Education, Science and Arts (1990) *Staffing for Pupils with Special Educational Needs*. London: HMSO.

Howard, C.M. & Lloyd-Smith, M. (1990) Assessing the impact of legislation on Special education policy - an historical analysis, *Journal of Education Policy*, 5, pp. 21-36.

ILEA (1985) *Educational Opportunities for All?* London: ILEA (Fish Report).

Jackson, B. & Marsden, D. (1962) *Education and the Working Class*. Harmondsworth: Penguin.

Jackson, B. (1964) *Streaming: An Education System in Miniature*. London: Routledge & Kegan Paul.

Karabel, J. & Halsey, A.H. (Eds) (1977) *Power and Ideology in Education*. Oxford: Oxford University Press.

Kirp, D. (1983) Professionalisation as a Policy Choice: British special education in comparative perspective, in J. Chambers & W. Hartman (Eds) *Special Education Policies: their History, Implementation and Finance.* Temple University Press.

Leach, B. (1989) Disabled people and the implementation of local authorities' equal opportunities policies, *Public Administration,* 67, pp. 65-77.

Lee, T. (1990a) *Carving Out the Cash for Schools: LMS and the new ERA of Education.* Bath Social Policy paper, No. 17. Bath: University of Bath.

Lee, T. (1990b) A cash flow that is likely to leave little in reserve, *The Times Education Supplement,* p. 18, 29 June.

Lewis, I. & Vulliamy, G. (1981) The Social Context of Educational Practice: The Case of Special Education, in L. Barton & S. Tomlinson (Eds) *Special Education: Policy, Practices and Social Issues.* London: Harper & Row.

Malek, M. & Kerslake, A. (1989) *Making an Educational Statement?* Bath: University of Bath.

Mills, C.W. (1970) *The Sociological Imagination.* Harmondsworth: Penguin.

NCC (1989) *A Curriculum for All: Special Needs in the National Curriculum.* York: NCC.

O'Connor, J. (1991) No buyer for market doctrine, *The Times Educational Supplement,* p. 6, 3 May.

Oliver, M. (1985) The integration-segregation debate: some sociological considerations, *British Journal of Sociology of Education,* 6, pp. 75-92.

Oliver, M. (1989) Disability and Dependency: a creation of industrial societies, in L. Barton (Ed) *Disability and Dependency.* Lewes: Falmer Press.

Oliver, M. (1990) *The Politics of Disablement.* London: Macmillan.

Pritchard, O. (1963) *Education and the Handicapped, 1760-1960.* London: Routledge & Kegan Paul.

Pumfrey, P. & Mittler, P. (1990) Peeling Off the Label, *The Times Educational Supplement,* pp. 29-30.

Pyke, N. (1990) Cuts blamed for rise in special needs referrals, *The Times Educational Supplement,* p. 19, 21 September.

Quicke, J. (1986) A case of paradigmatic mentality? A reply to Mike Oliver, *British Journal of Sociology of Education,* 7, pp. 81-86.

Ranson, S. (1990) *The Politics of Reorganising Schools.* London: Unwin Hyman.

Reid, I. (1978) *Sociological Perspectives on School and Education.* London: Open Books.

Reynolds, D. (1989) Effective Schools and Pupil Behaviour, in N. Jones (Ed) *School Management and Pupil Behaviour.* Lewes: Falmer Press.

Rieser, R. & Mason, M. (1990) *Disability Equality in the Classroom: A Human Rights Issue.* London: ILEA.

Rogers, R. (1986) *Caught in the Act.* London: Centre for Studies on Integration in Education.

Roaf, C. & Bines, H. (Eds) (1989) *Needs, Rights and Opportunities.* Lewes: Falmer Press.

Robinson, P. (1091) *Perspectives on the Sociology of Education*. London: Routledge & Kegan Paul.

Russell, P. (1990) The Education Reform Act: the Implications for Special Needs, in M. Flude & M. Hammer (Eds) *The Education Reform Act, 1988: Its Origins and Implications*. Lewes: Falmer Press.

Ryan, J. & Thomas, F. (1980) *The Politics of Mental Handicap*. Harmondsworth: Penguin.

Scull, A.T. (1982) *Museums of Madness: The Social Organisation of Insanity in Nineteenth Century England*. Harmondsworth: Penguin.

Tomlinson, S. (1981) *Educational Sub-Normality: a study in Decision-making*. London: Routledge & Kegan Paul.

Tomlinson, S. (1982) *A Sociology of Special Education*. London: Routledge & Kegan Paul.

Tomlinson, S. (1985) The experience of special education, *Oxford Review of Education*, 11, pp. 157-165.

Tomlinson, S. (1988) Why Johnny can't read: critical theory and special education, *European Journal of Special Needs Education*, 3, pp. 45 -58.

Warnock, M. (1982) Children with special needs in ordinary schools: integration revisited, *Education Today*, 32 (3) pp. 56-62.

Weiner, G. (1986) Feminist education and equal opportunities: unity or discord?, *British Journal of Sociology of Education*, 7, pp. 265-274.

Welton, J. (1989) Incrementalism to Catastrophe Theory: Policy for Children with Special Needs, in C. Roaf & H. Bines (Eds) *Needs, Rights & Opportunities*. Lewes: Falmer Press.

Whitty, G. & Mentere, I. (1991) The Progress of Restructuring, in D. Coulby & L. Bash (Eds) *The 1988 Education Reform Act: Conflict and Contradiction*. London: Cassell.

Williams, J. (1986) Education and race: the racialisation of class inequalities?, *British Journal of Sociology of Education*, 7, pp. 135-154.

Wolfensberger, W. (1975) *The Origin and Nature of Our Institutional Models*. Syracuse, N.Y.: Human Policy Press.

Chapter Five

On the Specificity of Racism

AHMED GURNAH

Does the mosquito thank you for your blood? (A Kiswahili proverb)

A central role for the sociology of education is justified by the 'undeniable effect' that schooling has on our behaviour and interaction and its ability to "modify or reinforce behaviour patterns, roles and status opportunities, values and structures" (Eggleston, 1974, p. 7). Thus sociologists can make either a general or specific contribution to educational analysis and at the same time influence social developments. Their descriptions and explanations may in the long run provide a basis for appropriate educational policies and programmes. Their work can potentially promote solutions to fundamental and vexed problems of how correctly to identify educational needs and create a meaningful learning context not just for pupils in schools but also for working class and second chance learners, especially black women and men. Sociologists can also increase the relevance of teachers' initial and inservice training and thus probably also help reduce institutional racism within the educational system.

The sociology of education in the last thirty to forty years has traced its own path, marking out a number of stages. So, for example, when interactionists such as Woods (1983) criticised functionalists (e.g. Glass, 1954), they added issues of meaning, classroom interaction and the importance of the curriculum to discussions of education and the economy. When Marxists (such as Bowles & Gintis, 1976) returned the discussion to social class and its reproduction through the classroom, they were questioning the complacency towards social democracy of both previous type of analysis. While feminists such as Deem (1984) were to remind us that educational analysis has tended to neglect girls and women.

This said, then, some sociologists have clarified particular philosophies and are therefore also capable of doing the same in education by interrogating its social origin and context. Others outline the social structure and analyse group or individual relationships within which educational philosophies are thought, thrive and inform learning. Sociological analysis is capable of providing a backdrop against which teachers may reflect and plan delivery (Burgess, 1986, p. 10). The discipline as a whole, therefore, participates in the collection and analysis of social data, (including educational data) and in its feedback to the classroom. Sociological findings thus can help in the design of a relevant curriculum.

But it is in the specific investigations on gender, class and racial inequalities and how to overcome them in the classroom, that sociologists can make and often do make a special contribution. They bisect ideas and ideologies and trace out the structuring influence which can be found in the process of learning. Modern sociologists habitually show the extent of this influence on teacher expectations and attitudes, assessment, achievement and training for employment (Brandt, 1986; Troyna, 1987; Tomlinson, 1990). They do so by examining group memberships, practices, and the culture that informs them; in the hope that, by these means, we shall reach a greater understanding of educational activities become better informed and thus be in a position to bring about change.

And yet, leaving aside right wing educational commentators who from the start are politically and ideologically hostile to the discipline, sociological research and the teaching of sociology of education also leaves some black people, educators *and* even sociologists themselves sceptical of these claims. Many find the research lack-lustre or its courses jejune, superficial and untheoretical. Bernbaum (1977) for example found sociology's preoccupations 'old' and 'traditional' - failing therefore to address important contemporary curricula issues. Instead of increasing relevance in education, sociological studies have also been found to justify the aims of particular pressure groups (Eggleston, 1974, p. 1). Critics have gone so far as to accuse the sociology of education of mystifying knowledge and undoing its own class projects (CCCS, 1981, p. 130). While Lawrence (1982) and Bourne (1980) are convinced that the sociology of race relations undermines the black agenda.

In this piece I want to extend Lawrence and Bourne's criticism by plotting two more key characteristics of sociology of education which I hope will contribute to its development. For within sociology there are still approaches which diminish our ability to analyse, in this case black people. Formalism and empiricism in sociology are such approaches. On the one hand, formalism is preoccupied with the realm of 'race' or 'IQ', definitions of 'racism' or 'ethnicity' or 'culture', to the exclusion of an honest look at the concrete lives and struggles of black people. Recent sociological debates tend not to be over what class action can be taken nor about how communal organisation can counter the exploitation or neglect of black people. Such debates tend to focus on definitions of 'race' or 'class', 'antiracism or multiculture'. Actual subjects of struggle and their activities, if you like, are put aside in favour of the exploration of overarching 'transcendental' definitions, in the mistaken belief, I think, that they will explain and direct every aspect of concrete black life. This platonic and rationalist influence in sociology constitutes its greatest analytical error (see Gurnah & Scott, forthcoming). By this I mean that mistakenly sociologists have appropriated a philosophical stance to social life. Instead of examining what is really the case, they tend to create a 'rational' model and assume social life must be like it. In other words, instead of studying society, they end up studying elegant 'concepts' and, via them, seek what may be expected by the theory to exist in society.

Sociological empiricists, on the other hand, flood us with 'facts' about black oppression, which can become repetitive or voyeuristic. For even when they give undeniable evidence of what that oppression looks like, they simultaneously also present accounts of how black people in western societies habitually are being degraded and humiliated. What is often missing in their accounts, are corresponding tales of black people's efforts to improve or reverse their condition.

I suspect, therefore, while fully convinced of the importance of sociology for educational analysis, that I am not at present convinced about sociologists' ability to deliver on the claims referred to earlier. For at base, formalism and empiricism are misleading influences on many sociological practitioners. Indeed, where black people's needs in education are concerned, sociologists appear quite misguided as I shall try to show.

As it is not my intention to conduct a review of sociology of education, but to make some very specific comments about the treatment of black people in sociological analysis, in the first section, I will structure my argument by reconsidering a number of key criticisms made of sociology and sociology of education in the 1970s. These criticisms in my view are still valid today and perhaps account for the failure of the discipline to address important contemporary general issues facing educational transformation. From my present location within a local educational authority I witness a plethora of reforms being introduced - from local financial management, school and college reviews, the restructuring of education provision and priorities to the implementation of the National Curriculum. Educational managers are doing all of this in their usual bureaucratic, plodding fashion without it seems much help given to them by the sociology profession. At a time when a major educational rethink is required, sociologists are nowhere to be found in large enough numbers to play a key analytical role. The question one is tempted to ask is whether this absence is a result of government hostility or whether sociology itself has constructed its own irrelevance. The ways in which sociology has treated issues concerning black people may be a case in point.

In the second section I consider therefore the possible reasons behind sociological neglect of genuine black concerns, such as those of adult literacy and community run provision. I consider also how sociology can contribute to black struggles by helping to highlight those needs identified by black working class men and women, analyse them and suggest the obvious practical implications of policy and legislation on attempts to respond to those needs.

Some Criticisms of the Sociology of 'Race Relations'

Eggleston writing in 1974 criticised sociological research for allowing, as a result of its theoretical vagueness, pressure groups to distort its findings. But according to the Centre for Contemporary Cultural Studies (CCCS, 1981), sociologists may have caused greater damage than merely providing raw materials for pressure groups. Sociologists had distorted their own work by paying too much attention to male experiences to the exclusion of female experience and also by undermining their professional class project. The more sociology influenced policy, "this paradox progressively deepened". Subsequently, rather than reduce inequalities, policies built on sociological findings produced similar failure "with monotonous regularity". "There was a dynamic of self-destruction" implicating "the very categories and methods of research" (CCCS, 1981, p. 130).

The desire to monitor results through comparable standard statistics, argued the CCCS, reduced class to social stratification, cultural process to measurable variables and created problems for the analysis of gender. Sociologists became conservative. They were unable to give explanations and disliked innovations which "risked losing the virtues of comparison" (Ibid, p. 130). Thus, specific masculine experience was presented as "the general case, from which the experience of girls was bound to appear as a deviation" (Ibid, p. 131).

Similarly, Errol Lawrence (1982) found sociologists incapable of questioning institutional 'commonsense' racism. Rather, they focused on identity crises, culture conflict and intergenerational conflict. They ignored black parental struggles both in Britain and in their country or origin (p. 95-6). Instead, black people were "characterised as passive, acquiescent victims of racism waiting to 'integrate' as reluctant 'traditionalists' " (p. 132).

Assisted by A. Sivanandan, Jenny Bourne (1980) presented a perceptive review of sociology of race relations. In an article entitled *Cheerleaders and Ombudsmen*, she announced that "there is a dangerous sociology abroad - a sociology of race relations ... dangerous to the black cause it seeks to espouse" (p. 331). She presented a number of arguments in opposition to what she called the sociology of 'enlightened capitalism'. Though the materials she criticised are sometimes about 20 years or so old, I believe that the themes she identified still remain in the contemporary sociology of black people. Her five objections to an abstract and distorting sociology are particularly useful starting points for my discussion on the formalism and empiricism in the field. These criticisms therefore are discussed below under the headings: objectification, statistics of cultural diversity, liberal moralism, colour prejudice, and control and imperialism. Each analysis is a fruitful field for critical analysis and presents a tradition which Bourne and other members of the Institute of Race Relations have been working on for many years, and which is particularly salient for the current project of reassessing the role of sociology of education.

Objectification

Bourne criticised the objectification (my term) of black people through sociological accounts which illegitimately turns them into agents of racism. One example she quoted was that of Judith Henderson who regretted on behalf of British people that "their national traditions of freedom and justice" were disturbed by black and white people coming to blows (p. 334). Thus, instead of examining the racism in white society, Henderson appeared to suggest that the issue was more to do with "educating blacks and whites for integration" (p. 339). Posed in that way, the problem then became, how many black people are there in Britain? What brought them here? How do they fit? Do they have stable leadership? Can they assimilate? And, what adjustments must black people make to become acceptable to white British people?

The numbers game became a popular preoccupation of the media in the 1960's and 1970's (see Cohen & Gardner, 1982). Academics also appeared to have felt that this was the most crucial issue for social analysis. When not led into this view by politicians such as Enoch Powell and Gerald Nebbarro (Foot, 1965 & 1969), the media at least cheered sociologists on and then confirmed that the logic of their utterances implied the need for black repatriation (see the *Question of Numbers*, BBC, 1971). Key Labour Party politicians also were not above exploiting the numbers game (Foot, 1969) or suggesting that controlling the numbers would be "good for race relations" (c.f. Bourne, 1980). The result could be found in the introduction of numerous pieces of legislation specifically designed to deny black British citizens from East Africa, the Caribbean, India, Pakistan and Bangladesh, their legitimate right of entry, domicile and employment in Britain (for example, the Commonwealth Immigrants Act 1962, 1968, and the Immigration Act 1971). Later on, the British state introduced nationality legislation which literally made black people from these countries second class citizens.

As a result of this focus on numbers, economists and sociologists (e.g. Castle & Kosack, 1973; Braham et al, 1981 p. 28-59) and statisticians (Runneymede Trust and Radical Statistics Group, 1982) " 'turned their attention to the push and pull' factors that brought black people to Britain", with projections of their growth. The effect, according to Bourne was one of "giving validity to Labour/Tory orthodoxy that numbers were the problem and that numbers and good race relations were organically linked". Perhaps inadvertently, but nonetheless effectively, sociologists had played their part in legitimising not just the objectification of black people but also the legislation against black entry and the oppression of black people from the Commonwealth and ex-colonies.

The fault seemed to lie in the fact that, once sociologists can explain to *each other's* satisfaction why *they* think black people came here and do what they appear to do, they are rarely troubled about whether it is a "defendable" explanation or if black people concur. Bourne argued that, sociologists sought 'understanding' according to their world view and subsequently assessed black people's 'fit' in British society. Sociologists of race relations in the 1950s and 60s, therefore led themselves down a number of 'blind' alleys. They became obsessed by 'their' (black people's) habitations and how they can be controlled. Could black people be considered to be 'out' or 'in' or could they ever overcome being 'dark strangers'? Would they, in short, ever assimilate? Even when assimilated, according to Sidney Collins, 'emergent' black groups remain maladjusted since they lacked leadership and were unstable. He felt that immigrants should not "continue to observe folkways alien to British society" (Bourne, 1980, p. 331-333).

Statistics of Cultural Diversity

To be stable and thus assimilable, according to this view, black people and communities must adjust. The Social Science Research Council thus funded a project to view "the process of adjustment through which coloured immigrants and their children were passing in order to establish indices of their relative permanence (or transience)" (Bourne, 1980, p. 339). Thus objectified, black people became indexes of someone else's analysis; living in a shadowy existence they were being denied expression by institutions, the state and sociologists alike. They become available for the collection of statistics of cultural diversity. Research, then, concentrated on "explaining customs, beliefs, behaviour, values and attitudes of immigrants to white society: Sikhs in Southall, Pakistanis in Bradford" (p. 336). Such voyeurism prompted a bitter response from Gus John:

> *Departments to study the immigrants spring up like mushrooms, financed by trusts and foundations. Yet the only relationship most of them have with black groups is that of visitors to the zoo. Their findings are never meant to enable the deprived to take action. (quoted in Bourne, 1980, p. 340)*

Ethnography and cultural statistics, furthermore, provided some social analysts with a resource from which to read off black occupational placement (Bourne, 1980, p. 343). Wallman, for example, commented that black people:

> *will not see, will not accept, will not succeed in the opportunity offered if it is not appropriate to their choice of work and their cultural experience. (quoted in Bourne, 1980, p. 344)*

93

Liberal Moralism

However, even those sociologists who had objectified black people recognised that obvious infringements against liberal stances of 'freedom and justice' had to be explained *and* condemned. It is, therefore, quite common to encounter, in sociological texts, (if not sound analyses) at least moral outrage against racism, or maybe more accurately against destabilisation of the given situation. Bourne reminded us that it is a combination of "Christian morality and a judicial concept of the reasonable man" that characterised the early work of the Institute of Race Relations (p. 334). But liberal outrage against racist behaviour often appears at the concrete level with both passion and mystification. For while these liberal sociologists refuse to accept or even notice racial differences, they do at the same time also *deny* black disadvantage. Apparently in Geoffrey Driver's view "even if there was racism in British schools, black children suffered no disadvantage that ethnicity could not overcome" (quoted in Bourne, 1980 p. 344).

Colour Prejudice

The real problem for both black and white people tends to be seen by sociologists as a question of prejudice. In the past this was presented in terms of 'dark strangers' in our midst and more recently as antipathy to colour prejudice. Once so presented, prejudice is not merely against 'black' people, but is to be found in reverse. Indeed, colour being the issue for sociologists, prejudice is to be found between different shades of colour, that is to say, between black people. Scarman set this scene in 1981 when he criticised black people for being 'racialist' towards each other (see Gurnah, 1987). Since prejudice is the issue, that can only be eliminated by education and legislation and by targeting a few misfits without, according to Nicholas Deakin, "compromising either the cultural integrity of our society or the values and principles which animate it" (quoted in Bourne, 1980, p. 337-338). Thus, formalists continue to define and empiricists to collate their cultural statistics, untroubled by the agitation of many black people.

Control and Imperialism

These sociological postures are controlling or imperialist in two ways. Sociological approaches to race relations assisted the British imperialist state to recruit and import labour in the 1950s to build up its industries and manage its white working class population at home (p. 332). But, also in another sense this control was of black people here and in their country of origin - achieved predominantly through educational and other definition processes. The British state used to import sons and daughters of Third World local rulers to Oxbridge and some key Redbrick universities and send them back well briefed. Meanwhile, the social scientist, perhaps unconsciously, promoted similar aims in Britain by his or her stance on black people living here. That stance defined black people as problems and removed their concerns and struggles from the analytical frame.

Bourne's observations were at the time especially astute and are particularly relevant to my criticisms of contemporary sociology of education. Her trenchant analysis of the effects of sociological analysis on the lives of black people is an especially important reminder of the relationship between sociological theorising and policy making. In the next section I intend to extend that analysis to take account of the sociology of education literature and draw attention to the way in which concerns of black people have been 'camouflaged' within this literature.

Formalism and Empiricism in the Sociology of Education

Sociology has not received much public attention or support from funding bodies and subsequently has not produced in my view much interesting work in recent years. Apart from the criticisms already made, I suspect that in the last ten years the discipline has suffered partly from government and funding agencies' prejudices about critical social sciences, and their preference for empiricist and scientistic studies in education. Sociology in particular, and sociology of education especially, has paid the price for its image as a critical discipline. That aside, sociological theory generally seems to be over preoccupied with metatheoretical debates stimulated by Jurgen Habermas and his followers. As a consequence, sociology of education or indeed education analysis as whole, has remained imprisoned within a stifling and unproductive liberal education ideology; and that includes many of the works which pass as progressive, critical or socialist. What exists as Marxist analyses (now even less fashionable) are often critiques of the establishment in education and rarely focus on or offer alternatives in learning.

As far as existing material in sociology of education is concerned, very little or hardly any of it mentions black people, but when it does, it analyses black people badly (e.g. Morris, 1972; Levitas, 1974; Sharp, 1980; Demaine, 1981; Meigham, 1981; Apple, 1982; Livingstone, 1983; Holmes, 1985). There are of course, notable exceptions (e.g. Barton & Walker, 1983; Reid, 1986). Chris Searle, in particular, over a number of years, has published excellent materials which celebrate black cultural achievements (Searle, 1982, 1984, 1986, 1991). Ironically, this absence of attention to black people in theoretical sociology has led to the development of the very lively sub-discipline of multicultural/anti-racist education, but at a price. Let us take some examples.

James Lynch's book (1983) provides a good example of how social analysts talk to each other (or in this case talk to budding white teachers), without any reference to black people of flesh and blood. The formalist assumption of this author leads him confidently to pronounce that it is necessary for education to identify:

> *the underlying ethic of a multicultural society before decision and policies ... can be proposed. Only then can discussion commence as to what kind of curriculum might be appropriate for schools. (p. 9)*

> *Given that the UK is a multicultural society, then all else should follow from that: its laws, its institutions, its schooling and its curriculum. (p. 10)*

He defines 'multicultural', multi-ethnic, multicredal, bilingual, bicultural, and ends up preferring multicultural. He insists that a multicultural educator is ethically bound to 'respect persons'.

Behind this apparent liberal tolerance lies at least three layers of camouflage that serve to hide the fact that black people are not at all the subject of this discussion. The *first* layer talks of 'multiculture', essentially in terms of serving the needs of white children in an environment which has radically changed from pre-war society. The *second* layer of camouflage, is to abstract the issues away from needs of black children altogether and present their parents' concerns in terms of a requirement to design a rational and moral curriculum. For then sociologists can confidently talk about their area of educational expertise without fear of serious challenge from non-professional black parents. That, in turn, allows for the *third* layer of camouflage which makes it easier for social scientists and educators to talk freely about, yet also define away, problems created in education by the presence of black learners.

Lynch (1983) is by no means the only one who takes this stance. A recent collection of articles edited by Robert Jeffcoate & Alan James (1981) revealed precisely this tendency, though in it are some chapters, for example by Bernard Coard and Farrukh Dhondy, which mention and focus on the experience of black young people. More recently Jon Nixon (1989) assumes that "racism is primarily a *system* of dominations and oppression" and that schools participate in continuing that system, with teachers' involvement (p. v). The practices of schools, Nixon argues "should be reconstructed around a serious and prolonged consideration of principle of equality for a multicultural society" (p. 1). Then Nixon repeats Lynch's programme of creating a rational and moral multicultural curriculum. Similar camouflaging takes place here too, with no analysis of black needs and how they will be met. The discussion of racism itself (I shall return to this) becomes a fourth camouflage.

Furthermore, these tendencies are not necessarily motivated by political considerations, as such. A number of self confessed left sociologists writing on black people and education also follow this same procedure in their writing. Godfrey L. Brandt (1986), for example, having reviewed various writings on different concepts in the first part of his book, then embarks on a similar mystification as his 'multicultural' colleagues, but now calling it 'anti-racist', and using a great deal of left sounding rhetoric.

But in this discussion, no less than in any other, he fails to address black people's needs directly.

Barry Troyna & Jenny Williams (1986) appear to wish to redress the social scientists' failure to analyse "decision making and policy formation in the sphere of education", especially on 'race' matters and thus reduce their political naivete (p. 1). While this is a legitimate and important task to pursue, I wonder how it can be done without a detailed 'analytical conversation' with black parents and young people. Much of this book appears to have the customary conversation with other academics about local education authority policies.

Part of the problem is that all too often sociologists, especially radical sociologists, talk of the 'problem of race', whatever that is, or focus on 'racism', which is real enough, without realising that a clear definition of racism or where it can be found *still* tells us nothing about black people. Rather, we are offered a discussion and a preoccupation with white repressive ideologies and practices which will apparently show us where things go wrong. But the discussion of such ideologies and practices, even if it were necessary, tends to be rather aloof and generalised. People are being asked to identify 'racism' in a simple equation with 'underachievement'. But it is not the general 'truth' equation of this kind that is of significance for analysis, rather it is the specific steps in the processes of how oppression takes place and adds up to this general actuality which is of analytical value. What is both more interesting and useful for identifying where solutions to reverse inequalities lie, are the various, small, and detailed and complicated steps, cycles, cultural habits and professional practices which produce this brutal equation. The little lies, the smartness of cultural deception, the historical procedures, the careerism of staff, the inflexibility of received knowledge, the defensiveness of the little informed, the training of teachers, the state and LEA resourcing design, the class and imperial attitudes, the recruitment and promotion of teaching and non-teaching staff, and many other seemingly unimportant routines all contribute to this equation.

Sociologists compare and argue, and provide a starting point for what Habermas calls 'argumentation', or a more honest discussion. But even if we reach the argumentative stage about the racism - underachievement equation, we are in my opinion still *not* dealing with the important issue at hand. The multicultural and antiracist literature does not just experience isolation from theoretical sociology but also suffers from its failure to tackle the real issue of racism. For me, the only substantial way into tackling racism is to address black people, their needs, aspirations, world views, and how they wish to live. If sociologists fail to do that, the rest becomes an expensive, irrelevant and tiresome dialogue amongst white (and some black) professionals.

In this context I found Beverley Shaw's (1981) book quite priceless. Black people are put under a subheading of 'children and their ethnic origin', definitions, education policy for, migration of, and ways of life. Shaw takes off with an old discredited chestnut of the 1950s:

in many countries the main divisions (or strata) in society seem to be created by ethnic (and religious) differences rather than by ones of occupation, income, status or power. (p. 119)

Shaw follows Reissman in the view that being black in America is an "inheritance of inequality in virtually every aspect of life". Though at first sight this may appear to represent sympathy (even if analytically sloppy), it actually also carries inevitability with it. Black people fail, that is their inheritance. He thought, in any case, there was "something of the general preoccupation" with "race problems" in Britain, copying America (p. 119).

The scene thus set, Shaw turns to the statistics of settlement and speculates on number of Pakistanis, Caribbeans, Indian etc, there will be in Britain in the future (p. 121). In seeking definitions of racial categories, Shaw prefers ethnic groups to 'black' people on the grounds that the latter was misleading because it lumped together diverse culture, religion and national origin (p. 121). He, therefore, totally misses its meaning for the collective struggles of black people in Britain.

Shaw, continues with his gallery to cliches by asking "What, then, is all the fuss about? Why should Enoch Powell have prophesied doom: like rivers of blood? Or Mrs Thatcher talk of swamping?" His answer is because black people (who are visible) tend to concentrate in poor areas (p. 121). He thus fails to give any sociological causation for this state of affairs.

It is, perhaps, little wonder that it is in such areas that the rival forces of the National Front and the Anti-Nazi League fight their mimic battles, to the discomfiture of the police and innocent bystanders. (p. 122)

His cliches become quite outrageous when he turns his focus to African and Caribbean communities. I shall let him speak for himself:

In West Indian society the long maintained white supremacy has been only too influential, bringing about a sense of Creole inferiority and encouraging a belief that the darker the skin the more inferior the status. (p. 122)

One of the legacies of slavery is the absence of a strong convention that parents (particularly fathers) be responsible for their children.

He ends by suggesting that not to treat all pupils the same "whatever their colour, ethnic or social background", is for him an "inverted racism" (p. 126) - yet for many of us this amounts to simply ignoring black people's oppressions.

Shaw's work reminds me of a less silly version of this analysis - the seminal text by Musgrove (1972), who gave statistics and talked of difficulties about numbers and the inappropriateness of black people's 'behaviour' which can cause 'administrative frustrations' (pp. 247-248). He also blamed racism on black people and denied them nationality rights:

it must be remembered that prejudice also exists amongst coloured immigrants both towards the British and towards each other. (p. 249)

Such texts raise a number of key issues for me. Firstly, they pose the question, in what ways can such comments pass as accurate sociological analyses of black people or their education? Secondly, lest we merely dismiss these authors as crude analysts, most contemporary sociologists still present similar arguments but now wrapped up in black and white radical rhetoric. A review of recent sociology of education research however would find similar tendencies to what I referred to earlier as formalism and empiricism (for a full discussion see Gurnah & Scott, forthcoming). The point about these observations is that such sociological analyses are, in my view, theoretical, generalised and prejudiced. They are therefore in danger of being misleading and not even descriptive of black people.

Conclusion

The main purpose of this article has been to present a critique of sociology of education especially in relation to black people's experiences and struggles. In the introduction I identified two highly significant characteristics of sociology of education, particularly in relation to the sociology of black people and education. I referred to these characteristics as first *formalism* with its preoccupations with defining for example, 'race', ethnicity and cultural diversity without due regard to the concrete lives and struggles of black people. Secondly sociological *empiricism* contributed to that process by collecting 'facts' (such as the numbers of immigrants and ethnic communities in Britain) that are used to account for black people's experiences.

Both approaches, I argued, represent a sociology which lacks a sense of history and an awareness of the struggles of black people. Yet when sociologists are historical and thus specific in their analysis of black people, they are well able to theorise about them, examine facts of their lives, and incorporate a sense of *their* world, without making them or the world they share with others vanish from our gaze. In short, a historical approach gives a voice to the subject, and makes sure, in the final analysis, that the voice is loud and clear and emanates not purely from the analysts' preferences or prejudices, but contains an authentic representation of what is important to the actors and to the struggles involved.

But an historical approach is also not sufficient, nor is a great deal of analytical perceptiveness, enough. For change we must stimulate reactions and a desire to subvert the existing order by black people and their supporters. Black people challenge and seek transformation. Sociology can, therefore, play an important role in clarifying the specific steps and cycles taken by black communities and in providing a systematic analysis which helps to evaluate the rhetoric that goes with such struggles.

The re-location of black people into sociological analysis also becomes crucial in the construction of successful social policy programmes. Too often, when not based on irrelevant sociological research, programmes are built upon widely held, but rarely informed views of what black people need, or views about which are the institutional and relational barriers that deny black people satisfaction. Some sociologists, particularly the radical ones, end up repeating black people's fighting rhetoric or merely extend their own social democratic educational frame (CCCS, 1981) to black people. The elimination of formalism and empiricism, therefore, becomes desirable for the correct evaluation of educational policy and programme for black women and men.

I have not provided an alternative in this article. Elsewhere (see Gurnah, 1987, 1989, 1990a, 1990b) I try to present materials about black people which gives full voice to their concerns and try to present 'their' world and the world around them as it affects their lives. A good sociological analysis does not simply present the subject's views correctly, but also offers a fair and balanced context which recognises a complex of interests and interpretations. Many contemporary sociologists in contrast, know very little about the black people they analyse - they do not speak their language or share their difficulties in coping in Britain. Few sociologists understand the brutalising effect colonisation has had on particular racial and national groups and individuals or the way it has set group against group. Instead, as innocents in this 'struggle' developed by 19th century European men to make judgments of black people now, some sociologists would also add black political rhetoric to give an authentic flavour to their writings.

Ironically a massive amount of writing on 'race' and education has appeared in the last 30 years discussing racism, cultural habits, numbers, immigration, and so on. Yet relatively little research has addressed the dire situation of black adults. It is not uncommon in most cities to find large numbers of elderly African and Caribbean people receiving no attention at all, from any social analysis or educational institutions. Nor is there much research on the experiences of black women, which is not seeking to score points.

Furthermore, the attention directed at young people, from these communities tends to focus almost exclusively on the effects of racism on young people's experience - yet subsequently offering only a superficial analysis of what racism consists of and how schools and colleges can tackle it. Neither strategy it seems appears truly relevant to the substantive needs of black young people. If the truth be told, the good work that takes place in educational institutions rarely is informed by sociologists of education. Quite often it comes about through direct parental and community organisation and interventions in those institutions and through the local authorities and voluntary groups.

With regard to non English speaking communities, Britain has lived with a scandal for 30-40 years, still not made public by research. In Sheffield, for example, male and female adults from almost all the black communities in the city are carrying illiteracy rates of between 60% - 80 amounting to between 8,000 - 10,000 people and nothing substantial was being done for them (Sheffield City Council, 1987, 1988)). The rhetoric of antiracism was strong, but only a handful of these adults were receiving education. Though English as a Second Language resources were meant to be made available to black pupils, schools were not above using the teachers appointed for this work to cover general duties. The resources were not always used efficiently and black students' failure rates continued. In its recent scrutiny the Home Office (1988) has shown that local education authorities have been misusing the funding made available to them by the government under the Section 11 of the 1966 Local government Act to provide education for black people. Yet in order to end this abuse of resources for black people by education authorities and institutions the government has now introduced a ridiculous monitoring regime. Educational writers could stop arguing over curriculum design and how to develop multicultural and antiracist resources, and concentrate on providing a sociological analysis of the specific needs of black people and whether teaching and non-teaching staff are adequately (or not) responding to them. Sociological research, therefore, could easily facilitate such monitoring procedures.

At present we are faced with some major changes in the education service, brought about by the Education Reform Act. There is much scope here for sociologists to make a genuine analytical and policy contribution, but only if they avoid formalism and the tendency to debate with each other about what they think they already know. In addition, they may need to refrain from the tendency to accumulate yet more statistics of disadvantage to satisfy an empiricist professional urge. Instead, as I have argued, sociologists should develop an analytical conversation, a dialogue, with black people, about their needs, and how as educators, we can satisfy them.

Acknowledgement

I wish to thank Clara Green for helping me prepare this manuscript.

REFERENCES

Apple, M.W. (1982) *Cultural and Economic Reproduction in Education*. London: Routledge.

Barton, L. & Walker, S. (Eds) (1983) *Race, Class and Education*. London: Croom Helm.

Bernbaum, G. (1977) *Knowledge and Ideology in the Sociology of Education*. London: Macmillan.

Bourne, J. (1980) Cheerleaders and ombudsmen, *Race and Class*, 21, pp. 332-352.

Bowles, S. & Gintis, H. (1976) *Schooling in Capitalist America*. London: Routledge.

Braham, P. et al (1981) *Discrimination and Disadvantage in Employment*. London: Harper & Row.

Brandt, G.L. (1986) *The Realisation of Antiracist Teaching*. London: Falmer Press.

Burgess, B. (1986) *Sociology, Education and Schools*. London: Batsford.

Castle, S. & Kosack, S. (1973) *Immigrant Workers and Class Structure in Western Europe*. Oxford: IRR.

Centre for Contemporary Cultural Studies (CCCS) (1981) *Unpopular Education*. London: Hutchinson.

Coard, B. (1981). What the British School System Does to the Black Child, in S.R. Jeffcoate & A. Jones (Eds) *The School in the Multicultural Society: a reader*. London: Harper & Row.

Cohen, P. & Gardiner, C. (1982) *It Ain't Half Racist, Mum*. London: Comedia/Carm.

Deem, R. (Ed) (1984) *Co-education Reconsidered*. Milton Keynes: Open University Press.

Demaine, J. (1981) *Contemporary Theories in the Sociology of Education*. London: Macmillan.

Dhondy, F. (1981) Teaching Young Blacks, in S.R. Jeffcoate & A. Jones (Eds) *The School in the Multicultural Society: a reader*. London: Harper & Row.

Eggleston, J. (1974) *Contemporary Research in the Sociology of Education*. Milton Keynes: Open University Press.

Foot, P. (1965) *Immigration and Race in British Politics*. London: Penguin.

Foot, P. (1969) *The Rise of Enoch Powell*. London: Penguin.

Glass, D. (1954) *Social Mobility in Britain*. London: Routledge.

Gurnah, A. (1987) Gatekeepers and Caretakers, in B. Troyna (Ed) *Racial Equality in Education*. London: Tavistock.

Gurnah, A. (1989) After Bilingual Support?, in M. Cole (Ed) *Education for Equality*. London: Routledge.

Gurnah, A. (1990a) Translating race equality politics into practice, *Critical Social Policy*, 27, pp. 110-124.

Gurnah, A. (1990b) Language for Autonomy, in Pam Cater et al. (Eds) *Social Work and Social Welfare*. Milton Keynes: Open University Press.

Gurnah, A. & Scott, A. (forthcoming) *The Uncertain Science*. London: Routledge.

Holmes, B. (Ed) (1985) *Equality and Freedom in Education*. London: Allen & Unwin.

Home Office (1988) A Scrutiny of Grants Under Section 11 of the Local Government Act 1966.

Jeffcoate, S.R. & James, A. (Ed) (1981) *The School in the Multicultural Society: a reader*. London: Harper & Row.

Lawrence, E. (1982) In the abundance of water the fool is thirsty: sociology and black 'pathology', in Centre for Contemporary Cultural Studies, *The Empire Strikes Back*. London: Hutchinson.

Levitas, M. (1974) *Marxist Perspectives in Sociology of Education*. London: Routledge.

Livingstone, D.W. (1983) *Class Ideologies and Educational Future*. Lewes: Falmer Press.

Lynch, J. (1983) *The Multi-Cultural Curriculum*. London: Batsford.

Meigham, R. (1981) *A Sociology of Education*. London: Holt Education.

Morris, I. (1972) *The Sociology of Education*. London: Unwin.

Musgrove, F. (1972) *The Sociology of Education*. London: Methuen.

Nixon, J. (1985) *A Teacher's Guide to Multi-Cultural Education*. Oxford: Blackwell.

Reid, I. (1986) *The Sociology of School*. London: Fontana.

Runneymede Trust Radical Statistics Group (1982) *Britain's Black Populations*. London: Heinemann.

Searle, C. (1982) *Sunflower of Hope*. London: Allison & Busby.

Searle, C. (1984) *Words Unchained*, 2nd Edn. London: Zed Press.

Searle, C. (1986) *All Our Words*. London: Young World Books.

Searle, C. (1991) *A Blindfold Removed*. London: Caria Press.

Sharpe, R. (1980) *Knowledge Ideology and Politics of Towards a Marxist Analysis of Education*. London: Routledge.

Shaw, B. (1981) *Educational Practice and Sociology*. Oxford: Martin Robinson.

Sheffield City Council (1987) Black Adult Literacy Campaign: A Discussion Paper.

Sheffield City Council (1988) Literacy, Fluency and Education.

Sheffield City Council (1988) A Partnership Broken.

Sheffield City Council (1988) Community Routes to Literacy.

Tomlinson, S. (1990) *Multi-Cultural Education in White Schools*. London: Batsford.

Troyna, B. & Williams, J. (1986) *Racism, Education and the State*. London: Croom Helm.

Woods, P. (1983) *Sociology and the School: an interactionist view point*. London: Routledge.

Chapter Six

Teachers' Responses to the Reshaping of Primary Education

ANDREW POLLARD

In this paper I aim to discuss both some of the early responses which primary school teachers have made to recent legislation in England and Wales and to begin to trace continuities between emergent issues and more long-standing sociological concerns.

Such a search for continuities in the midst of change is important, for the pace and extent of recent legislation, with multiple forms of innovation progressively impacting on primary schools, may at times seem to be setting entirely new agendas. This is far from the case and it is helpful to consider the relevance of the empirical and theoretical insights which have been developed by sociologists in the past.

Regarding the impact of the legislation itself, the key proposition I offer is that, whilst primary education is undoubtedly 'being reshaped' by external forces, considerable scope for strategic action by teachers and schools remains - scope which is being actively used.

The net result of such processes is impossible to predict at this particular point, a pivotal point at which teacher, parent and public responses remain relatively ill-defined and uncertain. However, it is certainly the case that any longer-term 'reshaping' will reflect the responses of children, parents, governors and teachers, whatever form these gradually acquire, as well as the more obvious forces of change emanating from central government. Of course, in making such arguments I am simply, in one sense, asserting and applying the key sociological insight about the interplay of agency and constraint in shaping change.

The paper beings with a consideration of the tension between government intentions behind the late 1980s legislation and previous primary school ideology. It then moves to an extended discussion of teachers' initial responses to various features of the Education Reform

Act.[1] The paper culminates in a section which traces the continuities in sociological concerns and speculates about the future agenda for sociological research.

Government Intentions and Primary School Ideology

The legislation of the late 1980s has brought changes in almost every aspect of primary education - including funding, accountabilty, management, enrolment, curriculum and assessment. Such changes have particular implications for the ideology of progressivism and 'child centredness', which, with its origins in the Plowden Report of 1967, has influenced the perspectives and commitments of primary school teachers for many years. The tension between these two contrasting value systems is a real one and is one key issue which is being played out in the early 1990s as the legislation is being implemented.

The government's explicit, publicity stated intention in introducing the Education Reform Act, 1988, was to 'raise standards'. Taking the inadequacy of existing standards as being almost self-evident and strongly influenced by the various pressure groups of the 'New Right' (Whitty, 1989), levels of achievement were to be raised by instigating a centrally directed national curriculum, associated assessment procedures and public reporting of children's educational results. These measures, it was claimed, would ensure curricular entitlement in all schools and provide parents and others with unbiased information about the achievements of schools and children.

Building on the Education Act of 1986, greater powers and autonomy were given to the Governing Body of each school, for schools were to operate in a competitive market in which they could act independently. It was believed that competition would cause schools to become more efficient.

There was also a clear intention to decrease the powers of local authorities, partly because it was felt that their traditional planning role would interfere with market mechanisms, but also because some local authorities were felt to be 'irresponsible' - for instance, having persisted with 'high spending' and interventionist initiatives such as those concerned with implementing Equal Opportunities policies.

The underlying assumptions were that standards were low, that professional educators and LEAs could not be trusted, that only the introduction of the market mechanism into education could repair the weaknesses. However, they contrast strongly with the thinking of many primary school teachers, teachers who, to greater or lesser extent [2], have been influenced by child-centred ideas and by the legacy of the Plowden Report (CACE, 1967).

Indeed, the Plowden Report set the dominant tone of much of the discussion of children's education in primary schools from its publication to the mid 1980's. It thus provides a context for any discussion of the challenges facing teachers at present.

Early in the Plowden Report, a child centred approach was advocated:

At the heart of the educational process lies the child. No advances in policy, no acquisitions of new equipment have their desired effect unless they are in harmony with the nature of the child. (Para 9)

The report, through descriptions of 'good practice', advocated activity and experience, both 'physical and mental', as the best means of gaining knowledge and acquiring facts. It was suggested that teachers should develop several 'centres of interest' around which the majority of children's work could be organised. Central to the teacher's role in the context were seen to be judgements about curriculum balance and pacing for each individual in the class. The emphasis on the development of individual children was supported by reference to the work of psychologists, Piaget in particular, and was seen as demanding sensitivity and observation from the teacher rather than intervention.

On the curriculum, the Plowden Report advocated an undifferentiated curriculum for the early years of learning and placed a particular emphasis on the importance of play. One of the hallmarks of the effective curriculum was taken to be its flexibility and responsiveness to children's interests, a way of working which placed great faith in the professional judgement of teachers in its implementation. However, it was anticipated that as children grew older the organisation of lessons with a focus on more conventional subjects became more appropriate.

Whilst there was an acceptance that education ought to equip children for the society into which they will grow up, a school was seen as ... "not merely a teaching shop. It is a community in which children learn to live first and foremost as children and not as future adults", (para 505). Christian Schiller, a leading commentator of the time and first Staff Inspector (HMI) for Junior Education, was influential in arguing that primary education was an important stage of education in itself, rather than simply a preparation for future stages.

The report recommended that, twice a year, teachers should hold private discussions with parents on their children's progress and that they should provide a written report annually. Parental choice of primary school was recommended wherever possible.

The authors of the Report envisaged close and complementary relationships between central government, LEAs, schools and parents. Thus a continuing interplay between local and national funding, maintaining the tradition of a national service delivered locally, was affirmed. Interestingly though, in recognition of the diversity of local circumstances and needs, the authors of the report advocated the establishment of 'educational priority areas' and local authorities were urged to adopt 'positive discrimination' by favouring schools in neighbourhoods where children were disadvantaged by socioeconomic circumstances.

There are many notable contrasts in the underlying assumptions of Plowden and the recent legislation. In the Plowden account flexibility and integration in the curriculum was to be encouraged, teacher judgement was be trusted, partnership with parents and with LEAs was supported. Educationalists, it was assumed, were working, with professional commitment, to improve the quality of children's learning. The assumptions associated with the present legislation are very different - the curriculum is to be standardised by Programmes of Study, the power of 'producers', such as teachers and LEA staff, must be curbed and replaced by that of parental and industrial 'consumers', teachers are seen to need tighter contracts and more effective management. Educationalists, it is appears to be assumed, should be sorted out with a strong dose of management and the stiff breeze of competition.

Of course, it would be wrong to assume that the Plowden Report reflected the way in which practice in primary school classrooms actually evolved during the 1970s and 1980s. Indeed, whilst the report appeared to be influential, it may have had rather less impact on actual practice. For instance, despite the extent to which child-centred ideas passed into the discourse of teachers, a large number of sociologists, educationalists and other commentators observed the apparent lack of the implementation of the kinds of practice espoused. The studies by Bennett (1976), HMI (1978) and Galton, Simon & Croll (1980), all suggested that most practice in English primary schools turned out to be more formal and teacher dominated than envisaged by Plowden. Only one tenth of teachers in the Bennett study and one fifth of teachers in the Galton, Simon & Croll (1980) study (or, depending on definition, about one tenth, Galton, 1989), might be described as corresponding to a 'Plowden approach' in terms of their practice. Similarly, the HMI Survey of 1978 indicated that most schools gave highest priority to teaching children to read, write and learn mathematics (1978, para. 8, 16) and felt it necessary to affirm the importance of a broad curriculum (1978, para. 8, 28/29).

Although such findings suggest that fully developed 'child-centred practice' was comparatively rare in classrooms, the idea remained an important rallying point for primary school teachers and as an important set of defining principles of professional commitment. Richards (1982 p. 16) asserted that ... "child centred ideology (was) the orthodoxy of primary education, at least as perceived by many policy makers, commentators and educationalists" - a point of view which received corroboration from the surveys of teacher aims by both Ashton (1975, 1981) and Broadfoot & Osborn (1988).

The evidence of the gap between espoused belief and action can easily be misinterpreted. The 'opportunities to teach', given the resource constraints in public education, are often problematic so that primary teachers have to cope as best they can (Woods, 1990; Pollard, 1985).

However, the Plowden Report encapsulated values which were vitally important to many primary school teachers in terms of their commitment and beliefs in children - the ideas of public service, of caring and nurturing, of responsiveness to need and of support for the disadvantaged. As Nias (1989) and Pollard (1988) have illustrated, such ideas formed an important part of the identity and sense of 'self' of many primary school teachers. Commitment to children comprised an area in which personal and professional interests coincided. Both public service and personal fulfilment were provided.

This pattern of commitment is vividly illustrated in Nias' report (1989) of her interviews with fifty primary teachers in mid-career. She asked them if they 'felt like a teacher' and, if so, to explain why. Forty two, out of the fifty, saw themselves as teachers and went on to describe the way in which they were able to 'be themselves', 'be whole and be natural' through the enactment of their role. Thus, despite the endemic tensions caused by disciplinary and instructional concerns, the overriding affirmation was of the personal, effective involvement and fulfilment which has often been associated with the relationships with children in primary classrooms.

Nias quotes one teacher as saying:

> *I've come to realise that if you really want to educate children you've got to share yourself with them, as a person. They've got to know about you, your interests, your life outside school, the sort of person you are. But most of all it means being open to them as a person, and that makes you vulnerable. Yes, being a teacher is being ready to be vulnerable. (Nias, 1989, p. 187)*

When the primary school teachers in her sample tried to explain what it was like to experience the wholeness and closeness of relationships with a group of children, they

> *... without exception, cupped their hands or made enfolding movements with their hands and arms. They spoke eagerly, enthusiastically, often leaning forward, their faces animated. ... They seemed to be displaying a deeply satisfying sense of belonging. (Nias, 1989, pp. 183-4)*

These data were collected before the recent education legislation and there are good grounds for believing that the pattern might not be repeated today - as the Education Reform Act of 1988 starts to take effect.

Teachers' Responses to the Education Reform Act

Primary teachers seem to have somewhat different approaches to current reforms of curriculum and assessment and consideration of these two issues can highlight some of the complex social factors at play in the production of teachers' responses to the new educational centralism.

Curriculum

The 'official' account of the responses of primary school teachers to the 1988 Act shows them moving forward constructively and professionally to implement the National Curriculum. Thus an HMI survey of 100 primary schools, conducted in the Autumn of 1989, concludes that

> *Overall, about two-thirds of the primary schools inspected were beginning to implement successfully National Curriculum requirements in core subjects for children in Year 1. (HMI, 1990, p. 12)*

and that

> *Most teachers were making a determined, conscientious effort to met their legal and professional obligations to the children and their parents. (HMI, 1990, p. 12)*

The National Curriculum Council has also begun an evaluation and monitoring programme and some of its Professional Officers have offered conference reports on the results of its pilot study of 33 schools in 8 LEAs during 1990 (Webb, 1990). The reported findings are broadly similar to those of HMI, with a consistent indication of teachers taking the reforms and trying, sincerely, to implement them.

Interview data from the Primary Assessment, Curriculum and Experience (PACE) project, based at Bristol Polytechnic and Bristol University, also confirms this generally constructive impression. In the first phase of this study, 148 Key Stage One teachers in 48 schools in 8 LEAs were interviewed about their views on the National Curriculum and assessment procedures and about changes in pedagogy, curriculum, relationships, role and job satisfaction which might result. The interviews took place during the Summer Term, in 1990. In the overwhelming majority of cases, the introduction of the National Curriculum was supported in principle and it was evident that a great deal of thought and work was going into its implementation. In some cases, it was clear that the full implications of the innovations had not been understood but only in a small number of cases was active opposition to the National Curriculum apparent.

The overall picture then is of teachers in primary schools accepting the broad terms of the National Curriculum and seeking to implement it.

Within this overall picture, however, there are a large number of more specific concerns. At the top of the list for most teachers is the issue of the pace of change. As Osborn & Pollard (1990) reporting the first findings of the PACE study, argued:

> *Major anxieties were expressed over the pace and extent of the changes. 'Too much has been happening too quickly' was the way some teachers put it. While they were developing new ways of working, particularly in the area of record keeping and assessment, more information would arrive which would supersede it, meaning that they had wasted their time. This fear of being swamped by change was particularly true of the documentation which accompanied the National Curriculum which was seen by most teachers as "simply overwhelming" - "far too much to assimilate, I have just had to give up on it for the time being" as one teacher put it. (1990, p. 1)*

This finding confirms, for the Summer Term of 1990, the pressure on teachers reported by HMI in 1989 using a survey of 1000 classes of 5-7 year olds.

A pressing problem for almost all of the schools was the lack of time for teachers to plan and prepare work, and in the case of subject coordinators to assist their colleagues at the end of the day. (1989, paragraph 10)

The pressure of reform combined with the generally conscientious approach of the majority of teachers was tending to produce extremely long working hours. Campbell & Neill (1990), in their study of the working habits of 94 primary teachers, most of whom were members of AMMA, found that the average hours worked per week was 49 hours, 35 minutes. The distribution of time between types of activity (see Table I) is also interesting and again indicates the extent of the development work, of one sort or another, being undertaken by teachers.

TABLE I. *Teachers' Use of Time*

Teaching	35%	
Preparation		31%
Administration	29%	
In-service	18%	
Other	6%	

(The total exceeds 100% because of overlapping activities).

Campbell & Neill, 1990, p. 33

Yet irrespective of the time pressure and hard work involved in the implementation of the National Curriculum, most teachers have welcomed the curricular clarification which it offers. Indeed, the need for curricular breadth and progression seems to have been largely accepted in principle. However, this has itself caused primary school teachers to become aware of some weaknesses in their subject knowledge, particularly in science and technology (Wragg, Bennett & Carré, 1989; Croll & Moses, 1990).

The PACE study found that teachers were attempting to increase significantly the classroom time spent on science and technology whilst less curriculum time was reported as having being spent on the arts (Osborn & Pollard, 1990). This point is evidently concerning HMI who draw attention to the "continuing need to offer children an appropriate range of experience in the arts and physical education" (HMI, 1990, p. 13).

The most striking feature of primary teachers' responses to the National Curriculum thus remains their general acceptance of it. Contributions from the primary sector to the work of the National Curriculum Subject Working Parties, which met to construct the National Curriculum, were certainly often forthright, but the overall feeling, subject by subject, has been remarkably positive. 'It's what we are doing already' or 'It's just good practice' are common responses. The result seems to have been that, up to the present time, primary teachers have tended to treat the challenges of implementing the National Curriculum as 'private troubles' (Mills, 1959). They have accepted its legitimacy and the 'reasonableness' of its expectations and have thus taken on the personal challenges which it brings. It is only gradually, as the curriculum requirements for History, Geography and other subjects outside the 'core' are being published, that the issue of curriculum overload, of over-prescription and of integration are beginning to surface as issues in a widespread way. Gradually the scale, complexity and impracticality of many aspects of the present National Curriculum therefore are being revealed. Awareness of the changes as 'public issues' is thus growing - a fact which now seems to be acknowledged by the National Curriculum Council in hasty moves to provide advice on curriculum integration and to rationalise the number of Attainment Targets in science and mathematics.

In contrast, teachers' responses to the new assessment procedures began in a far more assertive and combative way and it is to this issue that I now turn.

Assessment

Teachers' opinions on assessment issues differ from responses to the National Curriculum in that they have produced far more anxiety and resistance. Among the 50 headteachers interviewed by Croll & Moses (1990), 70% identified the need for more assessment, testing and record keeping as a major result of the implementation of the National Curriculum. Early results from the PACE study reveal similar concerns among classroom teachers. As Osborn & Pollard (1990) put it:

> Frustration and even anger was expressed by many over the amount of time now apparently demanded for record-keeping and assessment. There were fears that this was beginning to 'take over from teaching', that the heavy burden demanded in time and effort left too little time for planning, for responding to children, for display work and for all the things which were seen .. as 'real teaching'. .... As one teacher argued, "I am not prepared to become somebody walking round with a checksheet and I will fight it .... I think that my place is with the children, making a relationship with them. Its not fiddling around with bits of paper". (Osborn & Pollard, 1990, p. 2)

There have been two main problems here. The first is that primary school teachers, in general, are suspicious about the formal testing of children, particularly at the age of seven. This reluctance regarding the supposed certainties of assessment can be traced to the Plowden Report (CACE, 1967) and to awareness of the different rates of children's development, the need to foster self-esteem and to value the 'whole child'. Standardised procedures are therefore seen to threaten key tenets of child-centred ideology. Of course, this view can be, and is, articulated without reference to the evidence on the degree of ad hoc teacher testing that has always gone on (Gipps, 1983), but that is another story.

The second factor which generates anxiety has been uncertainty, for throughout 1989 and most of 1990, the School Examination and Assessment Council (SEAC) was not able to provide clear advice regarding assessment requirements. SEAC worked to a breathtaking eighteen month timetable for Key Stage One, attempting to conduct innovative development work on standardised testing procedures through three competitive consortia, to promote formative teacher assessment by working through Local Education Authorities (many of which were in no position to produce coherent training programmes), to have all teachers of Year 2 children trained and ready for standardised testing procedures by the Summer of 1991 and to institute recording and reporting procedures. It is little wonder that SEAC and LEAs were under extreme pressure and that the result was a great deal of anxiety and uncertainty among teachers.

Two events contributed to this anxiety. The first was the publication and national circulation of SEAC's *Guide to Teacher Assessment* in 1990. This document, which was intended to provide INSET support to schools, seriously failed to connect with primary teacher's views about learning or with the practicalities of the circumstances in which they work. For instance, it was suggested that 'lessons' are planned with direct reference to Attainment Targets and suggested, unproblematically, that the National Curriculum has set out the order in which children would learn. To teachers and advisers who retained child-centred beliefs and an awareness of the diverse patterns by which children learn, this was like red rag to a bull.

There was also enormous hilarity and anger over the impracticality of many of the suggestions which were made. In particular, the authors of the materials seemed to have no awareness of the demands of teaching with large class sizes and made a number of simplistic and naive suggestions. The credibility of the document was thus heavily undercut. SEAC was then humiliated by an article on the materials by Ted Wragg [3] in *The Times Educational Supplement* entitled 'Who put the 'Ass' in assessment?' and a large number of schools and LEAs actively discouraged the circulation or use of the *Guide*. It was not an auspicious start in reassuring teachers about their role in assessment.

The second event which actually induced anxiety was the Standard Assessment Task (SAT) Pilot Study, which was conducted in the Summer of 1990. In this study each of the three consortia piloted their materials and procedures for standardised testing. A 2% sample of children was used, drawn from a sample of schools across the country. It soon became apparent that the consortia had grossly over-estimated the amount of testing which they could reasonably expect teachers to carry out. Whilst the teachers were rushed off their feet and worked extraordinarily long hours, children who were not carrying out assessment tasks tended to be given occupational work. A vivid impression of the effects was provided by Torrance (1990) in an article drawn from letters sent to him by teachers who had been involved in the pilot. Amongst the things the teachers reported were the following:

> *It was an onslaught of new activity after new activity ... eventually we were just 'getting through'.*

> *The children ... could not understand it when they were left to get on with all these strange new tasks, sometimes as many as four a day, without the usual support and explanation.*

> *Some pupils were displaying extremely distressed behaviour. One child was found hiding in a corner in tears, with her piece of work torn up in her lap. Another developed a stutter.*

> *The standard of work produced in non-assessed activities has deteriorated steadily since the beginning of term. The children's behaviour is also deteriorating as the teachers can no longer give the class the attention they need and deserve.*

> *The developers of the .... SATs appear to have very little concept of how topics are approached in primary schools. What they have presented us with is a hotch-potch of loosely related themes, none of which can be developed properly.*

> *The assessment criteria were pretty useless, sometimes too specific, sometimes too unclear, sometimes open to different interpretations.*

> *Conducting SATs goes against everything else that happens in school and is as far removed from good primary practice as it is possible to get. We are constantly helping and encouraging children ... Then suddenly for half a term all this changes. They have a problem and we can't help them.*

There is a lot of anger and concern in these statements. Anger at the SAT developers and at those who have pressed for the innovation, and concern for the effects on the children. There is a sense that the teachers felt required to act in ways which they regarded as 'unprofessional', damaging and in conflict with their personal commitments and beliefs.

Of course, it is necessary to be careful in evaluating this evidence in that it was produced by an open invitation to write to Torrance about experience of the SAT trials. However, since SEAC permitted no independent evaluation or research on the trials, we have very limited ways of guaging the feelings of those who took part.

In any event, news of the SAT trials spread among primary school teachers and is likely to have amplified anxiety considerably. When SEAC made its recommendations to the Secretary of State in October 1990, the emphasis was on 'manageability' and both the time to be spent in assessment and the number of attainment targets to be addressed were very significantly cut back.

The situation regarding formative, 'Teacher Assessment' (TA) is a little different. This has been introduced into schools following LEA training programmes during 1990. Following the TGAT Report (1987) lead, emphasis has been placed on forming assessment judgment on the basis of 'gathering evidence' and on feeding through the enhanced understanding of children's thinking which teachers will then have. There is thus an account available regarding teacher-controlled formative assessment which is broadly consistent with child-centred philosophy and with the application of professional judgement. This has led many teachers to accept the principle of teacher assessment. However, the struggle with regard to the work-load and practicality of implementation and administration remains.

A major sociological issue which, at present, seems to be an explicit concern of relatively few teachers, is that of the possible influence of bias in testing procedures. Clearly vital equal opportunities issues are raised here but early findings on teacher implementation of assessment procedures from the PACE study do not show strong awareness. Of course, it could well be argued that this concern will become more prominent at later stages of the implementation of the assessment procedures. On the other hand, the present low awareness could suggest the continued existence of unwitting processes of stereotyping and labelling in primary schools which, as Sharp & Green (1975) highlighted, can occur even as a product of child-centredness. At present, such issues are largely being treated as technical ones and the concern is with the validity and reliability of the testing procedures. When the results are reported and it is possible to analyse patterns in the data, then the issue of inequality in educational achievement is likely to be highlighted and sociologists will have an important role to play. Monitoring such issues is one of the aims of the PACE study (Abbott, et al, 1989) and that of Gipps & Brown (1990).

The Management and Control of Primary Schools

If the curriculum and assessment procedures are the two most pressing aspects of the Education Reform Act to which classroom teachers have had to respond, that does not mean that they are unaware of other significant changes in the management and control of primary education. There are two issues of particular importance here, those concerned with accountability and those concerned with funding and open enrolment.

Accountability

Primary school teachers are aware of the rights and powers which the Education Reform Act has given to parents and governors. On the one hand, such innovations seem threatening and represent potentially a powerful focus of critique. On the other hand, some primary teachers who have subscribed to a belief in 'partnership' with parents and the community are able to interpret the new structures in those terms. Indeed, for some, the increased contact with governors and parents which the new formal structures are producing is being used as a means of forming alliances with which to promote the school's interests. Teachers who are opposed to the new reforms are, in one sense, helped in this by the failure of the innovations for governor and parent involvement to really take off. Once again, the difficulty derives from the difference between the assumptions on which legislation was based and the actual reality. In fact, it has been extremely difficult to recruit and retain school governors, given the scale of their new responsibilities. Similarly, the Annual Report meetings for parents which must now be held, have been sparsely attended. Indeed, interim evidence from the largest empirical study of parental opinion yet conducted (Hughes, 1990) suggests a large degree of parental satisfaction with the schooling which was provided in the primary schools which the respondent's children attended. The evidence thus belies the moral panics about 'standards' which have been so regularly created over the past decade and suggests that, to the extent that they are believed, the problem is normally thought of as existing 'somewhere else'. Indeed, throughout 1989 and 1990, education has been a high profile issue in public opinion polls, with many members of the public supporting greater investment and being generally appreciative of the difficulties faced by teachers - public support which is being carefully nurtured by the leaders of the various teacher professional associations.

On the issue of accountability then, it is far from clear whether the new arrangements will produce a greater degree of control of the education 'producers' by the 'consumers', as was the intention, or whether the result will be a gradual growth of alliances which will be used to lobby centralised bodies such as LEAs or the Government. Irrespective of the eventual outcome however, the situation in 1990 appears uncertain and destabilising to many teachers.

Funding and Open Enrolment

The Education Reform Act has introduced a requirement for the 'local management of schools' so that each school has its own budget and can determine its own expenditure priorities. Total funds available to each school are determined by a formula, the most important part of which is based on the number of pupils on roll. At the same time, Local Education Authorities are being required to devolve almost all their funds to schools direct, leaving very little available for centrally provided services.

The legislation also requires open enrolment of pupils and the results of pupil assessments are to be published at the end of Key Stage Two - a practice which is also strongly recommended by the Secretary of State at Key Stage One. The cumulative result of these measures is expected to be the creation of market competition between schools, and this, the government believes, will 'improve standards'. We do not know if this will be the case. However, there are grounds for suspecting that the measures may increase diversity and variation between schools so that inequality in provision will increase (Ball, 1990).

There is a great deal of concern with these issues, particularly among primary school headteachers, and the formation of 'clusters' or groupings of schools planning joint policies and actions is an increasingly common attempt at a collective response. Whilst it is too early to be sure of the eventual outcome of these processes, it is clear that the development of educational markets, enhanced by the 'opting out' of some schools to grant maintained status, has the potential to have major implications for social inequality.

It is an issue which sociologists need to monitor very carefully.

Continuities in the Sociology of Primary Education

There are a great many continuities in sociological research on primary schooling which it would be possible to identify, but, for the purpose of this paper, I am going to concentrate on just two - the nature and effects of teacher ideology and practice and the social consequences of differentiation processes in primary schools. These seem to be particularly pertinent at the present time. I will also consider some sociological issues which arise from this very significant period of policy formation, implementation and change.

The nature and effects of primary school ideology and practice has been a prominent theme in the sociology of education since, in the early 1970s, the seemingly enabling, humanistic and egalitarian philosophy of child-centredness began to be subjected to scrutiny. Of course, this was part of a larger trend in the sociological analysis of education, for the 1970s was a period of questioning and theorising much more generally. In particular, there was a challenge to the previously dominant quantitative, survey work which tended to focus on social class. In contrast to the emphasis on the role of education in terms of the social system as a whole, consideration of the curriculum and knowledge in terms of power and control was initiated. Young's collection of papers (1971) was especially significant in this.

One particular manifestation of this work was the interrogation of 'progressive' child centred ideology through work by structuralists such as Sharp & Green (1975) and, in another form, by Weberians such as King (1978). Their arguments highlighted the gap between the individualised, egalitarian rhetoric of child-centredness and issues such as stereotyping, labelling, and the existence of deficit models of home background - all of which, it was argued, would impact through teacher expectation, on children's academic achievements and thus on their life chances.

A second very significant area of work was the sustained theorising of Bernstein on pedagogy (e.g., 1975) which drew, in particular, on primary school practice for its examplars. Thus, his work on 'invisible pedagogy' and control raised the issue of the consequences of forms of pedagogy. In his more recent work he sees pedagogy as a 'symbolic ruler for consciousness' because of the way in which, in its various forms, it selectively and differentially positions individuals and establishes power relationships (Bernstein, 1986).

As we have seen earlier in this paper, primary school teachers are currently in a period of rapid change during which many aspects of their previously established ideology and practice are being called into question. The new rationalism of the National Curriculum, with its concerns with progression, differentiation and coherence and its framework of attainment targets, levels, programmes of study, etc, is creating a technicist approach to the management of a national curriculum. This contrasts sharply with the previous period of relative openness where teachers at least felt that they had the autonomy to create the curriculum which would be most appropriate for their children. Yet both approaches can make claims to the provision of entitlement, equal opportunities and 'high quality', 'effective' education.

In this context, we must note, as documented in this paper, the general support among primary school teachers in England and Wales for the introduction of the National Curriculum and this leads to the speculation that a new professional ideology is gradually emerging from the adaption of previous ideas of new circumstances.

Similarly, at the level of pedagogy, the National Curriculum and assessment procedures are undoubtedly having an influence, though we need more research, from projects such as PACE, before we can discern the precise forms of such changes. Even now though, it appears likely that more overt social differentiation of individual children will occur and this may be institutionalised in forms of classroom organisation and pedagogy.

Without a doubt then, the issue of the social consequences of teacher ideology and of forms of pedagogy in primary school classrooms will remain crucially important. Work which was initiated by sociologists in the 1970s will be revisited as a rich initial source of conceptual and analytical tools and applied to these new and changing circumstances.

Once again, the legislation of the late 1980s has created an enormous need for studies of its social effects in terms of differentiation. On an *a priori* basis, many sociologists would speculate that social differentiation will be increased. This might come about through forces and processes operating at many levels of the educational system - at the level of the state if Ministers and arms of government such as NCC and SEAC fail to prioritise equal opportunity issues; at the level of local 'markets' for school enrolments if LEA planning roles are neutralised and if 'sink schools' result from the government's determination to foster competition between schools (Ball, 1990); at the level of schools and classroom practice if it is found that teachers, in the process of implementing the new curriculum and assessment requirements, unwittingly create unequal opportunities for some children.

Issues concerning social differentiation have, of course, a very long history in the sociology of education. However, concerning primary education, as elsewhere, the issue has tended to be couched in terms of social class. Thus, in the post-war years, we had the empirical documentation of class inequalities both of the 'political arithmetic' school (e.g., Halsey, Floud & Anderson, 1961) and of more intuitive researchers such as Jackson (1964). Other good examples are provided by the work of Douglas (1964) on 'home and school' and by Klein's study of English cultures (1965). Such empiricism is reflected too in what was really the first systematic attempt to produce a sociology of English primary schooling by Blyth (1965).

As we have seen, analysis of differentiation issues took a different direction in the 1970s, with attention shifting to internal school processes, the influence of teacher knowledge, ideology and practices. However, the tendency to focus on social class remained and it was not until the 1980s that greater awareness of the importance of gender, race, special needs and disability in studies of primary schooling has really grown. Studies of gender led the way (e.g., Delamont, 1980; Clarricoates, 1981, 1987; Whyte, 1983; Evans, 1988) and continue to flourish. Greater degrees of theoretical sophistication also became available, with post-structuralists such as Walkerdine (1984, 1988) making particularly notable contributions in showing how restrictive the idealised image of 'the child' had become in primary school ideology.

Explicitly sociological studies of differentiation in relation to race issues in the primary schools of England and Wales are few and far between. Although since the publication of the Rampton Report (1981) and the Swann Report (1985), there have been a large number of more prescriptive publications (e.g., AFFOR, 1983; Willey, 1984; Nixon, 1985). However, important quantitative sociological studies have provided useful baseline data on educational achievement (Mortimore et al, 1988; Tizard et al, 1988) and more qualitative analyses are also now becoming available (e.g., Carrington & Short, 1989; Grugeon & Woods, 1990; Troyna & Hatcher, 1991). Such work will provide an excellent base for future social analyses of the impact of the Education Reform Act and other legislation on children of different racial backgrounds.

There is considerable room for further development in the sociological study of special needs and disability in primary education. At present, the field still remains dominated by the agenda set by the Warnock Report (1981). Studies range from the empirical analysis of views and provision such as that by Croll & Moses (1985), to the analysis of the politics of special education by Barton (1988). Meanwhile, the issue of how primary teachers think about pupil performance continues to attract attention (e.g., Carrier, 1990) and the direct experience of children in negotiating the complex bureaucracies of special needs provision is not forgotten (Branson et al, 1988). It is likely that such themes will be strongly reasserted in the post-ERA context, for the legislation showed very little awareness of special educational needs. Indeed, in many ways it has left a number of potential new hurdles to be overcome - such as the effects of assessment procedures, the prescriptive curriculum and competition between schools.

Overall, I would suggest that the sociology of education is in a good position, conceptually and methodologically to investigate such issues. There is a rich archive of previous work on which to build and move forward.

At the most fundamental level, the core sociological issue - of the relationship of the individual to society, of agency and constraint, control and order - will now, in my view, also achieve an enhanced place at the centre of studies of primary education. I suggest this because, given the degree of centralised control embodied in recent legislation, the issue is more prominent and explicit than it has been for many years.

For instance, this review of teachers' responses to the legislation, is just the beginning of the story of this particular period of change and contestation in this country. The responses of teachers, governors, parents, LEAs and children have yet to be fully played out and the present analysis can only be partial. Yet sociological research into how teachers respond to change is of vital importance, both for future educational developments in England and Wales and in view of similarly centrist 'restructuring' exercises gathering momentum in other countries.

In this case though, it is not really possible to consider 'continuities' in the sociological work on policy and change in primary education, for the issues have not received sustained attention in recent years. Although the politics of educational reform in the last fifteen years has generated a very strong interest in policy matters in education (e.g., Ball, 1989), the analysis rarely focuses on primary education, (Brehony's 1990, analysis of policy influences on the National Curriculum is an exception). The absence of a fully developed sociology of policy formation relating to primary education is a concern which sociologists must address.

Conclusion

The legislation of the late 1980s has brought about a period of rapid and multiple innovation in primary education. Yet the outcomes remain unclear as processes of adaption and contestation continue. The relevance of sociological theories of the dialectic interplay between individuals, interest groups and structural constraint represented by the state have, arguably, become of almost overt - even to relatively apolitical and socially unaware teachers and members of the public. When there is a pause from the immediate pressures, there is an unusually clear sense of history being made.

In this context, the influence of child-centred commitments by teachers continues to be very important in providing a bedrock of alternative criteria with which to evaluate innovations as they arise. Some teachers, according to Nias (1991), are so personally committed to such ideas that the required innovations and the changing nature of teaching as work are inducing a sense of bereavement as they 'grieve for a lost self'. Here then, we see the immediate continuity and importance of two of the themes of sociological enquiry which were reviewed in the introduction of this paper - the influence of child centred ideology and the nature of teaching as work. In the early stages of the implementation of the legislation, these issues are particularly prominent - with bewildering changes in the nature and demands of school work being set against the continuing residue of child centred, Plowden inspired, beliefs. One tangible result has been an unprecedented number of teachers taking early retirement. Morale, across the profession, is very low.

The phasing of the innovations is such that they will have a progressive impact, thus the actual effects in terms of classroom processes, child experience, curriculum balance and inequality have yet to be fully experienced and documented. One result of this is that some important sociological themes are not yet as prominent in public debate as they are likely to become in the future. There is likely to be increasing concern about the nature of children's future school experiences, about the curriculum and how children of particular races, sex, social class, disability or special educational need will be affected by the forms of pedagogy and school organisation which emerge.

However, it is too early to say, precisely, what the future patterns of experience and attainment will be. What is clear, however, is that the sociological insights and analyses which have been developed in the past, will have a continuing relevance.

As the impact of the legislation is really felt in the lives of teachers, pupils, families and their communities, sociologists have a major responsibility to document, analyse and theorise the overall social consequences and to feed such analyses back into public, policy-making debates.

Acknowledgement

I would like to acknowledge the contribution of Richard Eke in early discussions of the content of this paper and to thank the editors of this volume for their constructive comments throughout.

Notes

[1] As a result of this legislation, a number of new terms have been introduced into the educational language used in England and Wales. Among the most important for this paper are:

Key Stage One:	pupils aged 4 - 7 years,
Key Stage Two:	pupils aged 7 - 11 years,

'Years' to describe ages of pupils:

Reception:	4/5 years old
Year 1:	5/6 years old
Year 2:	6/7 years old

'Teacher Assessment': in which teachers gather continuous evidence and forms judgements regarding pupil attainment.
'Standard Assessment Tasks': which are standard, nationally prescribed activities intended to produce reliable evidence of pupil attainment.

[2] Primary school teachers do vary in the priority which they give to educational aims (Ashton, 1975, 1981; Broadfoot & Osborn, 1988) but it is arguable that the most secure yardstick around which such variation can be judged is their commitment to forms of child-centredness (Proctor, 1990).

[3] Ted Wragg is Professor of Education at the University of Exeter and writes a regular column for *The Times Educational Supplement*. Since the inception of the Education Reform Act the column has attracted avid and grateful attention from teachers because of its consistent mocking of government ministers and policy.

REFERENCES

Abbott, D., Broadfoot, P., Croll, P., Osborn, M. & Pollard, A. (1989) *Primary Assessment, Curriculum and Experience*, Working Paper 1. Bristol: Redland Centre for Primary Education, Bristol Polytechnic.

Abbott, D. & Croll, P. (1991) Whole School Change under ERA. Bristol: Redland Centre for Primary Education, Bristol Polytechnic. Presented at AERA, Chicago, April.

AFFOR (1983) *Issues and Resources*. Birmingham: AFFOR.

Alexander, R. & Willcocks, J. (1990) *Teachers and Children in PNP Classrooms*, Evaluation Report Eleven. Primary Needs Independent Evaluation Project. Leeds: University of Leeds.

Ashton, P. et al (1975) *The Aims of Primary Education*. London: Macmillan.

Ashton, P. (1981) Primary Teachers' Aims, 1969-77, in B. Simon & J. Willcocks (Eds) *Research and Practice in the Primary Classroom*. London: Routledge & Kegan Paul.

Ball, S. (1989) *Politics and Policy Making in Education*. London: Routledge.

Ball, S. (1990) Education, inequality and school reform: values in crisis! Inaugural Lecture. King's College, London. University of London.

Barton, L. (Ed) (1988) *The Politics of Special Educational Needs*. Lewes: Falmer.

Bennett, S. N. (1976) *Teaching Styles and Pupil Progress*. Shepton Mallet: Open Books.

Bernstein, B. (1975) Class and pedagogies: visible and invisible, *Educational Studies*, 1, pp. 23-41.

Bernstein, B. (1986) On Pedagogic Discourse, in J. G. Richardson (Ed) *Handbook of Theory and Research for the Sociology of Education*. New York: Greenwood Press.

Blyth, W. A. L. (1965) *English Primary Education*, Volumes I and II. London: Routledge & Kegan Paul.

Blyth, W. A. L. (1984) *Development, Experience and Curriculum in Primary Education*. London: Croom Helm.

Branson, J., Miller, D. & Branson, K. (1988) An obstacle race: a case study of a child's schooling in Australia and England, *Disability, Handicap and Society*, 3, pp. 101-118.

Brehony, K. (1990) Neither Rhyme nor Reason: primary schooling and the National Curriculum, in M. Flude & M. Hammer (Eds) *The Education Reform Act, 1988*. Lewes: Falmer Press.

Broadfoot, P. & Osborn, M. (1988) What professional responsibility means to teachers: national contexts and classroom constants, *British Journal of Sociology of Education*, 9, pp. 265-288.

Bruner, J. (1986) *Actual Minds, Possible Worlds*. New York: Harvard University Press.

Campbell, R. J. & Neill, S. St. J. (1990) *Thirteen Hundred and Thirty Days*. Final Report of a Pilot Study of Teacher Time in Key Stage 1, AMMA. Warwick: University of Warwick.

Carrier, J. G. (1990) Special education and the explanation of pupil performance, *Disability, Handicap and Society*, 5, pp. 211-226.

Carrington, B. & Short, G. (1989) *'Race' and the Primary School*. Windsor: NFER-Nelson.

Central Advisory Council on Education (1967) *Children and Their Primary Schools*, The Plowden Report. London: HMSO.

Clarricoates, K. (1981) The experience of patriarchal schooling, *Interchange*, 12, pp. 185-205.

Clarricoates, K. (1987) Child Culture at School: a clash between gendered worlds, in A. Pollard (Ed) *Children and Their Primary Schools*. London: Falmer Press.

Croll, P. & Moses, D. (1985) *One in Five*. London: Routledge & Kegan Paul.

Croll, P. & Moses, D. (1990) Perspectives on the National Curriculum in primary and secondary schools, *Educational Studies*, 16, pp. 187-198.

Delamont, S. (1980) *Sex Roles and the School*. London: Methuen.

Douglas, J. W. B. (1964) *The Home and the School*. London: Panther.

Evans, T. (1988) *A Gender Agenda*. London: Unwin Hyman.

Galton, M., Simon, B. & Croll, P. (1980) *Inside the Primary Classroom*. London: Routledge & Kegan Paul.

Galton, M. (1989) *Teaching in the Primary School*. London: David Fulton.

Gipps, C. (1983) *Testing Children*. London: Heinemann.

Gipps, C. & Brown, M. (1990) National Assessment in Primary Schools, Research proposal to ESRC. Mimeo.

Grugeon, E. & Woods, P. (1990) *Educating All: multicultural perspectives in the primary school*. London: Routledge.

Halsey, A. H., Floud, J. & Anderson, C. A. (1961) *Education, Economy and Society*. Glencoe: Free Press.

HMI (1978) *Primary Education in England*. London: HMSO.

HMI (1989) *The Implementation of the National Curriculum in Primary Schools*. London: HMSO.

HMI (1990) *The Implementation of the National Curriculum in Primary Schools: a survey of 100 schools*. London: HMSO.

HMI (1991) *Standards in Education, 1989 - 90*, Annual Report on HM Senior Chief Inspector of Schools. London: HMSO.

House of Commons Select Committee on Education and the Arts (1986) *Achievement in Primary Schools*. London: HMSO.

Hughes, M. et al (1990) *Parents and the National Curriculum*. Interim Report. University of Exeter, mimeo.

Jackson, B. (1964) *Streaming: an education system in miniature*. London, Routledge & Kegan Paul.

King, R. (1978) *All Things Bright and Beautiful?* Chichester: Wiley.

Klein, J. (1965) *Samples from English Cultures*, Volume I and II. London: Routledge & Kegan Paul.

Mills, C. W. (1959) *The Sociological Imagination*. New York: Oxford University Press.

Mortimore, P. et al (1988) *School Matters: the Junior Years*. Wells: Open Books.

Nias, J. (1989) *Primary Teachers Talking*. London: Methuen.

Nias, J. (1991) Changing times, changing identities: grieving for a lost self, in R.G. Burgess (Ed) *Educational Research and Evaluation*. Lewes: Falmer Press.

Osborn, M. & Pollard, A. (1990) Anxiety and paradox: teachers' initial responses to change under the National Curriculum, mimeo. Bristol: Centre for Assessment Studies, Bristol University. Presented at BERA, London, August.

Pollard, A. (1985) *The Social World of the Primary School*. London: Cassell.

Pollard, A. (1988) Primary School Teachers and their Colleagues, in S. Delamont (Ed) *The Primary School Teacher*. Lewes: Falmer Press.

Pollard, A. & Osborn, M. (1991) Classroom Change and Pupil Experience, mimeo. Bristol: Redland Centre for Primary Education, Bristol Polytechnic. Presented at AERA, Chicago, April.

Proctor, N. (1990) *The Purpose and Aims of Primary Education Today*. Lewes: Falmer Press.

Richards, C. (1982) Curriculum consistency, in C. Richards (Ed) *New Directions in Primary Education*. Lewes: Falmer Press.

Sharp, R. & Green, A. (1975) *Education and Social Control*. London: Routledge.

Task Group on Assessment and Testing (1987) *National Curriculum: a report*. London: DES.

Task Group on Assessment and Testing (1988) *Three Supplementary Reports*. London: DES.

Tizard, B. et al (1988) *Young Children in the Inner City*. Hove: Lawrence Erlbaum.

Torrance, H. Teachers' Experiences of Standard Assessment Tasks, mimeo. University of Sussex.

Troyna, B. & Hatcher, R. (1991) *Racial Incidents in Primary Schools*. London: Routledge.

Walkerdine, V. (1984) Developmental Psychology and the Child-Centred Pedagogy, in J. Henriques et al (Eds), *Changing the Subject*. London: Methuen.

Walkerdine, V. (1988) *The Mastery of Reason*. London: Routledge.

Webb, R. (1990) Address to members of the NAHT attending the National Primary Conference, Peterborough.

Whitty, G. (1989) The New Right and the National Curriculum, *Journal of Education Policy*, 1, pp. 329-341.

Whyte, J. (1983) *Beyond the Wendy House*. York: Longman.

Woods, P. (1990) *Teacher Skills and Strategies*. Lewes: Falmer Press.

Wragg, E. C., Bennett, S. N. & Carré, C. (1989) Teachers' subject expertise: results of a national survey, *Junior Education*, June, pp. 6-7.

Young, M. F. D. (Ed) (1971) *Knowledge and Control*. London: Collier-Macmillan.

Chapter Seven

Staying On and Staying In: comprehensive schooling in the 1990s

DAVID HALPIN

This chapter takes a somewhat different approach to others in this book in the sense that it does not work systematically through the changes to the comprehensive school system that are likely to be brought about as a result of the 1988 Education Reform Act and other recent and related legislation. Much of this sort of analysis is found in other chapters as well as in the author's earlier work (Halpin, 1989). Instead, this chapter focuses on two contemporary concerns - encapsulated in the slogans 'staying in' and 'staying on' - that deal with educational opportunity and distribution, on the one hand, and educational standards, on the other. In the course of doing this the chapter outlines and defends a particular point of view about the current context of comprehensive schooling and the need to formulate new policies to meet the challenges of the 1990s.

The chapter takes as its starting point the view that the development of a unified system of education and training for post 16-year-olds is good for young people and good for the country: good for young people because it would encourage more of them to continue their education after 16 years and thus increase their training and career opportunities and life chances generally; good for the country because it would contribute to a fairer society as well as meet some of the demands of our modern economy. The chapter also assumes that the integration of academic and practical studies in the secondary curriculum would foster an improved image for comprehensive schools and help to discourage certain parents from seeking alternative provision for the education of their children.

The structure of the chapter is as follows. The next section, after briefly discussing the current legitimacy crisis facing the comprehensive school reform, reviews significant social scientific and sociological research on its effects and achievements. Arising out of this review, the section concludes with a summary statement of ways in which the sociology of education could contribute to the present debate on the future of comprehensive schooling and the process of associated policy development. There then follows a two-pronged analysis of a new and particularly urgent challenge for the comprehensive school. This analysis is focused on examining ways in which the comprehensive school system might retain more pupils beyond the ages of 16 years and increase public confidence in its accomplishments and prospects. The argument at this point is supported and prompted by discussion of two secondary sources: David Hargreaves (1982) *The Challenge for the Comprehensive School* and the more recent *A British Baccalaureate* published last year by the Institute for Public Policy Research (IPPR). The chapter's concluding section, which points up part of a new policy agenda, reassesses the implications of the comprehensive community college for restructuring secondary schooling and speculates on its likely impact on staying on rates and public support for non-selective education.

Comprehensive Schooling and the Sociology of Educational Policy

Social scientific and sociological explanations of the nature, purpose and effects of schooling are noticeably absent from the present government's assessments of policy priorities for education. Instead, a particular form of New Right 'derisory' discourse (Ball, 1990, pp. 22-69) has largely replaced serious in-depth analysis of the consequences of, and need for, changes to the direction of educational policy. This is particularly so in the case of the comprehensive school reform, the early history of which, by contrast, was underpinned by policy formulation founded on empirical studies and social critiques that emphasised the inequalities of opportunity and wastages of talent endemic within selective systems of secondary education (e.g. Floud & Halsey, 1956; Douglas, 1964; Ford, 1969). Today, the more notable achievements of the comprehensive school reform (such as those documented by Moon, 1983) have been completely overshadowed by vitriolic attacks on its alleged failure to improve standards combined with suggestions that its products lack the skills and positive attitudes required for employment and citizenship.

To this extent, the comprehensive school reform is undergoing a fresh legitimacy crisis. Its future is, so to speak, 'on the line'; not simply because its long-standing critics have reasserted their influence on educational policy-making, but because one of the chief consequences of this process has been the introduction of new forms of secondary schooling that threaten the reform's historic mission. Moreover, despite the positive feedback elicited by numerous and recent questionnaire surveys about comprehensive education (e.g. MORI, 1989), increasing numbers of children and parents seem to be losing faith with non-selective secondary schooling, the former by continuing to leave school at the earliest possible opportunity, often with very few or indifferent qualifications, the latter by deserting LEA maintained schools for those in the independent sector and elsewhere.

A sense of proportion, of course, is necessary at this juncture. Pupil disaffection apart, it is clear that much of the parental anxiety about comprehensive schools has been manufactured by unfair adverse comment in the tabloid press. Furthermore, the actual percentage of parents choosing schools for their children from sectors other than those maintained by LEAs remains small. Even so, the effects of their actions are greater than the actual numbers involved would suggest. For they not only entail a continuing creaming of able children from comprehensives, whose presence has been shown to have an important bearing on their capacity to be 'effective', they also lend credence to the stereotypical view that non-selective schools are weak academically.

Given these trends, about which more will be written later, it is noteworthy that few of the sociologically informed studies of individual comprehensive schools (e.g. Ball, 1981; Burgess, 1983; Moon, 1983), or related surveys of the education systems of which they are a part (e.g. Benn & Simon, 1973; Monks, 1968 & 1970), engage directly with pupil and parental expectations of the schools they attend and choose. There are some exceptions, however, such as Corrigan's (1979) and Willis's (1977) enquiries into working class youth and Hargreaves' (1967 and 1972) investigations of social relations in secondary school; but all of this work is about pupils' adaptations to schooling and, as such, mostly ignores parental expectations of the same process.

Studies of the politics of public examinations and assessment apart (e.g. Whitty, 1985, pp. 120-146; Broadfoot, 1979), there also exist few sociological analyses of comprehensive schooling that articulate with the particularities of government policy for secondary education. Indeed, until only very recently, and notwithstanding the one or two isolated case studies of educational policy-making (e.g. Saran, 1973), the chief preoccupation of the sociology of secondary education has not been with government policy as such, but with the study of individual schools and classrooms in which particular areas of school life are explored in detail. Typical examples of this kind of work are included in two volumes edited by Woods (1978 & 1978a) and another with Hammersley (Hammersley & Woods, 1984), all of which examine aspects of teacher and pupil strategies and interactions in school. While extremely insightful, much of this ethnographic material is presented in a way that avoids discussing the social and political contexts within which schools are constrained to operate and teachers do their work.

Chronologically slightly behind this line of enquiry is another with a quite different focus and emphasis. Less interested in documenting the micropolitics of school and classroom life, this work makes problematic the nature of school knowledge by redefining the relationship between curricula and their institutional and societal contexts. Prompted by the rise of a radical 'new' sociology of education during the early 1970s, it also pursues the analysis of what secondary schools teach into studies of the structural location of schooling. In his sympathetic critique of this approach, Whitty (1985), no doubt prompted by a number of black and feminist challenges to the concept of comprehensive education (e.g. MacDonald, 1981; Deem, 1978; Wolpe, 1977; Troyna, 1984; Tomlinson, 1983), identifies an important omission in the 'new direction's' project to reconceptualise school knowledge, namely a failure to link sufficiently considerations of the relationship between secondary education and social class with questions of racism and sexism in pedagogy and curriculum organisation.

Attempts to develop such articulations in the 1970s and early 1980s were frequently inspired by neo-Marxist, and ultimately mainly theoretical, interpretations of secondary schooling. While contemporaneous with the products initiated by the 'new' sociology of education, this 'Marxist strand' was also partly a reaction to certain of the more naive political conclusions reached by some converts to the former traditions. The circumstances out of which this perspective first emerged are described by Whitty who writes that the "attraction of Marxism was ... linked to an increasing realization that social reality was not quite as fragile as students of the 1960s and the new sociologists of the 1970s had imagined. ... While phenomenological and ethnomethodological studies endlessly illustrated how reality was sustained at a micro-level, they offered little purchase on the nature of the broader context in which this took place" (1985, p. 22).

The espousal of Marxism by the sociology of education in this country is particularly noteworthy in the work of Dale and Esland (Dale, Esland & MacDonald, 1976), as well as Sarup (1978) and Levitas (1974). It also had a trans-Atlantic dimension, with, first, Bowles & Gintis (1976), and then Apple (1979), playing a pivotal role. Moreover, their respective, and very different, contributions typified the way in which Marxist analysis in the sociology of secondary education in this country gradually moved away from monolithic interpretations of state power in education towards an appreciation of the relative autonomy of schools and teachers to effect significant reform, sometimes in direct opposition to the wishes of central government.

Despite the amount and quality of much of this work, little of it engages directly with the origins, scope and effects of particular state policy initiatives for education. An exception to this generalization are the important contributions made by the Centre for Contemporary Cultural Studies during the late 70s and early 80s. Indeed, the Centre's publication, *Unpopular Education: Schooling and Social Democracy in England Since 1944* (CCCS, 1981), anticipates those more recent studies of educational politics promulgated by the sociology of education since the passage of the Education Reform Act 1988. Strongly influenced by continental neo-Marxist analysis, *Unpopular Education* offers a 'critical history' of educational policy-making since 1944 that discusses the competing pressures underlying educational change, the origins and character of the post-war educational settlement and the emergence of an aggressively populist Conservatism in the 1980s.

The sort of enquiries initiated by the CCCS were not taken up with the same degree of enthusiasm by mainstream sociologists of education until very recently. In the last few years, and largely it has to be said in the wake of, and as a reaction to, the success of the New Right in influencing the shape of educational reform, a plethora of short studies and longer reports on the predicted and actual effects of the Thatcher government's education policies have emerged (for example, Bash, 1989; Coulby, 1989; Chitty, 1989; Dale, 1990; Griggs, 1989; Flude & Hammer, 1990; Edwards, Fitz and Whitty, 1989; Hargreaves & Reynolds, 1989; Johnson, 1989; Jones, 1989; Whitty, 1990; Ball, 1990; Cultural Studies, Birmingham, 1991).

A number of other writers have focused on the extent to which the comprehensive education reform has been successful in its own terms and by comparison with the selective system it was designed to replace. Gray & Jesson (1989), for example, review the impact of comprehensive reforms on three key areas: on selection practices; on access to the 'grammar school' curriculum: and on educational attainment as measured by exam qualifications. After surveying an impressive number of research studies, Gray & Jesson conclude that the reforms have significantly delayed, though not abolished, some aspects of selection to 14, 15 and even 16 years of age; enabled an increased proportion of children to access higher standards of provision; but 'failed' to secure higher performance levels among more pupils than the previous selective system achieved.

Reynolds & Sullivan (1987) arrive at similar conclusions but suggest, too, that certain of the comprehensive schools they studied were able to achieve considerably greater levels of attainment with their pupils than others with similar intakes. Consequently, they argue that factors internal to some comprehensive schools (such as how they are managed; teacher expectations and their general ethos) must make them more 'effective'. They are not alone in their conclusions in so far as the search for 'effectiveness factors' has become an important feature of recent social scientific research on secondary education (see, for example, Rutter, Maughan, Mortimer & Ousten, 1979; Hopkins, 1987; Smith & Tomlinson, 1989; Reid, Hopkins & Holly, 1988). The concerns of these authors have also rubbed off on some politicians, particularly in the Labour Party, the recently concluded policy review of which led to a pre-general election promise that it would develop "a major programme to make schools more effective" (Labour Party, 1990, p. 30).

Making comprehensive schools 'more effective', of course, is a considerable and ambiguous undertaking. Some of the conclusions reached by the 'effective schools literature', moreover, need to be treated with caution. Certainly many of its lists of the characteristics of the 'effective' school (such as curriculum-focused school leadership, supportive climate within schools, clear goals and high expectations, ongoing staff development, parental involvement and support [Hopkins, 1987]) seem unremarkable, even self-evident. Occasionally they do no more than serve to remind us of certain commonsense values about good inter-personal relations and efficient organisation. Sometimes they entail the implication that school ineffectiveness is always either largely or entirely the responsibility of individual institutions and their staffs. Accordingly, some emphases within the effective schools movement unwittingly take on the role of 'blaming the victim', which in this case are schools and teachers struggling with the contradictions and pressures of their work.

This suggests that the sociology of education should be wary of engaging in policy analysis and development for secondary education if it entails the suspension of its debunking and critical functions. For while sociology can achieve many things, one of its central tasks must be to provide new intelligence about, and fresh insights on, existing social formations and institutions so as to foster enlightened and reflective social action. As our quick survey of trends within the sociology of education in the past twenty years indicates, there are a number of ways in which the discipline can continue to contribute to our understanding of the nature of comprehensive schooling and the debates on its future development. Three, in particular, spring quickly to mind. First, it should continue to monitor the actual effects of the reform on the educational life chances of children, especially those for whom schooling has been up to now one of disillusionment and failure. Further surveys, case studies and ethnographies all have important parts to play in this project. Second, it should consolidate and extend its work on the sociology of curriculum knowledge mainly by refocussing our attention on the problematic nature of academic and practical knowledge and their embodiment in particular courses of study linked to the government's National Curriculum legislation. Third, it should strengthen existing work in hand on the ways in which central government seeks to control both the structure of state secondary education and the careers of teachers who work in its schools. Moreover, by developing narrative accounts of the nature and source of contemporary education policy making - notably studies of the priorities of politicians, their advisers and civil servants and their translation into practical action - the sociology of education could assist those concerned to articulate and mobilise support for alternative policies.

A New Challenge for the Comprehensive School

We can remind ourselves of the power of social analysis in suggesting new policies for secondary education by reflecting on two of its contributions to recent debate about the future of the comprehensive school reform. In each case, a problem is first identified, then analysed and, finally, concrete suggestions put forward for improvement. Both, moreover, address a fresh challenge for the comprehensive school, namely how it is to keep on roll a greater proportion of young people after the age of compulsory attendance has been reached *(staying on)*; and how it is to increase parents' confidence in the quality of the education it provides *(staying in)*.

Our two sources are David Hargreaves's (1982) book, *The Challenge for the Comprehensive School* and the Institute for Public Policy Research's (IPPR) education and training paper, *A British Baccalaureate* (1990), on post-16 curriculum developments and qualifications. Neither of these sources is strictly a sociological account, though both draw upon social analysis in the course of developing their arguments. In particular, each, like the 'new' sociology of education of the early 1970s, problematises the nature of school knowledge. Their significance also lies in the manner in which they assume the relevance and need for comprehensive schooling and develop evidence-based arguments to improve the quality of its provision.

Although there is a gap of eight years between the publication of each of these sources, both stress the importance of the urgent need to reappraise the comprehensive school experiment. Hargreaves concludes, among other things, that, to succeed, the comprehensive school must first engage in a fundamental reform of its curriculum which he argues is presently too academic and subject based. In its place, and for all pupils of whatever ability and social background, he proposes a compulsory common core curriculum (11-15) organized around community studies and the expressive arts. Hargreaves envisages his core curriculum taking up about one half of pupil work in school, the remaining time being given to either 'remedial' options or "particular fields of study where pupils show a special interest or talent" (1982, p. 164). His proposals for the final year of compulsory schooling include the total abandonment of all 16+ examinations in favour of a programme of study for fifteen year olds that prepares them either for leaving school and entering employment or advanced study leading to further or higher education. While Hargreaves is anxious not to see comprehensive education restricted to pupils up to the age of 15, he is impressed by the idea of the tertiary college "which combines sixth-form 'A' Level work and vocational courses, whether academic or not, under the same roof" (1982, p. 165).

Like those of Hargreaves, the IPPR's proposals are based upon a high regard for the potential of the tertiary model for post-16 education. Unlike Hargreaves, the IPPR recommends the scrapping of all 'A' Level and its replacement by an Advanced Diploma (the British Baccalaureate) which integrates intellectual, practical and work-based skills through access to three areas of study: the social and human sciences; natural sciences and technology; and arts, language and literature. Central to the IPPR's analysis is the need "to develop an education system adequate to the economic and social demands of the next century". By getting rid of separate academic and vocation streams, it believes the system will be better placed "to help each individual realise their full potential" and ensure that "innovative capabilities (are) spread throughout the population" (1990, p. 4).

The sort of reforms Hargreaves and the IPPR have in mind for the education of post-16 year olds, of course, have implications for the 11-16 curriculum, the organisation of which is presently based upon subject departments complemented by electives that distinguish intellectual and practical knowledge. This arrangement not only foreshadows the demands of the traditional Sixth Form curriculum, it is partly a preparation for it as well. Thus, any adjustment to the 16 plus curriculum's form and content would render certain trends found elsewhere problematic. Accordingly, changes to post-16 education could act as a trigger to reconsider the shape and priorities of the curriculum earlier on.

Both Hargreaves and the IPPR are concerned to promote a more positive image for the comprehensive school, through, in one case, a reform of its early curriculum, in the other, by the introduction of less divisive and more relevant learning opportunities for post-16 year olds. Both are also committed to securing specific improvements in comprehensive schooling that impact directly on young people's sense of personal worth and rates of 'staying on'.

Staying On

The English education system is selective and specialised. Its selectiveness leads to relatively few people staying on at school ... and its specialised nature means those that do are not necessarily taking the subjects the country wants.

Thus concludes Smithers & Robinson (1989, p. 1) in their briefing paper for the Further and Higher Education Board of British Petroleum on increasing participation in higher education.

The IPPR says much the same:

In our view, Britain's education system is marked by low 'staying on' rates and poor comparative performance because it is <u>divided</u>. Most importantly, it divides 'academic' pupils from the rest through different institutions, different curricula, different modes of study and above all different qualifications which cater for the two groups. Our qualifications system resembles an educational obstacle race and is designed to 'weed out' the majority of pupils. We call this the <u>early selection-low participation system</u>" (1990, p. 4).

While roughly two-thirds of all 16-year-olds in the United Kingdom undertake some form of further education post-16, most (nearly 70 percent) do so on a part- rather than full-time basis. Significantly, approximately 20 percent of those which do choose to stay on for full-time study originate from, and remain within, the independent/private school sector. These figures compare very unfavourably with other advanced industrial nations. The United States, Belgium, Denmark, West Germany, Sweden, Japan and the Netherlands all manage to ensure that between 70 and 90 percent of the 16-18 range is participating in some form of full-time education and training (Central Statistical Office, 1990, p. 58).

To complicate matters, within the United Kingdom, there is considerable variation in the level of participation in further education. Recent figures (see Central Statistical Office, 1990a) show that Scotland has by far the highest proportion (77%) of 16 year olds staying on in some form of education and training, whether full- or part-time. But even within England, staying-on rates are also variable, overall participation being lowest in the South East, East Anglia and the South West. Other data suggest that variations in 'staying-on' rates are related to both gender and ethnic background. For instance, the large increase in the number of part-time further education students between 1980 and 1988 is mostly explained by the burgeoning number of young women who chose to stay on during that period rather than leave off their education entirely (Central Statistical Office, 1990, p. 58).

The 1989 *Youth Cohort Study*, confirms this trend, whilst indicating at the same time that young people from different ethnic and home social backgrounds are also more or less likely to stay on. Black young people, for example, with high prior examination attainments from non-manual home backgrounds have a probability of entering full-time education post-16 of almost 90 percent compared to 50 percent of their white counterparts (Gray, Jesson, Pattie & Sime, 1989, p. 19). This last finding reinforces the earlier analysis of Eggleston, Dunn & Anjali (1986) who concluded that black young people were "twice as likely as whites" to remain in continuing education (p. 219).

The Cohort Study's findings on the social origins of young people that choose to stay on also confirm that those from non-manual backgrounds are more likely to continue their education beyond 16 years. Interestingly, the lower rates of participation in further education recorded by children from non-manual backgrounds are the same irrespective of the examination attainment group from which they come. Data of these sort largely explain why, at the stage of entry to higher education, there is a massive imbalance in the proportion of candidates from different social classes, with those from the working class making up less than one third of the total admissions (see Farrant, 1981).

Why young people as a whole in the United Kingdom should be so disinclined to continue their education and training is not entirely clear. Variations in participation rates from one part of the country to another undoubtedly have something to do with the nature of local policies for education and training. But two other factors would appear to make as big a contribution to early school leaving in Britain: the experience of education pre-16, and the pull of the local labour market.

The experience of education pre-16 plays a significant role in discouraging certain young people from continuing in full-time education. Certainly, the old examination regime provided by Ordinary (O) Level seemed designed to produce failure for the majority and success for a minority. Indeed, Smithers & Robinson (1989, p. 3) estimate that a 40 percent failure at O Level was the 'going' rate. Even the old Certificate of Secondary Education (CSE), they argue, was designed to produce failures since, on average, less than 50 percent of pupils taking it were awarded grades A, B or C. At its worst, the examination system pre-General

Certificate of Secondary Education (GCSE) left approximately 10 percent of 16 year olds without any qualifications whatsoever.

With these data to hand, Smithers & Robinson conclude that

> *many young people do not stay on beyond compulsory schooling because they are not qualified to do so. The education system instead of rewarding achievements is a process of failure. How deeply depressing it must be to go through school knowing that at the end you will have little to show for it. Is it surprising then that so many youngsters should ... leave at the first opportunity when allowed to do so? (1989, p. 4)*

In this connection, it may be significant that the advent of the GCSE, with its emphasis on rewarding achievement, has coincided with a projected decrease in the number of young people leaving school at the minimum age. According to research published by the Department of Employment last summer (DoE, 1990), the staying on rate is expected to rise from its current level of 32% to about 42% by 1996. This rise, the Department predicts, is likely to be consolidated by the increased number of pupils that succeed at 'passing' the new GCSE examination.

Smithers & Robinson's conclusion that secondary schools 'fail' too many young people is a familiar one. So is Hargreaves' related attack on the *'culture of individualism'* that pervades secondary schooling and the way in which this exerts on many pupils a destruction of their dignity. To have dignity, Hargreaves explains, is "to have a sense of being worthy, of possessing creative, inventive and critical capacities, of having the power to achieve personal and social change" (1982, p. 17). No doubt many young people in the final years of compulsory schooling feel all or many of these things. But this is less likely to be the case for those who possess a strong sense of having persistently 'failed' its measures of success. It is less likely also for those young people who suffer forms of racial and sexual discrimination at school, both in the ways they are taught, and the form and content of what they are taught (see Davies, 1984; Wright, 1987). Any personal sense of worth such pupils acquire is, more likely, sometimes through membership of various youth sub-cultures, the values and attitudes of which can be antithetical to those projected by even well-meaning teachers. Given this oppositional reaction to school by some pupils, manifested in various forms of disaffection and indiscipline, it is hardly surprising that the world beyond its boundaries appears more attractive than staying on for more of the same.

Part of this attraction, of course, is the prospect of employment. For those 16-year-olds who have measured up reasonably well to the school's conception of success by achieving, say, a respectable clutch of 'good' grades in a number of GCSEs, the labour market provides a variety of short-term incentives to early school-leavers. There is evidence, for example, that in their efforts to beat a record shortage of teenage labour, a growing number of employers, particularly in retailing, were offering financial bounties and other perks to encourage job applications from young people in their final years of school (see Lees, 1990).

The Labour market also offers longer-term pay-offs to 16-year-olds who leave school. For those not bound for higher education, staying on at school can actually prejudice opportunities for training and associated career advancement because the former are restricted in many cases to young people in their teenage years. In other words, for some young people, to remain at school after 16 can reduce, rather than enhance, their chance of being in a job in two or three years time. To this extent, some trends within the youth labour market are in direct competition with the efforts of schools to retain their pupils beyond the age of 16.

Comprehensive schools, of course, are not able to regulate trends within the youth labour market. This will always remain the prime responsibility of government and employers. In this regard, the IPPR makes a number of suggestions as to what ought to be done by the central state to remove existing labour market incentives to early leaving. These include encouraging employers to switch their minimum recruitment age from 16 to 18 years, the removal of arbitrary age-limits for entry to jobs, the streamlining of apprenticeships so that these complement school studies post-16, and the provision of a work-based but *education-led scheme* for 16-18 year olds who leave school but who do not find a job or other training.

The IPPR's suggestions for improving and opening up intellectual and practical study post-16 through the creation of a unified qualification at 18-plus were outlined earlier. Their radicalism, which was not stressed enough then, centres on the proposal to reform the Sixth Form curriculum through the replacement of existing qualifications (Advanced Level, B/Tec, and the rest) by a common modular programme leading to the award of an Advanced Diploma. Underpining the IPPR's Advanced Diploma is a set of educational aims that emphasise 'flexibility', 'choice', 'breadth of study', the provision of 'knowledge necessary for all citizens in a democratic society', the integration of 'contextual' and 'specialist studies', the relation of theory to practice, and 'work or community-based experience' (IPPR, 1990, p. 26). While such emphases would strike a chord with a number of other proposals for reforming post-16 education, their distinctiveness lies in the commitment to abolish the separation of academic from other studies.

This commitment, if widely embraced, could have the effect of signalling to pupils that secondary schools operate with a much broader definition of 'success' than that indicated by academic achievement alone, thus hopefully encouraging a greater level of participation in full-time education after 16 years of young people who have other things to offer and whose studies are coordinated in a way that blurs the distinction between intellectual and practical achievement. It might also provide a model for the development of a genuinely comprehensive 16 plus curriculum, the impact of which ought to be felt throughout the secondary phase of schooling rather than be restricted to its post-compulsory stage. For if a common curriculum that integrates the academic with the practical is needed in order to attract more 16 to 18 year olds, it surely must be relevant too to the challenge of motivating and interesting pupils during the years of compulsory secondary schooling.

Staying In

But it is not just some pupils that have become disaffected by their secondary comprehensive schools. Increasingly parents, particularly those of academically able children, are showing signs that they also are concerned about the quality of education comprehensive schools provide and are beginning to seek alternatives. In the last ten years there has been a steady growth in the number of parents choosing to educate their children outside the state system (for details see Independent Schools Information Service, 1989). Other parents are also beginning to be attracted away from local authority comprehensive schools by new non free-charging independent colleges (City Technology Colleges) and DES-maintained schools (grant-maintained schools).

The drift towards growing parental take-up of private and other forms of secondary education, and the danger this poses to the future of comprehensive schooling, needs to be seen in the context of wider social and political forces, in particular the present government's attempt to introduce market principles into the style and pattern of its policies for the education service. This project has two main aspects. On the one hand, it is concerned to make education less dependent on state funding and increasingly reliant on private financial support and investment. On the other hand, it is designed to atomize decision-making in relation to the supply and demands of educational services through appeals to individual consumer or parental choice linked to greater competitiveness between providing institutions.

Both aspects threaten the future of comprehensive schooling in England and Wales. Certainly, moves to make comprehensives less reliant on state funding by encouraging parents to take more financial responsibility for their children's education (as, for example, in the areas of swimming instruction, musical tuition, and by the raising of funds in general through the activities of Parent-Teacher Associations) are likely to expose some schools whose catchment areas, especially those in the inner city, are less well-favoured and which do not have the same capacity as others to provide private aid of this kind.

But the threat posed to the comprehensive system by government support for the take up of private education outside the state (through its Assisted Places Scheme) and its attempts to introduce newer forms of state-maintained and privately funded schools is likely to be as great, not least because these initiatives have been developed within a 'grammar school frame of reference' which has wide appeal among those middle-class parents who want an academic education for their children and who are unconvinced of the comprehensive school's present ability to provide one.

While, in the short term, the actual number of able pupils that will be directly 'creamed' from the comprehensive sector as a result of the Assisted Places Scheme, City Technology Colleges and Grant Maintained Schools is likely to be very small, its symbolic value as a visible indicator of declining confidence in non-selective schooling should not be discounted. Reynolds & Hargreaves believe that initiatives of this sort, coupled with poor governmental support for, and powerful governmental ideological critiques of, the state system and its teachers, are likely only to increase the recent yet growing emigration of pupils, particularly able pupils, from the state to the private sector (1989, p. 4).

Towards Unified Provision: a new policy agenda?

David Hargreaves, of course, wrote *The Challenge for the Comprehensive School* some considerable time before the developments in government policy outlined here. Even so, one suspects that he would not alter much of his original argument if he were to begin to rewrite the book today. He would surely still plead strongly for a less academically oriented and subject-based core curriculum for the years of compulsory secondary schooling. But, equally, one could not imagine him proposing that comprehensive schools should abandon academic study altogether; for to do so would arguably further alienate those parents of academically able children which comprehensives wish, in some cases, to retain, in others, to attract back, and who clearly place considerable store by the academic aspects of school choice (Fox, 1985, p. 141; Edwards, Fitz & Whitty, 1989, p. 190) and the effects of that choice (Smith & Tomlinson, 1989, p. 61). It would also deny access to some working class children to the ladder of opportunity to higher education and certain careers.

Appeals to parents based on the principle of comprehensive education would hardly fare much better. What little we know about the nature of parental choice would seem to indicate that it is the proven quality of a non-selective school, not its ideological terms of reference, that inspires confidence (see, for example, Edwards, Fitz & Whitty, 1989, p. 196). The aim, therefore, must surely be for comprehensive schools to offer opportunities for academic study and success in ways that are neither narrowly intellectual and crudely elitist nor disassociated from the demands of practical living and the needs of society.

In theory, the philosophy of Local Management of Schools (LMS) ought to assist individual comprehensive schools in their efforts to develop a more positive image and increase public confidence in non-selective education. *Circular 7/88* in its opening statement of 'General Principles', for example, makes the point that the purpose of LMS is to facilitate improvement in the quality of both learning and teaching by "enabling governing bodies and headteachers to plan their use of resources ... to maximum effect ... and to make schools more responsive to their clients - parents, pupils, the local community and employers" (DES, 1988, p. 3). But the practice of LMS may create what Thomas (1990) has defined as an educational 'voucher economy' in which competition rather than cooperation between individual comprehensive schools is promoted.

Indeed, LMS, combined with open enrolment, could reinforce, instead of address and dissolve, the crude distinctions often made between 'good' (often associated simply with 'academic' achievement) and 'bad' schools within local systems of secondary education.

Under this new dispensation, local education authorities will be largely powerless to intervene. Furthermore, the new powers of appointment, suspension and dismissal of teachers conferred on governors under LMS will make it different for them to direct new, and redeploy existing, teachers to areas and schools where they are most needed, thus compounding the problems of those schools which do not recruit well and which are less well off financially as a result. Finally, if preliminary findings of recent studies of the practice of LMS are anything to go by (see Bowe & Ball, 1991, for example), teachers working in comprehensive schools may find that, as the importance of financial management and marketing takes hold, their involvement in corporate decision-taking and policy-making is reduced. This suggests that teachers' sense of professional worth and career development could undergo considerable shifts, and not all of them for the better, as LMS takes hold.

Whether, to follow the IPPR's suggestion, an increase in staying on rates would be assisted by the widespread development of tertiary colleges also remains an open question. Pupils whose sense of personal dignity has been badly dented by their experience of school pre-16 are hardly likely to be convinced that it will be restored by more education in an adjacent institution. Part of a more radical and long-term solution that articulates with the need to foster greater public confidence in non-selective schooling may lie in translating the IPPR's conception of a unified, common curriculum - one that successfully integrates academic with practical study - into institutional arrangements that possess the same characteristics but which dissolve age-specific educational provision. The Community College is a significant embodiment of this idea. Although it takes a variety of forms and stresses different aspects of the educational process (see Martin, 1987), the philosophy of community education upon which it is based is grounded in a fundamental commitment to public sector provision and the principles of comprehensive and continuing education.

Community education in practice, it has to be remarked, has not always lived up to these fine ideals (see Wallis & Mee, 1983; Cowburn, 1986). There have been, for example, problems with shared use of facilities, the democratisation of provision and access to educational opportunity generally. Despite these difficulties, there have been some important and exemplary developments such as the networks of community schools/colleges in Cambridgeshire, Coventry, Sheffield, Derbyshire, Leicestershire, Northumberland and elsewhere. While many of these have struggled to retain ways of working that combine schooling with training and continuing education opportunities, with the chief limiting factor often being the tendency of some school functions to dominate, the model, if properly implemented, might seriously challenge certain in-grained assumptions about 'staying in' and 'staying-out' as well as neutralise many of the worst predicted outcomes of present government policy for education.

Four aspects of this model stand out in particular and warrant consideration by education's policy promulgators as well as sociologists concerned to test its claims against practice. First, policies for community education undermine the aims of 'opting out' and anticipate the best features of LMS because they are designed to redirect educational priorities and practice in ways that bring education and community into a closer and more equal relationship. Second, they offer a basis and rationale for developing positive, coherent and user-friendly responses to the educational needs of all people in a locality. Third, they encourage the idea that education provision should work towards the harmonisation of intellectual and practical study and their integration with the pursuit of leisure. And, fourth, they signal that education should be regarded as a continuous process which people may take a break from but never leave off entirely. A community college based on such policies is arguably archetypical of a genuinely comprehensive education, which may suggest that the latter needs to be rescued from some comprehensive schools.

REFERENCES

Apple, M. (1979) *Ideology and Curriculum*. London: Routledge & Kegan Paul.

Ball, S.J. (1981) *Beachside Comprehensive: A Case Study of Secondary Schooling*. Cambridge: Cambridge University Press.

Ball, S.J. (1990) *Politics and Policy Making in Education*. London: Routledge & Kegan Paul.

Bash, L. (1989) Structural Contradictions, in L. Bash & D. Coulby, *The Education Reform Act: Competition and Control*. London: Cassell.

Bash, L. & Coulby, D. (1989) *The Education Reform Act: Competition and Control*. London: Cassell.

Benn, C. & Simon, B. (1972) *Half Way There*, 2nd Edn. Harmondsworth: Penguin Books.

Bowe, R. & Ball, S. (1991) Micropolitics of Radical Change: budgets, management and control in British schools, in J. Blase (Ed) *The Politics of Life in Schools*. London: Sage.

Bowles, S. & Gintis, H. (1976) *Schooling in Capitalist America*. London: Routledge.

Bristol Polytechnic Education Study Group (1989) Restructuring the Education System?, in L. Bash & D. Coulby, *The Education Reform Act: Competition and Control*. London: Cassell.

Broadfoot, P. (1979) *Assessment, Schools and Society*. London: Methuen.

Burgess, R.G. (1983) *Experiencing Comprehensive Education: A Study of Bishop McGregor School*. London: Methuen.

Central Statistical Office (1990) *Social Trends 20*. London: HMSO.

Central Statistical Office (1990a) *Regional Trends 25*. London: HMSO.

Centre for Contemporary Cultural Studies (1981) *Unpopular Education: Schooling & Social Democracy in England Since 1944*. London: Hutchinson.

Chitty, C. (1989) *Towards a New Education System: The Victory of the New Right?* Lewes: Falmer Press.

Corrigan, P. (1979) *Schooling the Bash Street Kids*. London: Macmillan.

Coulby, D. (1989) The Ideological Contradictions of Educational Reform, in L. Bash & D. Coulby (Eds) *The Education Reform Act: Competition and Control*. London: Cassell.

Cowburn, W. (1986) *Class, Ideology and Community Education*. London: Croom Helm.

Cultural Studies, University of Birmingham (1991) *Education Limited: Schooling & Training and the New Right Since 1979*. London: Unwin Hyman.

Dale, R. (1990) Political Change, Educational Change and the State, in R. Dale, *The State and Education Policy*. Milton Keynes: Open University Press.

Dale, R., Esland, G. & Macdonald, M. (Eds) (1976) *Schooling and Capitalism*. London: Routledge & Kegan Paul.

Davies, L. (1984) Gender and Comprehensive Schooling, in S. Ball (Ed) *Comprehensive Schooling: A Reader*. Lewes: Falmer Press.

Deem, R. (1978) *Women and Schooling*. London: Routledge & Kegan Paul.

Department of Education & Science (1988) *Education Reform Act: Local Management of Schools [Circular 7/88]*. London: HMSO.

Department of Education & Science (1990) *Press Release* [53/90]. 19th February.

Department of Employment (1990) Young People Leaving School, *Employment Gazette*, 98 (8).

Douglas, J.W.B. (1964) *The Home and the School*. London: MacGibbon & Kee.

Edwards, T., Fitz, J. & Whitty, G. (1989) *The State and Private Education: An Evaluation of the Assisted Places Scheme*. Lewes: Falmer Press.

Eggleston, J., Dunn, D. & Anjali, M. (1986) *Education For Some: The Educational and Vocational Experiences of 15-18 Year Old Members of Minority Ethnic Groups*. Stoke-on-Trent: Trentham Books.

Farrant, J. (1981) Trends in Admissions, in O. Fulton (Ed) *Access to Higher Education*. Guildford: SRHE.

Floud, J. & Halsey, A.H. (1956) English Secondary Schools and the Supply of Labour, in B. Cosin & M Hales (Eds) (1983) *Education, Policy and Society*. London: Routledge & Kegan Paul/Open University.

Flude, M. & Hammer, M. (Eds) (1990) *The Education Reform Act: Its Origins and Implications*. Lewes: Falmer Press.

Ford, J. (1969) *Social Class and the Comprehensive School*. London: Routledge & Kegan Paul.

Fox, I. (1985) *Private Schools and Public Issues: The Parents' Views*. London: Macmillan.

Gray, J. & Jesson, D. (1989) The Impact of Comprehensive Reforms, in R. Lowe (Ed) *The Changing Secondary School*. Lewes: Falmer Press.

Gray, J., Jesson, D., Pattie, C. & Sime, N. (1989) *Education and Training Opportunities in the Inner City [Youth Cohort Study]*. Sheffield: Training Agency.

Griggs, C. (1989) The New Right and English Secondary Education, in R. Lowe (Ed) *The Changing Secondary School*. Lewes: Falmer Press.

Halpin, D. (1989) The Present Image and Future of Comprehensive Schooling, *British Journal of Educational Studies*, 37, pp. 339-357.

Hammersley, M. & Woods, P. (Eds) (1984) *The Process of Schooling: A Sociological Reader*. London: Routledge & Kegan Paul.

Hargreaves, A. & Reynolds, D. (1989) Decomprehensivation, in A. Hargreaves & D. Reynolds (Eds), *Education Policies: Controversies and Critiques*. Lewes: Falmer

Hargreaves, D.H. (1967) *Social Relations in a Secondary School*. London: Routledge & Kegan Paul.

Hargreaves, D.H. (1972) *Interpersonal Relations and Education*. London: Routledge & Kegan Paul.

Hargreaves, D.H. (1982) *The Challenge for the Comprehensive School: Culture, Curriculum and Community*. London: Routledge & Kegan Paul.

Hopkins, D. (Ed) (1987) *Improving the Quality of Schooling: Lessons from the OECD International School Improvement Project*. Lewes: Falmer Press.

House of Commons (1988) *Parliamentary Debates*. 30th June, 524.

Independent Schools Information Service (1989) *Annual Census*. London: Independent Schools Information Services.

Institute for Public Policy Research (1990) *A British 'Baccalaureate': Ending the Division Between Education and Training*. London: Institute for Public Policy Research.

Johnson, R. (1989) Thatcherism and English Education: Breaking the Mould or Confirming a Pattern?, *History of Education*, 18, pp. 91-121.

Jones, K. (1989) *Right Turn: The Conservative Revolution in Education*. London: Hutchinson.

Labour Party (1990) *Look to the Future*. London: Labour Party.

Lees, C. (1990) Firms Scramble for Disappearing Teenagers, *Sunday Times*, 12th August.

Levitas, M. (1974) *Marxist Perspectives in the Sociology of Education*. London: Routledge & Kegan Paul.

MacDonald, M. (1981) Schooling and the Reproduction of Class and Gender Relations, in R. Dale, G. Esland, R. Fergusson & M. MacDonald (Eds) *Education and the State: Politics, Patriarchy and Practice*. Lewes: Falmer Press.

Martin, I. (1987) Community Education: Towards a Theoretical Analysis, in G. Allen, J. Bastiani, I. Martin & K. Richards (Eds) *Community Education: An Agenda for Educational Reform*. Milton Keynes: Open University Press.

Monks, T.G. (1968) *Comprehensive Education in England and Wales: A Survey of Schools and their Organisation*. Slough: NFER.

Monks, T.G. (1970) (Ed) *Comprehensive Schools in Action*. Slough: NFER.

Moon, B. (1983) (Ed) *Comprehensive Schools: Challenge and Change*. Windsor: NFER-Nelson.

MORI (1989) Opinion Poll, *The Independent*, 6th May.

Reid, K., Hopkins, D. & Holly, P. (1988) *Towards the Effective School*. Oxford: Basil Blackwell.

Reynolds, D. & Sullivan, M. (1987) *The Comprehensive Experiment: A Comparison of the Selective and Non-Selective Systems of School Organization*. Lewes: Falmer Press.

Rutter, M., Maughan, B., Mortimer, P. Ousten, J. (1979) *Fifteen Thousand Hours*. London: Open Books.

Saran, R. (1973) *Policy-Making In Secondary Education*. Oxford: Clarendon Press.

Sarup, M. (1978) *Marxism and Education*. London: Routledge & Kegan Paul.

Smith, D.J. & Tomlinson, S. (1989) *The School Effect: A Study of Multi-Racial Comprehensive*. London: Policy Studies Institute.

Smithers, A. & Robinson, P. (1989) *Increasing Participation in Higher Education*. London: British Petroleum Educational Service.

Thomas, H. (1990) From Local Financial Management to Local Management of Schools', in M. Flude & M. Hammer (Eds) *The Education Reform Act: Its Origins and Implications*. Lewes: Falmer Press.

Tomlinson, S. (1983) *Ethnic Minorities in British Schools*. London: Heinemann.

Troyna, B. (1984) Fact or Artefact: The 'Educational Under-Achievement' of Black Pupils, *British Journal of Sociology of Education*, 5, pp. 153-166.

Wallis, J. & Mee, G. (1983) *Community Schools: Claims and Performances*. Nottingham: Department of Adult Education, University of Nottingham.

Whitty, G. (1985) *Sociology and School Knowledge*. London: Methuen.

Whitty, G. (1990) The Politics of the 1988 Education Reform Act, in P. Dunleavy, A. Gamble & G. Peale (Eds) *Developments in British Politics 3*. London: Macmillan.

Willis, P. (1977) *Learning to Labour*. Farnborough: Saxon House.

Wolpe, A.M. (1977) *Some Processes in Sexist Education*. London: Women's Research and Resource Centre Publications.

Woods, P. (Ed) (1978) *Teacher Strategies*. London: Croom Helm.

Woods, P. (Ed) (1978a) *Pupil Strategies*. London: Croom Helm.

Wright, C. (1987) Black Students - White Teachers, in B. Troyna (Ed.) *Racial Inequality in Education*. London: Tavistock.

Chapter Eight

Whose Choice of Schools? Making Sense of City Technology Colleges

TONY EDWARDS, SHARON GEWIRTZ
& GEOFF WHITTY

In an earlier paper about our research on City Technology Colleges (Edwards et al, 1991), we described their diverse and puzzling origins and the consequent difficulty of explaining why they appeared when they did. They can of course be characterized as "instant policy-making" (Nash, 1988), "a costly gimmick by an opportunistic Secretary of State" (Chitty, 1989, p. 37), or as offering "an image of dynamic modernising reform that was especially helpful in the approach to the next general election" (McCulloch, 1989a, p. 178). And there are apparent grounds for short-term interpretations in the difficulties encountered in implementing Baker's promise to the 1986 Conservative Party Conference that twenty CTCs would be open within four years. For example, the claim that 'all or a substantial part' of the capital costs would be met by private sponsorship (DES, 1986, p. 8) had not been preceded by any careful estimate of what those costs might be, or by any prior recruitment of willing sponsors; subsequent funding difficulties have therefore forced the Government itself to become the major share-holder in the enterprise. The especial difficulty of finding sponsors and sites in the same places has also brought a considerable redefinition of the intended inner-city locations; indeed, none of the specific examples suggested by the DES (1986) - Moss Side in Manchester, Chapeltown in Leeds, Highfield in Leicester and St Paul's in Bristol - has either a CTC or a confirmed project for establishing one.

Such tactical miscalculations, however, are not in themselves evidence of mere opportunism. A policy initiative may have deep roots without being either thought through or competently planned, and this particular 'pilot project' has commonly been given a policy significance out of all proportion to its modest scale. Thus Chitty's reference to a 'costly gimmick' is contradicted by an extended warning not to treat CTCs in isolation and thereby 'seriously underestimate' their place in Government plans to "hand education over to the control of crude market forces...in the interests of the rich, the powerful and the articulate" (1987, p. 69). Elsewhere, the creation of CTCs has been described as a tactical expression of various deep Government strategies - for example, to reintroduce academic selection (Morrell, 1989), to undermine local authorities as the principal providers of educational services (McLeod, 1988), to blur the boundaries between public and private provision so as to produce radical changes in the 'culture and ethos of schooling' (Flude & Hammer, 1990), and to engage in a sweeping policy of 'conservative modernisation' (Dale, 1989b).

In this chapter, we first try to make sense of CTCs in the context of several different policy sets, each of which relates to main themes in the sociology of education. As a vigorous sponsorship of technical education in a country which has traditionally accorded it low status, it raises questions about how 'useful' knowledge is defined, especially for elites, and about the stratifying of educational routes into the labour market. As a declared enhancing of educational opportunity, it raises questions drawn from the political arithmetic tradition about who benefits - and does so in relation to more complex criteria for selecting suitable pupils than the traditional reliance on academic merit. The most radical aspect of the initiative, however, is its potential contribution to challenging 'monolithic' public provision, blurring the boundary between 'public' and 'private', and perhaps pointing the way to a free market of 'independent', competing schools. Analysis of the origins and implementation of CTCs therefore offers an opportunity to explore the relevance of sociological theory to an understanding of contemporary education policy through close study of a particular initiative.

That such varied and deep purposes have been attributed to CTCs indicates the impossibility of simply 'reading off' their significance from some primary underlying theme. Educational policies are likely to have various, not necessarily compatible, sources and objectives, and to attract support subsequently from interest groups who see opportunities to advance their own concerns. Nevertheless, we explore in the last part of the chapter an underlying tension which the promotion of CTCs both illustrates and highlights. It is a tension between the modernising and free market strands in Government policy. We argue that CTCs provide in many ways a model for how schools are intended to operate in a new market-oriented system. Yet as the product of conspicuous state intervention to create a suitably 'modern' version of secondary education, they may also be understood as recognising the limitations of the market to achieve that transformation of the labour force which advocates of modernisation perceive to be necessary. Finally, we refer briefly to collectivist or egalitarian objections to an educational free market which advocates of that market dismiss as invalid but which are drawn from the mainstream of sociological analysis of schooling.

The Sponsorship of Secondary-Technical Education

Although 'technology college' has a grander ring, and although a modern high-tech appeal is usually highlighted in their publicity, CTCs have an obvious resemblance to the technical schools described in the Ministry's pamphlet on *The New Secondary Education* (1947) as having 'the sphere of industry or commerce' as their 'particular link with the adult world', and as catering for the 'minority of able children' who respond best to a curriculum coloured in that way. Thus Pring (1989) notes that the DES guidance on how to select appropriate pupils for CTCs could have been taken directly from the Spens Report's (1938) advocacy of technical high schools. And it is because he regards them primarily as the latest in a series of unsuccessful attempts to establish a strong technical strand within secondary education that McCulloch (1989a & b) is so critical of the Government's apparent disregard of the lessons to be drawn from that 'usable past'.

From a sociological perspective, the main 'lessons' come from recognising the deep-rooted cultural resistance to 'technical' education as being anything other than inferior and subordinate to 'real' academic education, and the consequent obstacles to parity of esteem for any schools having that bias. They include a wariness about borrowing remedies for the neglect of technical education from countries which have traditionally given it much stronger institutional and cultural support (Naylor, 1985). And they suggest a need for scepticism about the efficacy of exhortations to greater 'relevance' which take no account of the longevity and persistence of the 'British disease' (Mathieson & Bernbaum, 1988). That scepticism includes doubts about whether employers will necessarily support schools set up explicitly to serve their interests, and whether it is realistic to blame the 'educational establishment' for a failure "rooted deeply within a specific culture and society" (McCulloch, 1989b, p. 210).

Although he traces the 'anti-industrial spirit' of Britain's cultural elite much further back, Corelli Barnett assigns much of the blame for "protracted decline as an industrial country" to the post-War welfare settlement perpetrated by the entire "enlightened establishment" (Barnet, 1986, pp.12-18). His indictment merits extended quotation for its vividness, but also because the 'Barnett thesis' has been widely accepted (for example Rae, 1989); indeed, it was cited by John MacGregor as one of his 'favourite books', and re-read when he succeeded Baker as Secretary of State (*The Times Educational Supplement*, interview 16 March 1990):

> While in 1940-1 Winston Churchill and the nation at large were fighting for sheer survival... members of the British cultural elite had begun to busy themselves with design studies for a 'New Jerusalem' to be built in Britain after the war was won...[A] century of cross breeding between the aesthetic

and moral strands in romanticism had made the 'enlightened' British establishment of the 1940s what it was: tender-hearted and high-minded...The marketing of the New Jerusalem took place in parallel inside Whitehall and outside in pulpits and print. There existed, moreover, a constant osmosis between Whitehall and the wider intellectual elite on the topic, thanks to shared membership of clubs, committees and dinner tables...Not one of the New Jerusalemites was an engineer, an industrialist or a trade unionist, not one of them had ever had the experience of running any kind of operation in the real world in which Britain competed commercially in peacetime...[They were] products of the closed loop of British elite education.

The diagnosis is much bleaker than Raymond William's (1965) description of a class-based gulf between the 'old humanist' and 'industrial training' traditions in English education, because it identifies not only the inappropriateness of 'elite education' to the modern world but the accompanying creation of a "segregated, sub-literate, unskilled, unhealthy and institutionalised proletariat hanging on to the nipple of state materialism" (Barnett, 1986, p. 304). Yet his own analysis of how 'enlightenment' had permeated the system might have made him cautious about one of its implications - that more competitive, modern forms of secondary education would arise from giving those with experience in the 'real world' what they want. For industrialists themselves exerted no consistent pressure for knowledge and skills directly relevant to an advanced economy, at least above the level of 'technician'. McCulloch's (1989a) socio-historical analysis leads him to attribute to the conservatism of employers and their organisations, rather than of educationists, the failure of technical schools to establish their fitness to prepare industry's 'officer class'. If access to high status jobs, in business and industry as well as in the 'liberal' professions, depended largely on traditionally academic qualifications, then secondary schools are responding to market forces rather than resisting them when they continue to emphasize such qualifications (Edwards, 1986). And as Olive Banks's (1955) sociological study indicated, it is correspondingly unrealistic to expect parity of esteem between types of secondary school, or types of curriculum, which normally give access to very different levels in the labour market. Thus Naylor's (1985) advocacy of a new wave of technical schools recognised that their predecessors had failed to attract 'really able pupils', and to win the status and resources which the West German *Realschule* commanded in a very different culture. Our own analysis of data collected in the course of research on the Assisted Places Scheme, a scheme embodying entirely traditional forms of 'academic excellence', suggests that 'the cultural pull of the public or grammar school curriculum (or rather the public perception of that curriculum) would distort the market with consequences which would not please the advocates of relevance as an organising principle for the curriculum' (Whitty, 1989, p. 337). As long as a 'good' education is popularly associated with a traditional academic curriculum, and as long as any form of 'technical' education is commonly perceived as 'second rate', parents are unlikely to opt for the kinds of school which 'modernisers' believe to be necessary for alleviating the 'skills shortage'- and the predominant preferences of employers will justify that parental choice.

In terms of the numbers directly affected, twenty CTCs will clearly have little impact on general skills shortages however energetically they are promoted in an effort to counter traditional consumer resistance. They can be seen, however, as a move towards closer correspondence with the particular production needs of an advanced economy increasingly dependent on information technology. More generally, CTCs may be seen as a response to changes in the mode of capital accumulation, reflecting a shift from the 'Fordist' school of the era of mass production to the 'Post-Fordist' school. In other words, CTCs may be the educational equivalent of what Stuart Hall & Martin Jacques (1989, p.12) characterise as the rise of "flexible specialisation in place of the old assembly-line world of mass production". The distinctive physical appearance of some CTCs, and their emphasis on 'niche marketing', provides some evidence for this view (Ball, 1990, pp.113-132). As a marketing strategy, the effects of CTCs may be considerable. Indeed, they can be seen not merely as a response to demand but as an attempt to create it among those in the process of choosing a secondary school.

Enhanced status for this new form of technical education is sought through various, sometimes contradictory, appeals - the emphasis on high technology, the special links with local industry which are presented as conferring tangible advantages in at least the local labour market, and the appearance of being an alternative, innovative and effective form of comprehensive school with at least a degree of selectiveness. Those CTCs which are not newly built are relatively lavish conversions of existing establishments. Located in areas where the surrounding schools are commonly perceived as suffering from poor repair and declining resources, their relative attractions are visible and easily publicized. For example, pupils entering the Solihull CTC in September 1990 were informed that "the technology of the future has already arrived at Kingshurst". Similarly, the 1989 recruitment leaflet for Gateshead's newly-built Emmanual College claimed that "this new concept in educational thinking" would consist of "some of the finest and most carefully planned buildings in the country" and "the most up-to-date equipment"; there would be "no shortage of vital resources to ensure the maximum progress for all our students". Such claims could not have been made by the maintained comprehensive schools with which Emmanuel was competing. Certainly the balance of relative advantage is very different from that experienced by even the 'successful' technical schools of the 1950s and 1960s in competition with neighbouring grammar schools. Whether it also enables CTCs to compete with the less tangible but powerful attractions of surviving (and usually 'independent') grammar schools remains to be seen. That uncertainty takes our analysis back to the historically 'second-class' status of technical education, and forward to more detailed consideration of the target groups for whom CTCs are primarily intended.

A New 'Ladder of Opportunity'

One of McCulloch's main lessons from the past is the need to be clear about the scope of technical-secondary education, and whether its primary function is to train the 'technological elite' or the 'technicians' of an advanced industrial society. The old technical schools aspired to the first, but were largely confined to the second. TVEI was presented in 1982 as a curriculum 'strand' suitable for a wide ability range, but David Young's particular target were those pupils, not the ablest but among the next 15% to 45%, for whom existing secondary education was "too academic and too unrelated to employment" and who should be trained to become the technicians of the new industrial age (cit. Chitty, 1987, p. 67; see also Evans & Davies, 1988: Young, 1990, pp. 23, 89-97). The CTCs were presented from the outset as fully comprehensive schools - as not merely another escape route for able children from 'failing' urban comprehensives, but as a general solution to problems of poor motivation and low achievement. Among their more evident sources was a conference on employment early in 1986, organised by Cyril Taylor (later Chairman of the CTC Trust) for the Centre of Policy Studies, from which came a proposal that "a hundred secondary technical schools" should be funded directly by the Government and concentrated initially in "deprived inner-city areas". That recommendation was identified as the conference's most important outcome (Taylor, 1986, p. 2). Its implementation would not only help to remedy the long neglect of technical education; it would also demonstrate that the Conservative Party, traditionally preoccupied with the most gifted, "also cares about education for the non-academically inclined majority of school children" (ibid. p. 30: Taylor, 1987). As "an injection of hope into depressed areas", as Angela Rumbold described them at the time of their announcement (*Guardian*, 15 October, 1986), CTCs were explicitly promoted (Young-fashion) as enhancing and even creating job prospects through their development of employable skills and attitudes across wide sectors and levels of the 'modern' labour market.

Ostensibly negating early predictions that they would become 'subsidized grammar schools in high technology clothes' (Glazier, 1986), the CTCs are statutorily obliged to show intakes 'representative of the community they serve', and not to seek promising recruits from beyond their designated catchment areas (DES, 1986). What forms that 'representativeness' is likely to take is considered later in this section. But some of those involved in the development of CTCs have appeared keen, beyond the call of statutory duty, to emphasize how much their effectiveness as 'beacons of excellence' will depend on their success with the same kinds of pupil who have been 'failed' by traditional comprehensive schools with their 'diluted' academic curriculum and didactic methods of teaching (Denholm, 1988; Taylor, 1988). From that perspective, they embody a familiar confidence that a more 'practical' approach, and a more direct relevance to the 'real world', would have particular benefits for less able and socially disadvantaged pupils. It will be interesting to explore, in the context of sociological analyses of class-biased forms of curriculum and pedagogy (Bernstein, 1977, 1990), the particular attractions of institutions explicitly committed to innovating in both. The task will be intriguing, because the emphasis on 'useful knowledge' and direct experience of technology is accompanied by certain aspects of 'progressivism' which have been identified as being more accessible to the 'new' middle class. For example, the first CTCs display or promise an unusual commitment to blurring disciplinary boundaries, to topic or thematic work across the curriculum, and even to that "creative activity carried out independently" which Anyon (1980) associated with "affluent professional" schools. In so far as they become distinctive in these respects, they raise familiar sociological questions about the 'strategic skills' or particular forms of 'cultural capital' required of 'successful' pupils (Bourdieu, 1986; DiMaggio, 1982; Edwards, 1987; Bernstein, 1990). They also raise questions about what used to be termed, misleadingly, the 'hidden' curriculum. In this case, socialization into an 'enterprise culture' is explicit as an objective and as a process. It is to be achieved not only through highlighting 'business understanding', 'enterprise' and 'self-reliance' in the formal curriculum, but also through the 'messages' carried in the 'business-like' organisation of the colleges. For example, some CTCs work an 'industrial day' (8.30a.m. to 5.30p.m.); the presence of sponsors and other local employers is made deliberately visible; and the physical environment may be designed, as it was by Valerie Bragg at Kingshurst, not to look like a school but more like a commercial or industrial organisation (Walford & Miller, 1991).

We turn in more detail, however, to even more familiar questions about the 'matching' of opportunity and merit, and the nature of secondary schooling as a channel of social selection. The "fresh opportunities for the children of our cities" which Baker proclaimed in 1986 could be presented as a policy response to the enduring evidence of the absence of equality of opportunity, and the ensuing wastage of talent. Yet previous 'ladders of opportunity' had been directed to conventionally 'academic' secondary education, and there is extensive sociological evidence that all such routes have been thinly populated by socially disadvantaged children. Thus our own study of the latest example showed that most holders of assisted places, while certainly from 'less well-off homes', were from homes with a substantial 'educational inheritance' (Edwards et al, 1989, Chapter 8: Whitty et al, 1989). But the schools to which they were admitted were essentially independent grammar schools of thoroughly traditional 'academic excellence'. If Ministers could have overcome their habitual suspicion of sociology, they might have found it useful in defence of CTCs to cite evidence that technical schools had been more egalitarian in access and outcomes than the grammar schools promoted at their expense (Halsey et al, 1980, p. 67; Heath & Ridge, 1983: Sanderson, 1987). The familiar sociological explanation of both findings is that the status culture embodied in grammar schools and independent schools is so distant from the assumptions, ambitions, tastes and styles of many working-class children (and their parents) as to seem 'not for the likes of us', or at least to involve considerable cultural uprooting for those selected. The CTCs, however, were presented explicitly as a break with tradition - as a 'new choice' of a new kind of school, with a distinctly 'modern' and by implication 'classless' appeal.

The especial relevance of that alternative to improving inner-city education figured prominently in Government publicity, often supported by references to the 'magnetic' effects of specialized high schools in the United States in attracting parents across boundaries of race and class. CTCs have certainly been described approvingly as 'a kind of technology magnet' (Stuart Sexton's foreword to Cooper, 1987; see also Hillgate Group, 1987, p. 39). But the comparison is inexact. Walford (1991) notes a "fundamental conflict" between the intention that CTCs should attract pupils into "a newly developed private sector" and so contribute to a "hierarchy of differentiated schools", and the American intention of attracting more white and middle-class pupils back into the public sector in the interests of social class and ethnic group integration. To that contrast in purposes has to be added the evidence that, in practice, magnets are disproportionately chosen by 'motivated and well-informed students/parents' with often serious effects on the schools around them (Rosenberg, 1989, p. 43; Blank, 1991; HMI, 1990).

Such evidence reinforces the common sociological conclusion that self selection is a powerful form of social selection. We noted earlier that CTCs are obliged to take a 'full' range of ability, and intakes 'representative' of the social class and ethnic character of their catchment areas (DES, 1986). There are formidable 'technical' problems in meeting those criteria, which a recent DES-sponsored study concluded were 'collectively unworkable' (Murphy et al, 1990, p. 11). The most obvious of these is the lack of data about ability, social class and ethnic distributions against which the intakes to particular CTCs can be assessed. What is clear is there is unlikely to be that nice balance between supply and demand which advocates of 'full' parental choice often seem to assume. As we note in the following section, CTCs were presented as offering real alternatives to inner-city parents in place of the existing choice between more or less effective versions of the same kind of school. In the classic formulation, they were to be 'different but equal', attracting those parents and pupils who positively wanted a secondary education with a distinctively science-technology bias. But as they were also promoted as offering enhanced educational and occupational opportunities, and had conspicuous relative advantages in buildings and resources, it is not surprising that demand has considerably exceeded supply. Thus opportunities have to be rationed. And whatever their commitment to being comprehensive, selection procedures which include written tests and an interview may well link the CTCs in popular consciousness with the 'quality' commonly associated with grammar schools, and produce in many of their pupils a strong sense of having been meritoriously chosen (Walford & Miller, 1991). The scrutiny of parental attitudes, and especially of a parental commitment to support seven years of full-time education, is also likely to produce a powerful social filter in urban areas with traditionally low staying-on rates at sixteen. The principal of Bradford CTC has justified a high acceptance rate for Asian applicants on the grounds that "the strong work ethic associated with such families is exactly the sort of quality which we are looking for" (Lewis, 1990). Thus, traditionally disadvantaged groups certainly cannot expect to be favoured indiscriminately, but only to the extent to which they display such desired characteristics. For all these reasons, CTCs are an obvious object for investigation in the 'political arithmetic' tradition of British sociology of education (e.g. Halsey at el, 1980).

Meanwhile, on the limited basis of their observations at Kingshurst in Solihull, the first of the CTCs to be opened, Walford & Miller (1991) have argued that CTCs will undoubtedly successfully sponsor members of the working class (or the 'deserving poor' as they once might have been called) out of their environment, but that they will have little positive impact on that environment and some negative consequences for those who remain in it. They claim that, while comprehensive schools attempted to overcome the historic links between diversity of provision and inequalities of class and gender, "City Technology Colleges have played a major part in re-legitimizing inequality of provision for different pupils" (p. 165). They also feel that, as CTCs become increasingly popular, they will wish to move up the traditional hierarchy of esteem and thus "deviate from [their original] role - as Kingshurst already appears to be doing" (p. 165).

Diversifying the System

It has been a common criticism of the 'common' secondary school that it offered nothing more imaginative, or more relevant to the needs and interests of many of its pupils, than a diluted version of the traditional academic curriculum (e.g. Young, 1990 p. 23). CTCs have therefore been presented as offering something different, not merely an improved model of the same kind. To questions about why they were necessary to promote technical education if TVEI is as successful as the Government itself claims, the answer that it was a 'logical' next step to move from a curriculum 'strand' to a pervasive curriculum orientation (Regan, 1990) is less relevant than is a more general intention to differentiate between as well as within secondary schools. Extending the 'CTC concept' to other curriculum specialisms, 'on the Magnet School model', has the dual function of increasing parental choice and increasing pressure on schools to develop distinctive forms of excellence (Hillgate Group, 1987, p. 39). CTCs are therefore presented by the Trust as the 'leading edge' of innovations in curriculum and the transforming effects of IT on teaching and learning. In the tradition of sociological studies of the boundary between permissible and impermissible curriculum innovations, it will be interesting to see how much room for manoeuvre the CTCs have within their obligation to 'keep to the substance' of the National Curriculum. Thus the curriculum plan commissioned by the DES from ORT in 1987 was seen as inappropriate by HMI, presumably because its emphasis on topic-centred 'educational events' into which a variety of disciplinary work would feed was contrary to that highly subject-centred National Curriculum which had already been decided upon. There are also problems for the neo-conservative Right, who have to balance their approval of CTCs as a 'new choice' for parents against their dislike of excessive 'relevance' and 'utility' in the curriculum, and their objections to all 'progressive' departures from 'proper' subjects authoritatively taught. Thus O'Hear, for example, warns that the products of CTCs may become the Bob Cratchits of the future, "tied to their computer screens without even the Victorian clerk's pride in his handwriting" (cited in Regan, 1990, p. 36; see also O'Hear, 1987).

Although their remit has already been extended to the performing arts, and would have acquired an ecological extension if the proposed CTC at Brighton had not foundered, the emphasis in CTCs is still on science and technology. As such, it raises fundamental questions about their future development. Where their primary purpose is seen to be the remedying of the historical neglect of technical education, then 15-20 new schools cannot do much to overcome national skills shortages unless great confidence is placed in their exemplary effects. Those for whom the strengthening of technical education is a (even the) priority are therefore likely to support the extension of CTCs into the public sector. The 'beacons of excellence' concept raises objections anyway that whatever might be 'learned' from well-funded institutions cannot be applied to the relatively impoverished comprehensive schools around them without comparable injections of resources. A funding formula which has made even twenty new 'state-independent' institutions hard to achieve is therefore being radically altered to encourage the transformation of existing voluntary-aided or maintained secondary schools into voluntary-aided CTCs. In place of the large capital costs which have so hampered the original initiative, the revised model envisages up to £1 million 'refurbishing' investment per school, shared between the LEAs, the DES and private sponsors. An expedient change in the present inhibition on changing their 'character' within five years would also allow schools to opt-out for grant-maintained CTC status. As Sir Cyril Taylor put it - "Better sixteen voluntary-aided CTCs than one orthodox college" (*The Times Educational Supplement*, 19 January 1990). But the 'orthodox' model has other attractions than the promotion of technical education. In particular, the independence from LEAs which some advocates of technical schools saw as a necessary condition for success in creating a real alternative to traditional 'academic' secondary education (Naylor, 1985; Taylor, 1986; Regan, 1990), was regarded by others as a significant contribution to restructuring the entire system.

In that context, the importance of CTCs was not as 'beacons of excellence' in (e.g.) curriculum innovation, but as prototypes for autonomous schools 'owned' by independent trusts and managed according to 'business principles' in a competitive system. They have also to be understood, therefore, as reflecting mounting political support for a revival of direct-grant schools, for special 'Crown' comprehensives to be taken out of LEA control and used as models for what could be achieved in urban areas, and for schools generally to be so funded that they would be thoroughly 'shaped, controlled and nourished' by customer demand (Hillgate Group, 1986 & 1987; No Turning Back Group, 1986: Cox, 1985; Flew, 1987; Sexton, 1987). It is in this context that Professor Brian Griffiths, a key member (and then head) of Mrs Thatcher's Policy Unit, is sometimes identified as a main progenitor of CTCs. There is no evidence in his case of any great concern for technical education. As a 'committed monetarist and privatizer', his influence on the 1987 election manifesto (especially marked on its education promises) was directed towards opening-up publicly provided services to competition and the free play of supply and demand (*Sunday Times* profile, 27 July 1987). Whatever their other disagreements, different groupings of the Right came together in their dislike of so-called monopoly provision, and that monopoly was perceived as being especially objectionable in the urban centres of what the *Sun* elegantly termed 'barmy burgherism'. Kenneth Baker's announcement of CTCs in 1986 was made during a warmly-received attack on LEAs, especially those Labour authorities which he claimed had subordinated their proper educational responsibilities to a futile pursuit of social justice or to blatant efforts at political indoctrination. "Education must be led by the users", and there was every reason to believe that a new appetite for it would be fostered by creating "new free alternatives outside the maintained system". At the following Party Conference in 1987, Thatcher's echoing of tabloid rhetoric again focused on the damage being done to children in the inner-cities who were having educational opportunity "snatched away from them by hard-left education authorities and extremist teachers", and the consequent necessity of challenging their 'monopoly'. The initial CTC prospectus expressed this premise in more delicate form, asserting that - "It is in our cities that the education system is at present under most pressure", and that parents had least choice (DES, 1986 pp. 2-3). The proposed locations of CTCs, following that diagnosis, were predominantly in areas which were either Labour-controlled or in (or near) marginal parliamentary constituencies. Like the 'right to buy' policy towards council housing, and the right of parents acting collectively to take schools out of LEA control, CTCs may be viewed as a means of giving some working-class voters in inner-city areas a direct 'stake' in Conservatism. But they also have a larger purpose, as part of an incremental strategy the ultimate (and not too distant) objective of which is an entirely 'free' market in educational provision.

That strategy requires no deft textual and sub-textual analysis. It is made explicit, notably by Sexton (1987). The objective is "a system of self-governing, self-managing budget centres obliged for survival to respond to the market" by the only true parent power "which is purchasing power". The first step towards that goal was to resurrect the direct-grant list, though by per capital funding channelled through parents rather than by payments directly to schools. The CTCs embody this tactic, their free places being a form of 'earmarked purchasing power' for the parents of those selected which can be regarded as a move either towards a voucher system, or (as Sexton does) towards a less controversial and unsettling way of achieving the same effects. Assisted places can also be seen in this way, and we may well have underestimated Sexton's own market-oriented reasons for promoting them so actively when we commented that their roots lay almost entirely in 'Old Tory' support for equality of opportunity for able children (Edwards et al, 1989, pp. 62-65). The second step in Sexton's strategy was to extend CTCs to 'all areas and types of school'. As we noted earlier, their attractions as a model extended far beyond curriculum specialization, and they foreshadow ways in which all schools are expected to operate in a competitive system founded on parental choice. Although they charge no fees, they are organisationally much closer to private than to maintained schools, including in the more limited representation given to parents and the non-participation of teachers on their governing bodies. Individual CTCs have already provided examples of 'plant bargaining' over pay and conditions, no-strike agreements, renewable performance-related contracts, performance related pay, salaries negotiated individually in relation to market demand, a prominent place for project directors and financial advisers drawn from business, and posts of responsibility labelled - like Kinghurst's curriculum 'area managers' - to further blur the boundaries between school and the 'world of work'.

Despite these marks of 'progress', CTCs are nevertheless only an interim measure - a 'staging post' along the way to a free market in which suppliers seek out what the consumers want, consumers seek out what they consider to be "best and appropriate for their purpose", and the 'national' curriculum is whatever "the market of parents, employers and society generally demands" (Sexton, 1990). That the free play of supply and demand may not produce that technologically-oriented secondary education which an advanced industrial society is seen to demand is the dilemma which we identified earlier, and which we now explore.

The Market, State Intervention, and Equity

In a book which can reasonably be regarded as a founding document of Thatcherism, Keith Joseph asserted his belief in the "overwhelming superiority" of the "blind, unplanned, uncoordinated wisdom of the market" to the planned, "rational" action of government (Joseph, 1976, p. 57). Leaving things to market forces would always be more effective than state intervention - provided of course that the free interplay of supply and demand was not impeded by the restrictive practices of bureaucratic or other interest groups. That declaration of faith accounts for the ideological disappointment on the neo-liberal Right that Joseph was not a more radical

Secretary of State for Education, and especially that he allowed himself to be persuaded by DES officials that education vouchers, however "intellectually attractive", were not practical (Seldon, 1986; Cox & Marks, 1988). 'Bureaucratic interest groups' were apparently still entrenched at the centre of policy-making.

The announcement of CTCs in 1986 came during the inauguration of a new radical phase in the Thatcherite Project, or what Leys (1989) calls its 'second stage'. At its heart was the 'revolution in consciousness' which Thatcher made explicit at a meeting with Parliamentary lobby correspondents shortly after the 1983 election; she wished her Administration to be remembered as the one which "broke decisively with the debilitating consensus of a paternalistic Government and a dependent people, which rejected the notion that the State is all-powerful and the citizens merely beneficiaries, which shattered the illusion that the Government could somehow substitute for individual performance" (cited in Kavanagh, 1987, pp. 251-252). The essential substitution was to be the replacement of producer interests by consumer interests. As a recent pamphlet published by the Institute of Economic Affairs explains, the general principle of consumer sovereignty:

> holds that each individual is the best judge of his or her needs and wants and of what is in their best interests. If there is some mechanism through which consumers can accurately express their preferences, and if there is a system of incentives for producers to respond to them, then resources will be directed away from activities which do not satisfy consumers to those which do. (Ashworth et al, 1988, p. 11)

Into this ideological context, CTCs fit untidily. They represent both an opening in the market to a 'new choice of school' and a shaping of that market by allocating enhanced choice to particular consumers for particular ends. By enhancing parental choice, they enhance competition, creating alternatives to urban comprehensives which are intended to raise standards around them both by example and by posing the threat of losing pupils unless standards improve. Being mostly situated in areas where secondary rolls are falling rapidly, CTCs can be seen as reinforcing that reliance on parental choice as a mechanism for closing 'ineffective' schools which is common on the Right. By placing such overt emphasis on family attitudes and aspirations in the selection of suitable pupils, they seem to reflect a neo-conservative approach to the distribution of welfare goods and services; "a CTC place for their child is a reward for parental commitment to family self-improvement, initiative and deservingness" (Dale, 1989b, p. 14). At the same time, however, CTCs also represent a state intervention in educational provision - a vigorous promotion of a new educational product at resource levels which have brought persistent complaints of unfair competition with neighbouring schools. An obvious counter-argument, that new products need special backing if they are to break into an established market, is reinforced by the kind of socio-historical analysis outlined earlier. The main conclusion of that analysis is that technical-secondary education has lacked competitive weight in this country, and so needs the high publicity and resourcing which CTCs have received. In other words, the market has been distorted by cultural values which will have to be challenged before it can be 'trusted' to deliver what is has signally failed to support before.

We have put this dilemma explicitly to some of those involved in the CTC initiative or its possible precursors, including open interventionists like Sir Cyril Taylor and Lord Young who had no doubt that bold government initiatives to promote technical education are essential. The dilemma can be illustrated most neatly from our interviews with Stuart Sexton and Bob Dunn, because they collaborated in a plan for direct-grant technical schools which was put to Joseph early in 1986 and then sent forward to his successor and because both identify themselves as being among the radicals of their Party. Given his frame of reference, Sexton's logic is entirely consistent (interviewed 3rd May 1990). Those who believe in the market have to rely on its judgments, and popularity with consumers is the test of what is needed as it is of the relative quality of competing suppliers. CTCs, like any other form of directly-funded school, are an interim measure only - a step towards that 'eventual free market' in which all schools prosper or fail according to their capacity to respond to demand, and market forces would define any 'gaps' in provision. Bob Dunn "shares Stuart's concern about the market", but was also - "more impatient...I want things to happen now" (interviewed 16 October 1990). His reading of English educational history had convinced him that persistent failures to establish secondary-technical education with the necessary scope and status had left a 'gap in provision' which needed very positive government encouragement (including financial inducements to LEAs) to overcome. His approach resembles Baker's insistence, when appealing to the CBI for sponsorship, that CTCs would create "a new appetite for full-time education and training" of an appropriately modern, technologically-oriented kind (cited *New Scientist*, 16 October 1986).

As we have already seen, it is often argued that the traditional academic bias of the 'education establishment' carries most of the blame for the disparaging of 'practical' alternatives. This is the view held strongly by Lord Young, hence his "dawn raid on education" in 1982 when TVEI was announced (Young, 1990, pp. 89-97). But as we noted earlier, there is substantial evidence that consumer choice has operated powerfully in favour of the traditional secondary curriculum. CTCs therefore have to create rather than respond to a specialized demand, hence the apparent tensions between opening up the system to more competition, offering a new choice to 'deserving' pupils and parents, and shaping that choice in the interests of the state and capital.

These tensions are, to some extent, resolved by Dale (1989b) in his analysis of CTCs as "the most representative emblem" of a broad strategy of "conservative modernisation". Briefly, it is a policy of simultaneously 'freeing' individuals for economic purposes while controlling them for social purposes; indeed, in so far as economic 'freedom' increases inequalities, it is likely to increase the need for social control. A 'small, strong state' limits the range of its activities by transferring to the market, which it defends and legitimises, as much welfare provision as possible. In education, the new reliance on competition and choice is not all-pervasive; instead, "what is intended is a dual system, polarised between what I will call market schools and minimum schools" (ibid, p. 8). As part of the market system, CTCs contribute to capital accumulation by promoting knowledge and skills directly relevant to an advanced industrial economy, by emphasizing the benefits to pupils willing to invest in themselves by acquiring such cultural capital, and by their demonstration of how autonomous, competing schools should operate.

Dale's analysis of how a 'new' form of schooling corresponds to larger processes of economic and social reproduction prompts further questions about the 'minimum' schools drawn from traditional sociological investigation of educational equality. For example, CTCs are part of a retreat from public provision of 'common' secondary schooling to parental choice between varieties of uncommon schooling. What kinds of parents will make that choice, with what advantages for their children and at whose expense? Can alternative forms of secondary education be 'equal but different', when so much past evidence is against it? Preoccupation with escape routes for deserving individuals precludes much consideration of their effects on those left behind, and CTCs represent a new 'ladder of opportunity', admittedly of self-consciously 'modern' construction and with a much broader definition of those who 'deserve' the chance to climb it. From that traditional perspective, any resulting inequalities are made acceptable by the 'merit' of those justly helped to 'succeed'. But they are also part of an incremental strategy intended to produce the 'true democracy' of the market, in which real alternatives exist and all parents have the power as well as the formal right to choose between them, The claim that individual consumer choice is 'fairer' as well as more efficient than collective provision is often supported by an argument with particular resonance for sociologists - namely, that it replaces "incorrigible differences in cultural power" by "corrigible differences in purchasing power" (Seldon, 1981, p. xxi). In this context, 'purchasing power' clearly includes that earmarked purchasing power now represented by an assisted place, a free place at a CTC or grant-maintained school, or a per capita funded free place at whichever school a child has been openly enrolled. But wherever demand exceeds supply, cultural power comes back into play. We noted earlier that selection for over chosen CTCs is determined by unusually wide-ranging definitions of 'merit', the likely outcome being intakes which are not culturally 'representative' of the catchment areas. And while an 'individualist' perspective may direct attention to the consequences for those chosen, any 'collectivist' analysis has to extend beyond the immediate impact on the size and quality of intakes to schools within the catchment area. It has to include the wider prospect of 'open' competition between schools very differently equipped to compete, of parental choice 'shaped in the social and spatial mould' of older inequalities (Echols et al, 1990; Adler et al, 1989).

Conclusion: CTCs and the sociology of education

Throughout this chapter, we have tried to make sense of CTCs in relation to major themes in current education policy and major concerns in the sociology of education. At the level of policy formation and implementation, we have identified individuals and interest groups whose choice they were, and the main purposes for which they were intended. We have tried to avoid imposing an unreal tidiness on an initiative with quite varied origins and objectives, while recognising that serious miscalculations in planning it might well have led to the abandonment of a policy with weaker motivations and ideological attractions. It is clear that the complexities of an initiative of this sort are often difficult to reduce in any straightforward way to contradictions between the functions of the capitalist state, as Dale (1989a) recognises. While an analysis in those terms can help to illuminate some of the underlying influences on current education policy, some of the particular tensions associated with the CTC initiative can as helpfully be explored through traditional sociological approaches to the study of educational opportunity and the so-called 'new' sociology of education's concern with the differential status of various forms of school knowledge.

Our own analysis reflects a strong sociological scepticism about the power of specific educational initiatives to challenge deep-rooted practices and priorities, and about the relevance to one educational system of the 'lessons' drawn from the very different conditions of another. As we argue, the failure to establish anything resembling the Realschule in status and resources cannot be attributed simply to the protective inertia of the 'educational establishment' because it also reflects a preference for traditional academic education among the very interests which more 'modern' alternatives might seem obviously to serve. In that context, Dale's (1989b) analysis of CTCs perhaps understates the tension between modernisers arguing for 'relevance' and 'practicality', and neo-conservative defence of education 'for its own sake'. It also carries the risk of imposing a coherence derived from giving primacy to the requirements of production on an initiative which is both diverse and contested. Like Stephen Ball, we accept the 'messiness' which comes from the 'infusing' of education policy with 'economic, political and ideological contradictions'. A large part of the messiness of the CTC initiative comes from persistent tensions between 'old humanists', 'industrial trainers' and 'public educators' (Williams, 1965), and some more recent tensions within these groupings identified by Ball himself (1990, p. 5ff). Mapped on to these tensions is the one we have explored in the latter part of this paper between 'planned' and 'market' remedies for the particular educational deficiency to which CTCs claim to be addressed.

Sociological investigation of class-biased forms of curriculum and pedagogy, and of arguments over the curriculum as arguments over the whole basis of social order, are therefore highly relevant to understanding the origins and prospects of CTCs. For Ball, CTCs are themselves a terrain of struggle between the "discourse of vocational progressivism" and "the elitist conceptions of knowledge prosletysed by the old humanists" (Ball, 1990, p. 118). He argues that "to some extent" the notion of CTCs resolves, at the discursive level, the tension between the industrial trainers and the cultural restorationist wing of the old humanists by embodying "high-tech, high standards and efficiency" and (in theory) private funding (p. 129). But, given the tensions between social and cultural reproduction that have been a major theme in English educational history, as well as recent sociology of education, it seems unlikely that any such resolution will be other than short lived.

In this connection, we have highlighted the particular tension, recently explored by Bernstein (1990), between the useful, 'modern' knowledge supposedly embodied in CTCs and the traditional regard for the autonomy of school and its proper hierarchy of subjects which is evident in the thinking of many on the Right. We also noted the dilemma, not always recognised by their supporters, that CTCs also embody commitments to (for example) curriculum integration and to active, collaborative learning which are often identified as characteristic of 'progressivism'. In so far as these come to represent an 'invisible pedagogy' marked by weak classification and framing, they will add an intriguing dimension to a traditional sociological interest in the social and cultural backgrounds of pupils attracted to (and successful in) this 'new choice of school'.

Finally, it is quite clear that the contradictions and tensions identified here will remain a significant theme of our current research project on CTCs, as we trace through the implementation of the policy at school level. Furthermore, they are likely to remain at the centre of the wider research agenda for the sociology of education for the foreseeable future.

REFERENCES

Adler, M., Petch, A & Tweedie, J. (1989) *Parental Choice and Educational Policy*. Edinburgh: Edinburgh University Press.

Anyon, J. (1980) Social class and the hidden curriculum of work, *Journal of Education*, 162, pp. 67-92.

Ashworth, J., Papps, I & Thomas, B. (1988) *Increased Parental Choice*. Warlingham: Institute of Economic Affairs Education Unit.

Ball, S. (1990) *Policy and Policy Making: Explorations in Policy Sociology*. London: Routledge.

Banks, O. (1955) *Parity and Prestige in English Secondary Education*. London: Routledge & Kegan Paul.

Barnett, C. (1986) *The Audit of War*. London: Macmillan.

Bernstein, B. (1977) *Class, Codes and Control:* Volume 3 (2nd revised Edn). London: Routledge.

Bernstein, B. (1990) *The Structuring of Pedagogic Discourse: Class, Codes and Control,* Volume 4. London: Routledge.

Blank, R. (1991) Educational effects of magnet schools, in W. Clune & J. Witte (Eds) *Choice and Control in American Education,* Volume 2. Lewes: Falmer Press.

Bourdieu, P. (1986) The Forms of Capital, in J. Richardson (Ed) *Handbook of Theory and Research for the Sociology of Education.* New York: Greenwood.

Chitty, C. (1987) The commodification of education, *Forum,* 29(3), pp. 66-69.

Chitty, C. (1989) CTCs: a strategy for elitism, *Forum,* 31(2), pp. 37-40.

Cooper, B. (1987) *Magnet Schools.* Warlingham: Institute of Economic Affairs Education Unit.

Cox, C. (1985) Many attractions of the magnet, *The Times Educational Supplement,* 15th March.

Cox, C. & Marks, J. (1988) *The Insolence of Office.* London: Claridge Press.

Dale, R. (1989a) *The State and Education Policy.* Milton Keynes: Open University Press.

Dale, R. (1989b) The Thatcherite Project in Education: the case of the City Technology Colleges, *Critical Social Policy,* 9 (3), pp. 4-19.

Denholm, L. (1988) A powerful reproach to the system, *The Times Educational Supplement,* 28 October.

Department of Education and Science (1986) *City Technology Colleges: A New Choice of School.* London: DES.

DiMaggio, P. (1982) Cultural capital and school success, *American Sociological Review,* 47, pp. 189-201.

Echols, F., McPherson, A. & Willms, D. (1990) Parental choice in Scotland, *Journal of Education Policy,* 5, pp. 207-222.

Edwards, T. (1986) Education and training 16-19: rhetoric, policy and practice, in A. Hartnett & M. Naish (Eds) *Education and Society Today.* Lewes: Falmer Press.

Edwards, T. (1987) Language codes and classroom practice, *Oxford Review of Education,* 13, pp. 237-247.

Edwards, T., Fitz, J. & Whitty, G. (1989) *The State and Private Education: an Evaluation of the Assisted Places Scheme.* Lewes: Falmer Press.

Edwards, T., Gewirtz, S. & Whitty, G. (1991) From Assisted Places to City Technology Colleges, in G. Walford (Ed) *Private Schooling: Tradition, Change and Diversity.* London: Paul Chapman.

Evans, J. & Davies, B. (1988) The Social Context of Educational Opportunities in New Vocational Education Initiatives, in D. Gleeson (Ed) *TVEI and Secondary Education: a Critical Appraisal.* Milton Keynes: Open University Press.

Flew, A. (1987) *Power to the Parents.* London: Sherwood Press.

Flude, M. & Hammer, M. (1990) Opting for an Uncertain Future: grant-maintained schools, in M. Flude & M. Hammer (Eds) *The Education Reform Act: Its Origins and Implications.* Lewes: Falmer Press.

Glazier, J. (1986) CTCs - so what's new?, *Education*, 5 December, p. 488.

Hall, S. & Jacques, M. (1989) *New Times: the Changing Face of Politics in the 1990s.* London: Lawrence & Wishart.

Halsey, A., Heath, A. & Ridge, J. (1980) *Origins and Destinations: Family, Class and Education in Modern Britain.* Oxford: Clarendon Press.

Heath, A. & Ridge, J. (1983) Schools, Examinations and Occupational Attainment, in J. Purvis & M. Hales (Eds) *Achievement and Inequality in Education.* London: Routledge.

Her Majesty's Inspectorate (1990) *Teaching and Learning in New York City Schools.* London: HMSO.

Hillgate Group (1986) *Whose Schools? A Radical Manifesto.* London: Claridge Press.

Hillgate Group (1987) *The Reform of British Education.* London: Claridge Press.

Joseph, K. (1976) *Stranded on the Middle Ground.* London: Centre for Policy Studies.

Kavanagh, D. (1987) *Thatcherism and British Politics.* London: Oxford University Press.

Lewis, J. (1990) Bradford CTC responds, letter in *Education*, 1 June.

Leys, C. (1989) *Politics in Britain: from Labourism to Thatcherism.* London: Verso.

McCulloch, G. (1989a) *The Secondary Technical School: A Usable Past?* Lewes: Falmer Press.

McCulloch, G. (1989b) CTCs: a new choice of school?, *British Journal of Educational Studies*, 37, pp. 30-43.

McLeod, J. (1988) CTCs: a study of the character and progress of an educational reform, *Local Government Studies*, January/February, pp. 75-82.

Mathieson, M. & Bernbaum, G. (1988) The British disease: a British tradition?, *British Journal of Educational Studies*, 36, pp. 126-174.

Morrell, F. (1989) *Children of the Future.* London: Hogarth Press.

Murphy, R., Brown, P. & Partington, J. (1990) *An Evaluation of the Effectiveness of CTCs' Selection Processes.* Report to the Department of Education and Science.

Nash, I. (1988) CTCs forced to change tack, *The Times Educational Supplement*, 17 June.

Naylor, F. (1985) *Technical Schools: a Tale of Four Countries.* London: Centre for Policy Studies.

No Turning Back Group (1986) *Save Our Schools.* London: Conservative Political Centre.

O'Hear, A. (1987) The importance of traditional learning, *British Journal of Educational Studies*, 35, pp. 102-114.

Pring, R. (1989) Fifty years on, *British Journal of Educational Studies*, 37, pp. 17-29.

Rae, J. (1989) *Too Little Too Late?* London: Collins.

Regan, D. (1990) *City Technology Colleges: Potentialities and Perils.* London: Centre for Policy Studies.

Rosenberg, B. (1989) Public school choice: can we find the right balance?, *American Educator*, pp. 1-14 & 40-45.

Sanderson, M. (1987) *Educational Opportunities and Social Change in England* London: Faber & Faber.

Seldon, A. (1981) *Wither the Welfare State.* London: Institute of Economic Affairs.

Seldon, A. (1986) *The Riddle of the Voucher.* London: Institute of Economic Affairs Education Unit.

Sexton, S. (1987) *Our Schools: a Radical Policy.* Warlingham: Institute of Economic Affairs Education Unit.

Sexton, S. (1990) Free market's better values, *Guardian,* 14 August.

Taylor, C. (1986) *Employment Examined: the Right Approach to More Jobs.* London: Centre for Policy Studies.

Taylor, C. (1987) Qualifying pupils for the Year 2000, *Daily Telegraph,* 17 August.

Taylor, C. (1988) Climbing towards a skilful revolution, *The Times Educational Supplement,* 21 January.

Walford, G. (1991), City Technology Colleges: a private magnetism?, in G. Walford (Ed) *Private Schooling: Tradition, Change and Diversity.* London: Paul Chapman.

Walford, G. & Miller, H. (1991) *City Technology Colleges.* Milton Keynes: Open University Press.

Whitty, G. (1989) The New Right and the national curriculum: state control or market forces?, *Journal of Education Policy,* 4, pp. 329-341.

Whitty, G., Fitz, J. & Edwards, T. (1989) Assisting Whom? Benefits and Costs of the Assisted Places Scheme, in A. Hargreaves & D. Reynolds (Eds) *Education Policies: Controversies and Critiques.* Lewes: Falmer Press

Williams, R. (1965) *The Long Revolution.* Harmondsworth: Penquin.

Young, Lord (1990) *The Enterprise Years: A Businessman in the Cabinet.* London: Headline.

Chapter Nine

Reconstructing Professionalism: ideological struggle in initial teacher education

JOHN FURLONG

The 1980s was period of quite dramatic change for initial teacher education. At the beginning of the decade initial teacher education was a relatively quiet backwater of the education service, controlled and organised autonomously by higher education. By the end of the decade government control had increased considerably, those responsible for initial teacher education losing a substantial proportion of their professional autonomy. However, as I will attempt to demonstrate in this chapter, the government was not merely interested in increasing control; it also attempted to use that control to reconstruct fundamentally the character of initial education and thereby the nature of teacher professionalism. As a consequence, during the 1980s, initial teacher education was transformed from that quiet backwater into a major site for ideological struggle between the government and other groups with an interest in education.

The aim of this chapter is to utilize a sociological framework to begin to explore the nature of the changes that have taken place; it will focus on the ideological 'struggle for meaning' in this one area of educational policy. In the last few years, many sociologists have utilised a concept of ideology to reveal the coherence as well as the contradictions in contemporary educational policy. Writers such as Demaine (1988), Whitty (1989), and Ransom (1990) have, for example, analysed the ideological thrust behind the 1988 Educational Reform Act; others have examined teacher education (Whitty et al, 1987; Crozier et al, 1990). However, while it is important to analyse the ideology behind government initiatives, this is really only part of the story if we want to understand policy change. A fuller sociological account demands that we also analyse how particular initiatives - or 'texts'

- engage with a particular area of practice. How they are responded to - accepted, challenged, by-passed and in some cases transformed by those outside government. In the words of Fiske (1987):

The text can no longer be seen as a self sufficient entity that bears its own meanings and exerts a similar influence on all its readers. Rather it is seen as a potential of meanings that can be achieved in a number of ways. Of course this potential is proscribed and not infinite; the text does not determine its meanings so much as delimit the arena of struggle for that meaning by marking out the terrain within which its variety of readings can be negotiated. (p. 269)

In analyzing the character of ideological struggle surrounding recent government initiatives, I will focus on two key documents or 'texts' that have been the main vehicles for increasing government control. During the last ten years, a considerable number of government, Department of Education and Science (DES) and Her Majesty's Inspectorate (HMI) reports, advice and consultative documents have been issued on teacher education (DES, 1983, 1988, 1989a; HMI, 1983, 1987, 1988a, 1988b). However, two stand out as having particular significance. They are Circular 3/84 (DES, 1984) issued by the DES in 1984 and Circular 24/89 (DES, 1989b) issued in 1989. What is significant about these two texts is their constitutional status. Through them, for the first time, the government attempted to define the content and structure of initial teacher education in this country: they had statutory authority. The DES had always had formal responsibility for granting new teachers Qualified Teacher Status (QTS) but until 1984 they were happy to do so simply on the recommendation of initial training institutions. All students who had satisfactorily completed a course of training were automatically granted QTS by the DES. Circular 3/84 changed that practice fundamentally. From that date on, QTS was only to be awarded to graduates of courses that conformed to the criteria laid down in the Circular. If training institutions did not conform to the new criteria, they could in effect, no longer train qualified teachers. In order to make sure that training institutions did indeed conform to the criteria, a new government appointed body - the Council for the Accreditation of Teacher Education (CATE) - was established. In the years immediately following the issuing of the first Circular, CATE formally inspected every initial teacher training establishment in England and Wales. In 1989 a second circular, Circular 24/89, was issued, revising and extending government control through new criteria. A recent government announcement suggests that a further circular is to be issued in early 1992 (Clarke, 1992).

Describing the means of increased government control is therefore easy enough; it has been achieved through these two circulars and CATE. Examining the way these procedures have been used to reconstruct initial teacher education is a more complex matter and demands an analysis of the ideological struggle that has surrounded the two circulars. In understanding that struggle it is necessary to recognise that policy on teacher education, as in any area of social policy, is highly complex. It is made up of a number of distinct strands or issues that have been the focus of controversy and debate for many years. Together they make up a complex 'discourse' of teacher education. In this chapter I intend to focus on four such dimensions in the policy discourse. They concern the role, character and significance accorded to

'Main subject' study

The 'educational disciplines' (psychology, sociology, philosophy and history)

Practice

Pedagogy

This recognition that a policy area such as teacher education is multi-dimensional has two implications for understanding the struggle surrounding particular policy texts. The first is that texts seldom engage with every dimension of a policy area at the same time. Usually they are selective, focusing on one or two dimensions, leaving other areas untouched. However, if radical transformation is to be achieved, eventually every dimension must be confronted. As I will demonstrate, government interventions have progressively been felt in each of these different dimensions of training.

The second implication is that each dimension of a policy area, each "sphere of social practice has its own structures, dynamics and history" (White 1987, p. 140). As will become apparent below, each aspect of teacher education policy has itself been subject to longstanding ideological debate. New policy texts do not therefore enter into a vacuum and if we are to understand how they have been responded to, it is necessary to consider the recent history of each of these dimensions of policy.

Educational Ideologies in Initial Teacher Education

Before examining recent policy changes in detail it is necessary to consider the character of ideologies themselves. What exactly are ideologies and how do they relate to educational thought and policy making? The concept of ideology is itself deeply contested and may have one of a number of different meanings. In this chapter I intend to take a broad definition of the concept seeing ideologies as historical and intellectual movements or traditions. As such they involve sets of beliefs, values and practical experiences as well as research findings about the character of human nature and society and the role that education should play in relation to these.

Ideologies are therefore complex intellectual traditions that are integral to the way that each of us understands and interprets the world. And, as White says, "the point of ideological criticism is not to find unadulterated truth or unbridled manipulation 'beneath' or 'behind' a given text or system of representation, but to understand how a particular system of representation offers *us* a way of knowing or experiencing the world (White, 1987, p. 141).

Because ideologies are broad intellectual traditions they may have implications for the education of pupils and for the professional formation of teachers. Many different ideologies have been influential in education but it is possible to identify five that have been particularly important in debates about initial teacher education; these are:

Educational Conservatism

In this tradition the central aim of education is seen as the preservation of a refined cultural heritage. The curriculum is considered a "repository of worthwhile activities and values into which learners need to be initiated in an orderly systematic way" (Conner & Lofthouse, 1990, p. 77) In the words of the Hillgate Group (1989) education "depends on....the preservation of knowledge, skills culture and moral values and their transmission to the young".[1] The task for initial teacher education is to develop professionals who are themselves experts in their own subject area. Such professionals also need to have the practical didactic skills necessary to induct the next generation into established bodies of knowledge. Educational conservatism found its most vocal expression in the Black Papers issued from 1969 onwards as well as more recent pamphlets issued by the New Right (Hillgate Group, 1986, 1987); one can also see the influence of this line of thinking in the establishment of the National Curriculum. However, as a tradition of thought it is much older stretching back to Plato and including writers such as Mathew Arnold, T.S. Elliott, F.R. Leavis and G.H. Bantock.

Liberal Education

The aims of liberal education are fundamentally different. Where as educational conservatism is concerned with the preservation of a particular cultural heritage, liberal education acknowledges the significance of initiation into traditions of belief, practice and value but sees the purpose of this as the development of the learner as a rationally autonomous individual. This concern with rational autonomy influences both the selection of what is to be taught as well as the strategies for teaching. Bailey (1984), for example, argues that education should be centrally concerned with learning which is both fundamental and general for only in this way can autonomy be promoted and the child freed from the constraints of the present and particular. Given its aims, liberal education also stands in marked contrast to more utilitarian approaches. Education, if it is worth its name, must not be determined solely by the 'needs' of society, but by what is required in order to bring about the development of the autonomous person. As far as teacher education is concerned, liberal educationalists have argued that student teachers must themselves have a full and rounded liberal education. Professional teachers must themselves be rationally autonomous adults if they are to develop this characteristic in their pupils.

Teacher education must also address the pedagogic and curriculum planning skills necessary to foster rational autonomy in pupils. An unanalysed notion of 'teaching skills' is insufficient.

Progressive Education

Progressive education, which has been influential in many aspects of schooling, has much in common with the liberal tradition; it too focuses on the development of the individual. There are however important differences of emphasis. The founding fathers of progressivism (Rousseau, Pestalozzi and Froebel) all believed that education must begin with the child; all children, they asserted, are unique and moreover, their nature is essentially different from that of adults. If it is to be effective, education must be adapted to the unfolding nature of children's interests and developmental needs. This emphasis on developmentalism has influenced a great deal of British educational thought, particularly in the primary sector (Alexander, 1984). Its influence is also readily apparent in many examples of curriculum development in the secondary sphere too. The progressivists' view of the professional teacher is someone who has a deep understanding of the ways in which children develop. Initial teacher education must therefore develop such an understanding. It must also focus on forms of pedagogy and curriculum planning that will allow students to adapt their teaching methods to children's interests and developmental needs.

Social Reconstructionism

What is distinctive about social reconstructionist thought is that its starting point is political. It is committed to achieving equality and justice in society at large and teachers are seen as key change agents in that process. This concern with equality has been expressed both in terms of support for particular educational policies (e.g. special needs, equal opportunities policies, mixed ability grouping) and for particular curricular initiatives (e.g. anti-sexist and multi-cultural teaching). In pursuing these policies teachers must come to see themselves as 'transformative intellectuals', transforming the consciousness of children and enabling them to develop critical thinking (Hill, 1989). In the words of Giroux & McLaren (1986), they must "treat students as critical agents, question how knowledge is produced and distributed, utilise dialogue, and make knowledge meaningful, critical and ultimately emancipatory". The task for initial teacher education, is to develop students as 'transformative intellectuals' by giving them 'critical' education and helping them develop the pedagogic skills necessary for promoting critical thinking amongst their pupils.

Liberal education, progressivism and social reconstructionism are therefore broad intellectual traditions that have, in the post war period, been influential in many aspects of British educational policy, including initial teacher education. The influence of educational conservatism on teacher education policy is more recent. However, despite the importance of the ideas advanced within each of these ideologies, I will suggest that Circulars 3/84 and 24/89 are influenced by a further ideology - that of technical rationality.

Technical Rationality

In the last 30 years, many of those in the Frankfurt School (Marcuse, 1964; Habermas, 1972) have concerned themselves with exposing the growing domination of industrialised societies by technical rationalist belief systems and forms of knowledge. According to Carr & Kemmis (1986), the technical interest "is the interest of human beings in acquiring knowledge that will facilitate their technical control over natural objects. The knowledge resulting from this interest is typically instrumental knowledge taking the form of scientific explanations" (p. 135). Technical rationality can therefore be seen as combining an emphasis on utilitarianism with an interest in applying rationalist 'scientific' principles to human affairs such as education. Under the influence of utilitarianism, technical rationalists define the aims of education in terms of what is useful. Children's education should aim to prepare them for the world of work and their other future roles in society. In similar vein, it has been argued that initial teacher education should be narrowly functional, emphasising only what will be professionally useful for teachers. This utilitarianism has gone hand in hand with the application of rationalist and even scientific principles to teaching and learning. As a consequence, the problem for education is seen as how to develop the most effective means to achieve given ends. Very often, in teacher education and else where, this has meant an emphases on task analysis, skill training and 'scientifically' based testing.

The view of the professional implicit in technical rationality is of someone who is both efficient and 'neutral'. For technical rationality, more than any other ideology, creates the impression of disinterestedness and objectivity in education. It implies that there is a common framework for people with fixed goals. In the words of Popkewitz (1987) it "flattens reality and obscures the struggles which fashion and shape our world" (p. 12). Yet underneath, such approaches often remain deeply ideological. The 'neutral professional' is in reality asked to deliver an education that is increasingly defined by a political process over which the individual teacher has little control. As Marcuse says "Technology is always a historical-social project: in it is projected what a society and its ruling interests intend to do with men and things" (Marcuse, quoted in Roderick, 1986).

It is these five ideologies that have informed post war policy in initial teacher education; they represent the ways in which, through initial teacher education, the professionalism of successive generations of teachers has been constructed. In the remainder of this chapter I will argue that the government, through Circulars 3/84 and 24/89, have attempted substantially to re-construct initial teacher education, and hence the professionalism of the next generation of teachers, in accordance with technical rationalist principles. However, I will also argue that if we are to understand how practice in initial teacher education has in reality been changed by these circulars we must recognise the continued significance of other ideological positions, especially the ways in which they inform the context of teacher education and the way in which those with an interest in teacher education have responded.

'Main Subject' Study

The first dimension of teacher education policy to be considered concerns 'main subject' study. Whether it takes place within a BEd degree or another first degree, nowadays virtually all commentators agree that 'main subject' study forms the essential first basis of professional preparation. However Circulars 3/84 and 24/89 have attempted to impose a technical rationalist ideology on main subject work; re-defining its aims more precisely in relation to the school curriculum and setting minimum as well as maximum limits on course time to be devoted to it. What is interesting about this aspect of policy is that as far as the teacher education profession is concerned these initiatives have so far proved relatively uncontroversial.

The rise in importance of main subject study in initial teacher education came with the Robbins Report in 1963. That report recommended that teacher education should be expanded massively and relocated within the higher education system. The ideological arguments deployed were primarily political but there were also educational justifications too. Students who were training to be teachers had a right to a liberal education like any other student. But a full liberal education was also seen as an essential prerequisite for being an effective 'progressive' teacher. Students who were not themselves fully personally developed through their education would not be able to respond effectively to the developmental needs of the children that they taught. The aim of main subject teaching in the newly launched BEd degree was therefore to educate students in their chosen subject "to as high a pitch as can be attained throughout the whole duration of the course" (Eason, 1971).

In understanding current struggles it is important to recognise that the liberal educational ideals of this earlier period are still supported by many in the teacher education profession today. The strength of the liberal education arguments is perhaps best demonstrated by the fact that until the intervention of the two recent circulars, main subjects did not necessarily have to relate to the school curriculum. Art history could, for example, be justified as a main subject because of its contribution to a student's liberal education. In the same way, those accepting students onto secondary PGCE courses took a very relaxed attitude to the content of students' first degrees. For many PGCE tutors, the quality of a student's first degree was just as important as its content.

At one level government support of this liberal educational ideology was short lived. Just 9 years after the Robbins Report, the James Report (1972) adopted a fundamentally different ideological stance, recommending that teacher education should be unashamedly specialised and functional. However the James Report merely made recommendations; it had no statutory authority and it was not until the intervention of Circulars 3/84 and 24/89 that a different approach to main subject study became mandatory. For example, Circular 3/84 defined, for the first time, the proportion of undergraduate courses to be devoted to 'subject studies'; all B.Ed students should have at least 2 years of their course devoted to subject studies "at a level appropriate to higher education". However, in sharp contrast to the liberal educational aims of the Robbins Report, the justification for this requirement, set out in the White Paper 'Teaching Quality' (DES, 1983) was entirely instrumental.

This requirement would recognise teachers' need for subject expertise if they are to have the confidence and ability to enthuse pupils and respond to their curiosity in their chosen subject field. (para 64.1)

More recent policy statements have further consolidated this technical rationalist thrust. For example Circular 24/89 insists that in the B.Ed degree one quarter of the two years devoted to main subject study should be concerned with 'application' to school teaching. Although such courses must still be at a level 'appropriate for higher education', the declared aim is merely one of providing "a breadth and depth of subject knowledge exceeding beyond the demands of programmes of study or examination syllabuses in schools" (Annex A, para 4.5). On PGCE courses, students must now have a degree "appropriate to the primary or secondary school curriculum and to the subject or subjects and age range for which they will be trained" (Annex A, para 7.5).

The most vociferous response to government policy on this issue has not in fact come from the teacher education profession; rather it has come from various New Right commentators. They too have been centrally concerned with the role of main subject knowledge in the professional formation of teachers but their stance has been more critical stemming as it does from a conservative ideology. First they have challenged what they see as the drift in official policy away from an emphasis on solid subject preparation. For them, sound academic knowledge is the basis of good teaching. If our cultural heritage is to be passed on to our children then teachers must themselves be thoroughly educated in the disciplines they teach. In the words of Lawlor (1990) "Although the good teacher is unique, he shares one characteristic with every teacher: a deep knowledge and mystery of his subject" (p. 7). This is a view echoed by O'Hear (1988); for him the main qualities of a good teacher "are knowledge and love of the subject being taught" (1988). For both of these commentators, the key to more effective training is a return to an emphasis on academic learning. Indeed for Lawlor the central deficiency with current programmes is that too much attention is devoted to the issue of how to teach; such an emphasis, she suggests, actually undermines the importance of the subject itself.

In contrast to these views, the response of the teacher education profession has so far been relatively muted. Why is this the case? The answer would seem to be that the two circulars have not in themselves centrally challenged the role and character of main subject study. The circulars have certainly employed a utilitarian rhetoric but they remain silent on the content of such course. Some changes at the margins have of course been necessary - the few B.Ed main subjects that were not related to the National Curriculum have been dropped; graduates without an appropriate degree can no longer apply for the PGCE. But despite this, main subject lecturers on B.Ed degrees have so far retained substantial scope for the pursuit of liberal educational ideals. Moreover, in so doing, such lecturers have found common cause with New Right commentators supporting a conservative position.

However recently issued guidelines from the National Curriculum Council (NCC, 1991) suggest that the scope for pursuing these aims may soon be seriously curtailed. For example the NCC suggest that newly trained primary teachers need to have sufficient subject knowledge in *all* 'core' subjects "to teach and assess pupils across the full range of National Curriculum levels appropriate to the key stage(s) for which they are being trained" and to have sufficient subject knowledge in other 'foundation' subjects in which they are not specialists, to teach and assess pupils "with support and guidance of colleagues". If adopted by the government as mandatory, these suggestions would seriously curtail the time available for in depth work in a single specialist subject. Moreover, it is suggested that at least some of the time devoted to the main subjects should be focused on the content of the National Curriculum. Such a proposal (supported by the most recent HMI report on initial teacher education, 1992) makes a significant bid to define the very content of main subject study.

The technical rationalist thrust of this latest initiative fundamentally challenges both liberal educationists and those of the New Right who advance a conservative ideology. So far the guidelines are merely advisory; it would seem however to be the hope of the NCC that at some stage they become mandatory by being included in future versions of circulars.

The Educational Disciplines

One of the most deeply contested areas of initial teacher education policy concerns the role of the educational disciplines of sociology, psychology, philosophy and history. The status of these subjects has been challenged both by the government and New Right pressure groups but the response has been an interesting one involving accommodation, resistance and at least some temporary transformations.

The history of the development of the role of the educational disciplines within initial training in Britain in many ways parallels the

171

development of main subject study. During the 1950s the educational disciplines, especially developmental psychology, were to some degree represented in the teacher education curriculum but from contemporary surveys it seems that the approach was highly selective and seldom academically rigourous (Taylor, 1961; Bernbaum, 1972).

Once again it was the moves to make teacher education courses 'degree worthy' in the post-Robbins era that signalled the rapid growth in the status of these subjects. Existing approaches to educational theory were challenged by those in universities who were to validate the new degrees. As a consequence new disciplinary specialists were recruited to replace generalist education tutors. These new lecturers (many of whom are now significantly in senior positions in the profession) saw themselves as "equipping students for intelligent and informed discourse about educational issues, sharply distinguished from practically expertise" (Bell, 1981, p. 13). These moves were justified from at least three different ideological positions. In the first place the academic study of the disciplines was justified on liberal educational grounds; studying the disciplines was conceived of as "part of the education of the scholar, who happened to want to be a teacher" (Bell, 1981, p. 13). But some disciplinary study was also justified in terms of progressivism. This was particularly true of developmental psychology which was the first subject to gain a stronghold in the new degrees but it was also true, if to a lesser extent, of sociology, especially in the study of 'educability'. Finally, disciplinary study was advocated from a social reconstructionist point of view. Education could only contribute to the development of a better, more morally justifiable world if teachers were themselves educated to think critically about their work.

In recent years a forceful challenge to the educational disciplines has been made by New Right critics from a conservative perspective; they attack both the liberal and social reconstructionist aims of disciplinary teaching. The Hillgate group (1989) for example suggest that most 'education' courses are "intellectually feeble and biased". They are overly concerned with topics such as race, sex and class and even 'anti-imperialist' education. These 'preoccupations' appear "designed to stir up disaffection, to preach a spurious gospel of 'equality' and to subvert the entire traditional curriculum" (p. 5). Even if they were taught in a more unbiased way, the Hillgate group question how much history, psychology, sociology and philosophy could be acquired in a course of 'education', "and to what intellectual effect". Moreover, they argue that such learning is of little or no help in the classroom. The disciplines are "second order knowledge, which gives the teacher himself nothing that he can transmit to the children and no special skill in the difficult task of teaching them" (p. 4).

The government has certainly heeded these criticisms. Disciplinary teaching as such is now virtually extinct. And while some of the topics traditionally covered by sociology, psychology and philosophy remain politically too important to abandon entirely, the circulars have attempted to transform them through the promotion of a technical rationalist approach. The first shots against the disciplines were fired by the James Report (1972) which doubted whether disciplinary study in initial teacher education was useful except in so far as it could offer direct practical help in teaching. However, in itself such a conclusion did little to weaken the influence of the disciplines, especially in the university sector. The CNAA and some universities slowly moved away from straight disciplinary teaching but in the 1970s there was nothing in official policy to insist that they did. Conservative policy during the 1980s has pursued a similar technical rationalist line but has progressively devised strategies to insist that it is followed.

For example in both circulars, the contribution of the disciplines in terms of the topics covered is acknowledged. Indeed on the surface it might seem that much of the disciplinary agenda remains - multicultural education, equal opportunities, learning difficulties, personal and social education. However the inclusion of other topics under the heading of Educational and Professional Studies suggests that the agenda for this aspect of training is *politically* rather than an educationally derived. (Witness for example the recent addition of the European Dimension to the list; the inclusion of Education for Mutual Understanding in Northern Ireland.)

The educational disciplines therefore retain utility only to the extent that they address topics of political importance for the government. New Right critics have been successful in adding to the agenda (see for example the concern with the 'economic base of a civilised society' and with teaching controversial issues 'in a balanced way'). However, whatever the ideological origin of individual items, they are all constructed as 'professional' issues. If the disciplines are employed they can no longer be taught in a straightforward way; they must become the servants of professional studies. As Circular 3/84 says "Even if these elements (Educational and Professional Studies) are not formally integrated within the structure of the course they should be planned so as to achieve this common purpose" (Annex, para 10). This approach is taken even further in Circular 24/89 where the aims of such courses are defined in terms of developing students' competencies on "key professional skills" (Annex A, para 6.1). In order to achieve this, Circular 24/89 insists that all such courses are "clearly linked to students' school experience so as to enable them to develop both a full range of competencies and the ability to analyse and evaluate their own performance" (Annex B, para 6.1). Once again the government has indicated that future regulation will define competencies in ever more detail (Clarke, 1992). By insisting on this technical rationalist approach, complex and contested issues are to be transformed to a list of competencies. As a consequence the original ideological and educational aims of disciplinary teaching are suppressed.

The response of the profession to a decade of challenge has been an interesting one involving accommodation, resistance and some degree of transformation. Certainly the 1980s saw a slow demise of pure disciplinary teaching, particularly in the PGCE. Today few if any PGCE students receive courses of lectures in sociology, psychology, philosophy or history. Instead disciplinary theory has entered into a new and important dialogue with 'practice'. Throughout the 1980s the teacher training profession was experimenting with a variety of strategies to bring 'theory and practice' into new relationships. In those experiments the role and character of disciplinary based knowledge has been a key issue. Before documenting these responses to the challenge to the educational disciplines it is therefore necessary to examine the next dimension of teacher education policy - that of 'practice'.

Practice

The most contested dimension of initial teacher education policy concerns the role of practice. Debates over the proper character of practical training for students have a long history in this country stretching back to the 1830s when the first training institutions were built with model classrooms and 'galleries' for observers (Wragg, 1990). In more recent times the McNair Report of 1944 challenged the orthodoxy of the day by suggesting that schools should have equal responsibility with teacher education institutions in the practical training of students. Despite strong support in some sections of the profession those proposals did not become mainstream policy for forty years; practice, particularly in the post-Robbins era, had relatively low status.

By the time we move to the 1970s however, it is possible to trace a growing emphasis on practical training. In the first instance the need to strengthen practical training was largely interpreted from a technical rationalist point of view as the need to develop systematic skill-based approaches. In the 1980s however, practical training was interpreted rather differently; what was needed it was suggested was more time in school and a closer partnership between teacher education institutions and schools (Booth et al, 1990). Today, virtually all commentators appear to agree on the significance of this approach. The government position is clearly stated in Circular 24/89.

> *Close cooperation between schools, local education authorities and initial teacher training leads to better training of students for their future careers and provides valuable staff development for institutions and schools. (Annex, B para 1.1)*

The emphasis on practice in Circulars 3/84 and 24/89 is thus a technical rationalist one. Moreover in comparison with other dimensions of teacher education, both circulars are explicit and detailed about the role and duties of practical training, signifying that for the government this aspect of teacher education is of prime political significance.

As a result of these two circulars students spend much more time engaged in practical work in school and that time seems set to increase substantially in the future (Clarke, 1992). In addition teacher education institutions have their courses overseen by external committees where teachers, LEA officials and industrialists have a majority voice; tutors themselves have to regularly update their school experience by undertaking 'recent and relevant' work in schools; teachers must be involved in the planning and implementation of courses; they must also have a central role in the selection as well as the final assessment of students; the number and timing of student days in schools during their course is explicitly defined. Finally and most comprehensively, virtually all of the parts of courses that take place in teacher education institutions - subject application work, curriculum studies and educational and professional studies "should be closely linked to students' practical experience in schools" (Annex A, para 2.4)

One reading of recent history on this issue could be the gradual emergence of a professional and political consensus on the significance of practical training and the form that it should take. My interpretation would be rather different. Certainly throughout the 1970s a number of voices were arguing for a greater emphasis on practice (Wilkin 1987, 1990). However, it is also apparent that until well into the 1980s these remained minority voices. As the SPITE (1982) survey of university PGCE courses and the HMI (1987) survey of public sector institutions revealed, examples of closer liaison between schools and teacher education institutions were rare in the early 1980s. The political intervention of Circular 3/84 was, I would suggest, a significant one. Most institutions did not move in the direction of a closer involvement with schools until they had to. Moreover, the response to the government's insistence on a greater practical emphasis in teacher education has been very varied; different parties have taken up the circulars in very different ways. Three broad approaches can be identified. These are

Apprenticeship models
Competency models
'Reflective teacher' models

An apprenticeship model of training is probably as old as teaching itself but official policy in this area has given new legitimacy to those advocating such an approach. Recent years have seen two groups of commentators supporting apprenticeship models though they do so from different ideological positions. The most radical proponents of apprenticeship training have been New Right commentators arguing from a conservative position. For example the Hillgate group argue that there is a long tradition going back to Aristotle that some skills, including many that are difficult, complex and of high moral and cultural value, are best learned by the emulation of experienced practitioners and by supervised practice under guidance. "In the case of such skills, apprenticeship should take precedence over instruction and even when formal instruction is necessary it can never be a substitute for real practical training" (p. 9). Lawlor (1990) makes a similar point: "Graduates would be sent to school to train on the job, designated to an experienced mentor - a senior teacher in the subject" (p. 38).

But the New Right are not the only ones to have advocated an apprenticeship model. Recent proposals by Hargreaves (1990) and Warnock (1985, 1988) for the establishment of 'training schools' to be run on similar lines to 'training hospitals' are also built on a notion of apprenticeship training. Their arguments are strictly utilitarian. Although more abstract forms of knowledge are important in teaching, they are not, they argue, necessary in initial teacher education. In the first instance students should learn the craft of teaching by mastering a series of practical 'competencies' laid down in a national curriculum for teacher education.

This mention of competencies links to a rather different response to the current emphasis on practice; this has been the rediscovery of the scientific or systematic tradition in initial teacher education. Not surprisingly those advocating such approaches do so from a technical rationalist perspective. Systematic training has a long history in this country though it reached the height of its popularity in the 1970s with interaction analysis (Flanders, 1970; Wragg, 1984) micro-teaching (Stones, 1976) and some interest in American Competency Based Teacher Education. Recent government initiatives have however rekindled an interest in competency training (TES, 1990).

Circular 3/84 represented the first national attempt to define the essential elements of initial teacher education; Circular 24/89 took the process further by attempting to define what teachers should be able to do at the end of their course. The government has indicated that this approach is likely to strengthen further new regulations for teacher training (Clarke, 1992). But the greatest stimulus to the development of a competency approach is the introduction of the Licensed Teacher Scheme. As it stands at present, Licensed Teachers do not need to have the normal entry qualifications of a degree. Neither do they have to undergo a formally structured training programme; rather, training is to be adapted to their individual needs as assessed by their employers. In circumstances where entrance qualifications and the content of training are variable, one response is to move towards the introduction of 'exit criteria' and the definition of competencies (Whitty, 1990). This is certainly the solution advocated by Hargreaves (1990) and accords well with the highly influential National Council for Vocational Qualifications.

The final response to the growing emphasis on practice, and the one most widely supported by the teacher education profession itself, has been the adoption of the 'reflective teacher' model. As Calderhead (1989) notes, there is great difficulty in defining with any precision what reflective teaching actually is and there are important differences between those who have advanced the concept in initial teacher education; compare, for example, the different approaches derived from the writings of Dewey (1933), e.g. Pollard & Tann (1987); Schon (1983, 1987), e.g. Furlong et al, 1988); and Habermas (1972), e.g. Carr & Kemmis (1987), and Whitty et al (1987). However, as a broad approach, it stands in marked contrast to technical rationalist approaches such as apprenticeship and competency models in that it insists that a professional activity such as teaching cannot be reduced to craft knowledge. Teaching involves complex skills, but those skills are not merely practical; they also have cognitive, moral and affective domains. Given that it stands in opposition to technical rationalist views of teacher education, the notion of the reflective teacher has become an important rallying cry for those in teacher education committed to liberal, progressivist and social reconstructionist ideologies. It has been taken up particularly vigourously by those committed to some continued role for the educational disciplines in initial teacher education. The promotion of such models has been the major strategy whereby those in the disciplines can respond to the increased emphasis on practice in the two key circulars. The challenge of the reflective teacher approach is to find a more effective means than in the past of raising cognitive, moral and affective issues in relation to students' own teaching.

Just as there are then many different conceptions of what the 'reflective teaching' actually involves, there are also different views of how it can best be achieved through initial teacher education. The early 1980s saw considerable experimentation with forms of simulation and other 'school-focused' teaching approaches (Bishop & Whitfield, 1972). Spurred on by the emphasis on practice in Circular 3/84, the mid- 1980s saw the widespread adoption of IT-"NSET- a research based approach built on collaboration between students, teachers and lecturers (Ashton et al, 1982). The later 1980s saw growing support for various forms of 'school-based' teacher education (Furlong et al, 1988; Benton, 1990).

The debate as to precisely what reflective teaching actually is and how it can be achieved through initial teacher education goes on. So far, the adoption of the reflective teacher model has been a relatively effective strategy through which those in initial teacher education committed to liberal, progressivist and social reconstructionist ideologies can respond to the technical rationalist demands of government initiatives. However, as Crozier et al (1990) points out, it is an essentially unstable concept which is vulnerable because of its internal divisions. How well it will survive if the central emphasis on competencies increases remains an open question.

Pedagogy

The final strand in the teacher education debate relates to the form of pedagogical training students should receive. Pedagogy is concerned with the promotion of effective learning on the part of pupils and following Schulman (1986) pedagogical preparation can be seen as involving the development in students of three different forms of 'knowledge'. Firstly there is content knowledge which for prospective teachers involves "going beyond the facts or concepts of a domain. It requires understanding the structure of the subject matter" (p.9). Secondly there is pedagogical content knowledge: "The particular form of content knowledge that embodies aspects of knowledge more germane to its teachability" (p.9). Finally there is curriculum knowledge which involves knowing the full range of curricular strategies available for teaching a particular topic. Although they are rarely discussed in this way, a great deal of what goes on in initial teacher education courses can be characterised as concerned with these aspects of pedagogy. Within the PGCE these issues form the heart of 'methods' or 'curriculum' courses while within the BEd they inform 'professional studies' courses and to a lesser extent 'main subject' teaching as well.

Within the teaching profession generally, the character of pedagogy is deeply contested. (See for example Ball's, 1985, case study of debates within English). Moreover, debates about pedagogy have been most frequently conducted between those responsible for initial teacher education. As a result, student preparation on pedagogical issues is often explicitly ideologically informed. However, until recently the government was agnostic about such matters. HMI advice was given but advice seldom turned to directives; the debates were almost exclusively professional ones. However, recent developments have however started to challenge this position.

Pedagogical training in the 1950s and early 1960s was dominated by a progressivist, child-centred orientation; indeed according to Bell (1981), child-centredness was raised to the level of a moral principle. The new academic emphasis introduced to teacher education by the Robbins Report of 1963 led to a growing cross fertilisation between subject specialisms and the educational disciplines - firstly psychology and then sociology. This had the consequence of further reinforcing progressivist ideals in subject teaching and pedagogical training. The influence of developmental psychology was apparent in many examples of curriculum development in the 1960s and 1970s (see for example Nuffield Science, Schools Council History). In the 1980s a growing strand of social reconstructionist thought crept into pedagogical debates influenced by sociological categories. Syllabuses on world history emerged, new strategies for encouraging girls into science were devised (Kelly, 1981) and the possibility of anti-racist mathematics was discussed (Woodrow, 1989). In fact none of these later movements achieved more than minority support, nevertheless they did challenge the progressivist orthodoxy in many subject areas. Whether they disproportionately influenced the curriculum for students in teacher education is hard to assess. What they did do, was increasingly attract the attention of New Right commentators.

Until very recently, discussion about the role of pedagogy in initial teacher education has been rare. Circular 3/84 did not address the issue. Pedagogical preparation therefore remained part of the private domain of individual lecturers who introduced students to their own view of pedagogy be that broadly or narrowly conceived. More recent initiatives have, however, begun to challenge some aspects of that autonomy by attempting to introduce a technical rationalist perspective. For example Circular 24/89 specifies in some detail the amount of time that should be devoted to pedagogy in courses but remains relatively silent on content; only the most general aims are outlined (Annex A, para 4.7). However elsewhere this circular states that curriculum courses must take account of the statutory orders for all National Curriculum subjects as they are introduced and the relevant non-statutory guidance from the DES and National Curriculum Council (NCC).

The NCC has recently issued 'guidelines' (NCC, 1991) drawing out the implications of their work for initial teacher education. This document defines lists of 'Skills in assessment, recording and reporting achievement' and 'Skills in curriculum planning and review'. In addition it gives detailed guidance on how courses should prepare students to be able to review the whole curriculum, 'understand curriculum continuity' and 'develop information technology capability'. Such guidelines could be seen as representing the first stages of a National Curriculum for teacher education on pedagogy.

Whether Circular 24/89 will in the end represent a major ideological challenge to those responsible for pedagogy is hard to assess at this stage. However, the fact that most lecturers have responded to the National Curriculum with relative equanimity indicates that the majority of them will continue to find space within NCC guidelines to pursue their existing ideological aims without too much difficulty.

By contrast the New Right commentators, arguing from a conservative perspective have explicitly challenged recent government policy on pedagogy. For example Lawlor (1990) characterises pedagogy as "modish educational theory" (p. 42). For her, the fetishism with pedagogy at the expense of subject knowledge is the main weakness of teacher training and the explanation for what she claims to be declining standards in British schools.

> *Teaching remains alone amongst the professions in having switched emphasis from mastery of the subject to the practice of teaching. But this emphasis on practice is in fact far from practical. Teachers are not encouraged to develop the style of teaching which time and experience prove best for them. Rather there is imposed on them, in training courses and later, a single method of teaching often at the expense of the subject itself. Such a style does not rest on any agreed tradition nor on its having been tested successfully over generations but rests rather, on a series of fleeting fashions and accidents".*
> *(p. 8)*

Whether such arguments influence the next round of initiatives on initial teacher education remains to be seen.

Conclusion

This sociological analysis of teacher education has revealed that the overall thrust of recent government policy has been a technical rationalist one. However it has also demonstrated that if we examine the Circulars 3/84 and 24/89 in relation to each of the key dimensions of initial teacher education, we can see that the attempt to introduce such an approach is extremely varied. In the area of 'main subject' study, technical rationality is still quite limited though the new NCC guidelines may progressively reduce lecturers' opportunities to pursue their own aims. The impact on pedagogy has also been limited so far. Circular 3/84 did not address the issue at all and Circular 24/89 outlines only the most general 'competencies'. To date, teacher educators are therefore still largely in control of this aspect of the curriculum. However the explicit challenge to the relevance of any pedagogical training by New Right critics (Lawlor, 1990) may mean that future government directives address this issue more explicitly. Pedagogy is now on the political agenda.

The areas where there has been a more direct attempt to introduce a technical rationalist approach are in relation to the educational disciplines and practice. Here the prescriptions of Circulars 3/84 and 24/89 are explicit and detailed. Even so it has been possible for those in teacher education to reinterpret the criteria in these circulars so as to preserve some of their own ideological commitments. The most explicit example of this has been the widespread support for the notion of the 'reflective practitioner'. Such an approach has allowed teacher educators to conform to the new emphasis on practice while at the same time maintaining a commitment to progressivist or social reconstructionist principles.

The central point of this sociological analysis has therefore been that the impact of government policy is uneven. Those in the education system responsible for the implementation of a particular policy often retain some autonomy. As the case of teacher education demonstrates, subordinates will only conform to the imposition of policies that challenge their fundamental commitments if they have to. Teacher educators have in the last decade struggled to continue to pursue their own professional ideals both in the spaces left untouched by government directives and by attempting to transform those aspects of policy that must be obeyed. They are likely to continue to do so though it could be that further reform promised by the government will specifically reduce the 'spaces' in which teacher educators can offer resistance (Clarke, 1992).

In conclusion it is important to ask why the government has attempted to reconstruct teacher education along technical rationalist lines. Why have they attempted to promote a different model of the professional teacher? The answer would seem to lie in the changing relationship between the state and the teaching profession as a whole.

As Grace (1987) has argued, throughout the history of state education, successive governments have recognised that teachers are a key professional group that must be managed and directed. In the post war period up until the mid 1970s, the means used by the state to control teachers was one of granting them limited professional autonomy. Organised teachers, such as members of the NUT, gave up aspirations for political and economic advance in return for control over the curriculum. Teachers, Grace argues, were de-politicised and incorporated by being granted a form of 'legitimised professionalism'. Teacher educators were granted professional autonomy too; the autonomy to form the next generation of teachers in line with their own educational ideals. As we have seen, for the most part those ideals were constructed from progressive, liberal or social reconstructionist ideologies. In the late 1970s, partly as a result of challenges by those adopting a conservative ideological position, the compromise between the profession and the state began to break down and relations increasingly became characterised by the politics of confrontation. By the end of the 1980s, teachers had largely lost their control of the curriculum, lost their salary negotiating rights, and were subject to appraisal and new contracts. It is in this context that we must place the government's attempts to take control of teacher education.

Recent government initiatives on teacher education, I would suggest, represent an attempt to reconstruct the very notion of professionalism itself. During the post war period, as a result of professional autonomy, teacher professionalism was increasingly characterised by deep commitment to a limited number of educational value systems or ideologies. Through initial teacher education, each new generation of teachers developed similar ideological commitments. Circulars 3/84 and 24/89 have tried to challenge this view of professionalism. Their language is neutral, speaking of professional relevance and competencies. However, behind that neutral language there is clear evidence of an agenda of topics to be covered which is primarily *politically* derived. On the surface therefore that agenda may represent a particular political compromise. At a more fundamental level, through their promotion of a technical rationalist approach, these circulars aim to remove ideas of teacher education from their ideological base, thereby constructing a different form of professionalism amongst the next generation of teachers.

The view of professionalism advanced by these circulars is not one that is based on a deep commitments to particular value systems; rather it is of a teacher who is a competent practitioner, able effectively to implement those policies advocated by the government of the day.

Future governments will have different political priorities and the list of competencies to be acquired will change. However, in the foreseeable future, it seems unlikely that governments of any political persuasion will retreat from the attempt to take a tighter control of initial teacher education. The central question that remains, for sociologists and for others, is how much space and resilience there will continue to be within the system for those who wish to advance different views of professionalism.

Note

[1] The PGCE is the one year Post Graduate Certificate of Education taken by graduates wishing to train as teachers.

Acknowledgements

I would like to thank Madeleine Arnot, Len Barton, Ruth Furlong, Terry McLaughlin, Sheila Miles, and Margaret Wilkin for comments on earlier drafts of this chapter.

References

Alexander, R. (1984) *Primary Teaching*. London: Cassell.

Ashton, P.M.E., Henderson, E.S., Merritt, J.E. & Mortimer, D.E. (1982) *Teacher Education in the Classroom*. London: Croom Helm.

Bailey, C. (1984) *Beyond the Present and the Particular: A Theory of Liberal Education*. London: Routledge.

Ball, S. (1985) in I. Goodson (Ed) *Social Histories of the Secondary Curriculum: Subjects for Study*. Lewes: Falmer.

Bell, A. (1981) Structure, knowledge and relationships in teacher education, *British Journal of Sociology of Education*, 2, pp. 3-23.

Benton, P. (1990) *The Oxford Internship Scheme: Integration and Partnership in Initial Teacher Education*. London: Calouste Gulbenkian.

Bernbaum, G. (1977) *Knowledge and Ideology in the Sociology of Education*. London: Macmillan.

Bishop, A. & Whitfield, R. (1972) *Situations in Teaching*. Maidenhead: McGraw Hill.

Booth, M., Furlong, J. & Wilkin, M. (1990) (Eds) *Partnership in Initial Teacher Training*. London: Cassell.

Calderhead, J. (1989) Reflective teaching and teacher education, *Teaching and Teacher Education*, 5, pp. 43-51.

Carr, W. & Kemmis, S. (1986) *Becoming Critical: Education, Knowledge and Action Research*. Lewes: Falmer Press.

Clarke, K. (1992) Speech to the North of England Conference, January.

Conner, C. & Lofthouse, B. (1990) *The Study of Primary Education: A Source Book, Vol. 1*. Lewes: Falmer Press.

Crozier, G., Menter, I. & Pollard, A. (1990) Changing Partnership, in M. Booth, J. Furlong & M. Wilkin (Eds) *Partnership in Initial Teacher Training*. London: Cassell.

Demaine, J. (1988) Teachers' work, curriculum and the New Right, *British Journal of Sociology of Education*, 9, pp. 247-264.

DES (1983) *Teaching Quality*. London: HMSO.

DES (1984) *Initial Teacher Training: Approval of Courses (Circular 3/84)*. London: DES.

DES (1988) *Qualified Teacher Status, Consultation Document*. London: DES.

DES (1989a) *Future Arrangements for the Accreditation of Initial Teacher Training: a consultation document*. London: DES.

DES (1989b) *Initial Teacher Training: Approval of Courses (Circular 24/89)*. London: DES.

Dewey, J. (1933) *How we Think*. Boston: D.C. Heath.

Eason, T.W. (1971) Main Subject Courses, in J.W. Tibble (Ed) *The Future of Teacher Education*. London: Routledge.

Fiske, J. (1987) British Cultural Studies and Television, in R.C. Allen (Ed) *Channels of Discourse*. London: Routledge.

Flanders, N. (1970) *Analysing Teaching Behaviour*. London: Addison Wesley.

Furlong, V.J., Hirst, P.H., Pocklington, K. & Miles, S. (1988) *Initial Teacher Training and the Role of the School*. Milton Keynes: Open University Books.

Giroux, H. & McLaren, P. (1986) Teacher education and the policies of engagement: the case for democratic schooling, *Harvard Educational Review*, 56, pp. 213-238.

Grace, G. (1987) Teachers and the State in Britain: a changing relation, in M. Lawn & G. Grace (Eds) *Teachers: The Culture and Politics of Work*. Lewes: Falmer Press.

Habermas, J. (1972) *Knowledge and Human Interests*. London: Heinemann.

Hargreaves, D. (1990) Another radical approach to the reform of initial teacher training, *Westminster Studies in Education*, 13, pp. 5-11.

HMI (1983) *Teaching in Schools: The Content of Initial Teacher Training*. London: DES.

HMI (1987) *Quality in Schools: The Initial Training of Teachers*, London: DES.

HMI (1988a) *Initial Teacher Training in Universities in England, Northern Ireland and Wales*. London: HMSO.

HMI (1988b) *The New Teacher in School*. London: HMSO.

HMI (1992) *School-based Initial Teacher Training in England and Wales*. London: HMSO.

Hill, D. (1989) *Charge of the Right Brigade: The Radical Right's Attack on Teacher Education*. Brighton: Hillcole Group.

Hillgate Group (1986) *Whose Schools? A Radical Manifesto*. London: Claridge Press.

Hillgate Group (1987) *The Reform of British Education: From Principles to Practice*. London: The Claridge Press.

Hillgate Group (1989) *Learning to Teach*. London: The Claridge Press.

James (1972) *Teacher Education and Training (The James Report)*. London: HMSO.

Kelly, A. (Ed) (1981) *The Missing Half: Girls and Science Education*. Manchester: Manchester University Press.

Lawlor, S. (1990) *Teachers Mistaught: Training Theories or Education in Subjects?* London: Centre For Policy Studies.

Marcuse, H. (1964) *One Dimensional Man*. Boston: Beacon Press.

McNair, A. (1944) *Teachers and Youth Leaders (The McNair Report)*. London: HMSO.

NCC (1991). *The National Curriculum and the Initial Training of Teachers*. York: National Curriculum Council.

O'Hear, A. (1988a) *Daily Telegraph*, 12 December 1988. p. 8.

O'Hear, A. (1988b) *Who Teachers the Teachers?* London: Social Affairs Unit.

Pollard, A. & Tann, S. (1987) *Reflective Teaching in the Primary School*. London: Cassell.

Popkewitz, T.S. (1987a) (Ed) *Critical Studies in Teacher Education: Its Folklore, Theory and Practice*. Lewes: Falmer Press.

Popkewitz, T.S. (1987b) Ideology and Social Formation in Teacher Education, in T. Popkewitz (Ed) *Critical Studies in Teacher Education: its Folklore, Theory and Practice*. Lewes: Falmer Press.

Ransom, S. (1990) From 1944 to 1988: education, citizenship and democracy", in M. Flude & M. Hammer (Eds) *The Education Reform Act 1988: Its Origins and Implications*. Lewes: Falmer.

Robbins (1963) *Higher Education (The Robbins Report)*. London: HMSO.

Roderick, R. (1986) *Habermas and the Foundation of Critical Theory*. London: Macmillan.

Schon, D.A. (1983) *The Reflective Practitioner*. London: Temple Smith.

Schon, D.A. (1987) *Educating and Reflective Practitioner*. New York: Basic Books.

Schulman, L. (1986) Those who understand: knowledge growth in teaching, *Educational Researcher*, 15 (2) pp. 4-14.

SPITE (1982). Patrick, H., Bernbaum, G. & Reid, K. (1982) *The Structure and Process of Initial Teacher Education Within Universities in England and Wales (The SPITE Report)*. University of Leicester: School of Education.

Stones, E. (1976) Teaching teaching skills, *British Journal of Teacher Education*, 12, pp. 59-78.

Taylor, W. (1969) *Education and the Training of Teachers*. London: Faber & Faber.

The Times Educational Supplement (1990) What makes a good teacher? 7 September.

Warnock, M. (1985) *Teacher Teach Thyself*. London: BBC Publications.

Warnock, M. (1988) *A Common Policy for Education*. Oxford: Oxford University Press.

White, M. (1987) Ideological Analysis and Television, in R.C. Allen (Ed) *Channels of Discourse*. London: Routledge.

Whitty, G. (1989) New Right and the National Curriculum: state control or market forces? *Journal of Education Policy*, 4, pp. 329-341.

Whitty, G. (1990) *Building the Bridge: Profiling the Student Teacher. The Surveyor's Report*. Unpublished paper presented at DES conference 'Building the Bridge: Profiling the Student Teacher', York, January.

Whitty, G., Barton, L. & Pollard, A. (1987) Ideology and Control in Teacher Education, in T. Popkewitz (1987a) (Ed) *Critical Studies in Teacher Education: Its Folklore, Theory and Practice*. Lewes: Falmer Press.

Wilkin, M. (1987) The Sociology of Education and the Theory-Practice Relationship in Teacher Training, in P. Woods & A. Pollard (Eds) *Sociology and the Teacher*. London: Croom Helm.

Wilkin, M. (1990) The Development of Partnership in the United Kingdom, in M. Booth, J. Furlong & M. Wilkin (Eds) (1990) *Partnership in Initial Teacher Training*. London: Cassell.

Woodrow, D. (1989) Multicultural and Anti-racist Mathematical Education, in P. Ernest (Ed) *Mathematics Teaching: The State of the Art*. Lewes: Falmer Press.

Wragg, E.C. (1984) (Ed) *Classroom Teaching Skills*. London: Croom Helm.

Wragg, E.C. (1990) Two Routes into Teaching, in M. Booth, J. Furlong & M. Wilkin (Eds) (1990) *Partnership in Initial Teacher Training*. London: Cassell.

Chapter Ten

The Reform of Higher Education

GEOFFREY WALFORD

The Development of Higher Education

Britain's present higher education system is almost entirely the creation of the post-war years. Although the universities can trace a path back to the twelfth century, by 1938 there were still just 16 universities serving only about 50,000 students. These universities catered for a small, largely male, elite who either already had wealth and privilege or were destined to take their place at the top of the power structure in due course.

The three decades following the end of the war were dominated by expansion, rising to 205,200 university students in 1967, and 277,000 in 1977. This change meant that the universities moved some way from their former role as highly elite institutions and became, if not 'mass' institutions on the American model (Trow, 1974), at least somewhat more open to a variety of ideas, purposes and people. They also became more dependent on government funding such that, in 1969/70, 73 per cent of university funding came directly from the government through the University Grants Committee, and fees accounted for a further 7 per cent (Halsey, 1988, p. 281).

During the 1950s and 1960s there had been a broad party-political consensus that there was a need to expand higher education both to meet the perceived national needs for a skilled and knowledgeable workforce, and to provide for increased demand for places. Mandatory grants covering fees and maintenance were thus introduced in 1962, older universities were expanded, new universities created and former university colleges and colleges of advanced technology were promoted to full university status. This rapid expansion was well under way before the

Robbins Committee reported in 1963, but that report was used to justify the changes to any who still had doubts.

To most academics and administrators the model student at the time was someone who was young, working full time on a three year degree course, and living away from home in accommodation provided by the institution. Universities were thus provided with generous accommodation for students and the newly created ones were purposely sited away from major centres of population. However, such residential universities were expensive to fund, so that when the Robbins Report recommended that all higher education should come under the university umbrella, the Labour government balked at the prospect. Instead, in 1965, it reaffirmed and restructured the pre-existing dual system of provision of higher education which had gradually developed. The result was a well-funded university sector, and a local authority and voluntary controlled public sector where several hundred colleges and 30 new polytechnics offered degree courses. The rhetoric was that the two halves were to be different but of equal status, but it was clear that it was hoped that the local authority public sector would be cheaper to run than the universities, more amenable to public and local control, and more responsive to the needs of industry and commerce.

The end of the unrestricted expansionist period was marked by the 1972 White Paper, put forward by Margaret Thatcher as Secretary of State at the DES, which revised downwards the predicted student numbers and announced a two per cent reduction in funding per student. This contraction was continued by the Labour governments of 1974 which, facing an energy crisis, rapid inflation and pressure from the IMF, abandoned the quinquennial system of funding for the universities and made cuts of about eight per cent per student between 1974 and 1979.

The Years of Crisis Prior to 1988

When Margaret Thatcher's first government was returned in 1979 it was committed to reducing government expenditure on education, increasing efficiency, and re-directing the educational system further towards the perceived needs of industry. That this policy was to be applied with vigour to higher education quickly became evident, for subsidies for overseas students were rapidly reduced and a decision was made not to fund any expansion in higher education to take account of a demographic peak in the number of 18 year olds due to occur in 1983. Instead, the government actually cut university funding by about 17 per cent over three years (Kogan & Kogan, 1983; Sizer, 1987a & b; Walford, 1987), and left it to the University Grants Committee to distribute the cuts to individual institutions. The government's idea, however, was that the UGC was to be selective and directive, and that there was to be an increase in the proportion of students studying science, technology and engineering at the expense of those studying arts and social sciences.

In implementing these 1981 cuts the UGC made one very important decision which is now usually seen as having been an error. It decided that the unit of resource would only partly worsen. This meant that between 1981 and 1985 the universities admitted fewer students than the government might have wished and, in consequences, the polytechnic and colleges seized the chance to expand to take up the increased demand. One of the quirks of the binary system at that point was that while central government could control its own expenditure on universities, it had no direct powers to restrict the amount of money provided by local education authorities to support the public sector polytechnics and colleges. Additionally, many of the colleges and polytechnics were under the control of Labour councils which, with many of the institutions themselves, wished to widen access and support a growth in student numbers. The government's attempts to reduce expenditure on higher education were thus thwarted by the local authority sector's willingness to expand to meet the new demands made on it by students. Between 1979 and 1988 the number of full-time students in higher education in Great Britain rose by nearly 116,000, but the proportion in universities fell from 57 per cent to 50 per cent of the total. Practically all of the expansion in full-time student numbers took place in the polytechnics and colleges, and most importantly to the government, it was achieved at a far lower cost per student than would have occurred had these extra numbers been accommodated within the universities. Between 1981/82 and 1986/87 the student:staff ratio for polytechnic higher education teaching moves from 9.7: 1 to 12.4: 1, with the average class size rising from 13.7 to 16.4 (DES, 1989a).

These lower costs were welcomed by the government and seen as an indication of greater efficiency in the public sector. It is worth nothing that the expansion in part-time students also mainly occurred in the public sector. While the universities have been slow to move away from their 'traditional' students on three year courses, the polytechnics and colleges have made determined efforts to broaden access to more women, working-class students, mature students and students from ethic minority backgrounds.

The universities dealt with their financial crises by trying to attract more overseas students, gaining more research and development funding from industry and shedding staff. By 1984, more than 4000 academic staff and 5000 non-academic staff received payments from a special scheme designed to encourage early retirement or 'mobility' out of university life. Universities closed or amalgamated departments and restructured faculties in their attempts to deal with the cuts (Walford, 1987).

After all the uncertainty, disruption and animosity that such changes engendered the universities were given little time to adjust, for by 1983 the government had become convinced that they were inefficient, wasteful and unresponsive. They were seen as not offering value for money, being too distant from the wealth creating sectors of industry and commerce, and being too dependent upon government funding. In short, it wished to reprivatize what had become a public service, to force the universities to become more independent and to compete in the market for students, research contracts and other services (Walford, 1988, 1990).

Before universities could be allowed to compete against each other in the market, it was perceived that they would have to change their organizational structures and methods of working to become more managerial. The cuts in finance meant that there had to be far greater forward planning and decision making. Greater power had thus accrued to those administrators and senior academics able and willing to spend sufficient time in committees and back-room micropolitics. By the mid 1980s, Registrars such as Geoffrey Lockwood at Sussex (Lockwood & Davies, 1985) were tackling the 'management challenge' of universities, and found their ideas accepted by Vice-Chancellors and University Councils faced with impending economic bankruptcy.

A series of reports published during the mid 1980s emphasised this new managerial emphasis. The Jarratt Report (1985) argued that the Vice-Chancellor should be seen as the chief executive, and Governing Bodies were to act more like Boards of Directors. More fundamentally, the Jarratt Report explicitly put the good of the institution before that of individual academics or their disciplines, and regarded universities as being 'first and foremost corporate enterprises to which subsidiary units and individuals are responsible and accountable'. But, as Kogan (1989) persuasively argues, this was to misunderstand the nature of higher education:

> The well being of the institution is important only because it ensures the good work of the individuals within it. Any academic enterprise which does not have powerful academic departments and powerful individual academics who cherish their academic discipline above all else, will be second rate or worse (p. 76).

A corresponding emphasis on managerialism can be seen in several other major documents. Within the polytechnic and college sectors the National Advisory Body produced its Management for a Purpose in 1987, which had many similarities with the Jarratt Report. The Croham Committee (1987) recommended performance indicators for universities' finance, management, teaching and research, and major changes in the way universities should receive money from the UGC. As funding was progressively reduced, so more time and effort was put into distributing the ever decreasing slices of cake.

The Development of the Sociology of Higher Education

The contraction of universities and the expansion of the public sector institutions brought with them major changes for staff and students. The work of thousands of university academics was disrupted or curtailed, as their courses and departments closed. Many retired earlier than they had planned and there were few opportunities for young aspirants. In the polytechnic and colleges sector, academics found their work loads increased, and their conditions of work worsened. Criteria for acceptance of students appear to have become idiosyncratic, and students who survived the lottery found themselves in larger classes with fewer facilities. The problems within higher education were widely recognised by those involved in higher education yet, strangely, there was little academic study or comment. We have accounts of the broad outlines of what happened, but we do not have reliable research evidence on, for example, how institutions and individuals have adjusted to the new managerialism, or what the effects of the changes have been on students, academics and administrators.

In 1983 the Editors of the *British Journal of Sociology of Education* decided to encourage such contributions by calling for papers for a proposed 'Symposium on the Current Educational Crisis'. They saw the need to look at the effects of the changes in higher education on educational opportunity and disadvantaged groups, and saw a real threat to the continued life of sociology and sociology of education as disciplines. They asked for papers within the sociology of education which illuminated the crisis in higher education, and which examined the threat to the disciplines. They expected to receive case studies of what was happening in various institutions and accounts of how these changes were effecting those involved. However, a few issues later, in 1984, Ivan Reid, on behalf of the editors, was forced to write:

> In the future, historians of education may well be surprised by the dearth of material in academic journals of our time about the dramatic changes implemented in British higher education in the early to mid-1980s. The editorial board of the BJSE anticipated this surprise following the almost non-response to their editorial invitation for such material ...

In the end, the journal published a symposium of four short pieces - 15 pages in all - none of which was based on research (Reid et al, 1984).

In practice, this lack of academic research and comment by sociologists of education on institutions, and on higher education in general, is not restricted to the early years of the 1980s - there is little academic work on the sociology of British higher education at all, and the work that has been done has been concerned with a limited range of issues. For example, during the first ten years of the life of the *British Journal of Sociology of Education*, articles concerned with higher education accounted for only about five per cent of the total published (excluding some concerned with teacher education). One of these was concerned with female academics (Acker, 1980), one with postgraduate students (Walford, 1983), one with student culture in an urban community college in the USA (Weis, 1986) and only one dealt with organizational change and the rise of managerialism within a case study institution of higher education, how the changes affected individuals and how these changes might be understood in terms of wider social restructuring. That study was Australian (Henry & Lingard, 1989)!

It is also not the case that sociologists of education have published many articles on higher education in other journals. During the same decade the main higher education contributions to *Sociology* were a presidential address on 'Research policy in British higher education' (Platt, 1986) and a special issue on teaching research methodology in 1981. Within the journals specifically devoted to higher education, such as *Studies in Higher Education, Higher Education* and *Higher Education Review*, some of the articles were certainly informed by sociological thinking but they are still few and far between, mainly concerned with a narrow range of issues, and often conducted over a rather leisurely time scale. In the main, they do not offer insights into aspects of current educational reform.

In order to understand why this should be so, it is worth briefly examining how the sociology of higher education developed within Britain for, interestingly, higher education was one of the main interests of those involved in the development of the sub-discipline of sociology of education. In Britain, some of the earliest sociological work which might be considered to be sociology of education was the work on education and social mobility conducted by David Glass (1954) and his co-workers at the London School of Economics. This broad range of 'political arithmetic' work centred mainly on the work of schools, in particular the inequalities of selection, where the research was used to direct policy away from selective schools and towards comprehensives. But there was also a focus on higher education. A. H. Halsey was one of the group at LSE who had a key influence on the way in which the sociology of education developed. He was co-author of the first major review of the sociology of education (Floud and Halsey, 1958), co-editor of one of the first 'Readers' in the sociology of education, *Education, Economy and Society* (Halsey, Floud & Anderson, 1961), became the first Professor of Social and Administrative Studies at Oxford University, and continues to have a key role in the sociology of education. About a quarter of the articles in this first Reader were concerned with higher education, showing the degree of prominence that it then had in the developing subdiscipline. These articles included some by Eric Ashby, David Riesman, Burton R Clark, Arnold Anderson, Martin Trow and A. H. Halsey. Areas of interest included: the functions of higher education and various types of higher education institution; student selection, access and achievement; and the role academics and nature of academic life.

Halsey has continued to undertake research on both schools and higher education, but his research on schools has tended to be more closely linked to policy-making. For example, he directed the Educational Priority Areas action research programme in the late 1960s and early 1970s which developed from government action in this area (Halsey, 1972). Meanwhile his research on higher education, being conducted at the same time, was less directly policy relevant. In 1964, Halsey & Trow continued the political arithmetic tradition and conducted the first major sample survey of university academics. This large scale study, published in 1971 (Halsey & Trow, 1971), was to be the first of what has now become a series of three studies of academics in higher education: the second was conducted in 1976 and included university and polytechnic teachers (Halsey, 1979, 1982), while the third was conducted in 1989, with the results so far only being published in a series of articles in *The Times Higher Education Supplement* in January/February 1990. This series of surveys has provided a great deal of information on academics and how they see their world, but the nature of its methodology means that change is only considered in broad terms and resulting general trends. These surveys are fascinating exercises intellectually, but not ones which directly link to policy.

In a similar way, in 1970 Halsey was one of a team of academics at Oxford who was a driving force behind a national multi-purpose survey which came to be known as the Oxford Social Mobility Survey. This study examined the educational histories of a representative sample of men aged 20 to 60 and led to a major book and many articles on schools and higher education (for example, Halsey, 1977; Halsey, Heath & Ridge, 1980, 1984). The study placed itself firmly in the political arithmetic tradition, brought new sophistication to the interpretation of data, and may be seen in part as an attempt to reassert the importance of this theoretical framework within the sociology of education. Although their data and analysis were restricted to men only, the authors were able to show, for example, that entry to university during the period under study was still strongly influenced by social class and that further expansion of higher education would be necessary before significant numbers of working class students could be expected. However, they were also unable to find unequivocal evidence for genuine school effects on A level performance or university entry (Halsey et al, 1984). They found that, once background variable were taken into account, the effect of differing school type was small and argued that the differences were most likely to be due to unmeasured variations in family background.

In Halsey's second Reader, *Power and Ideology in Education* (Karabel & Halsey, 1977), still about a quarter of the articles were concerned with higher education, with the topic area being generally similar to those in the earlier Reader. Articles were concerned with: student selection, access and achievement; social mobility; various types of higher education institution; and some on cultural reproduction and transmission. Interestingly, one article considered the student movement of the 1960s and early 1970s in the context of the industrialization of higher education (Miles, 1977). The collection also included Pierre Bourdieu's well known 'Cultural Reproduction and Social Reproduction' which includes higher education within its analysis.

Although French, Pierre Bourdieu is a key figure in the way British sociology of education developed in the 1970s. The Annual Conference of the British Sociological Association in 1970 was devoted to sociology of education. The 'new' sociology of education that sprang from that conference, at its simplest, revealed that many of those involved in that conference wished to move beyond the 'black box' political arithmetic framework that had dominated the sub-discipline to that point. Michael

Young (1971) proclaimed the need for 'new directions', and pointed towards a need to study the content of the curriculum and the organization of knowledge. He, and his contributors, wished to explore the processes that linked macro changes to micro variables. That collection of nine articles included two by Bourdieu, (1971a & b) both of which were more concerned with higher education than schools. Bourdieu's pathbreaking work with Jean-Claude Passeron (Bourdieu & Passeron, 1977) also concerned itself with higher education as well as schools, and Bourdieu's voluminous recent work has included a monograph devoted to the nature of French academics and academic life, *Homo Academicus* (1988). Unfortunately, there is no comparable British academic who was closely involved with the 'new' sociology of education and who combined an interest in culture, knowledge and higher education. The result was that the sociology of higher education remained largely untouched by the 'new directions'.

Michael Young's call to explore the structure and organization of knowledge was not answered strongly even at the school level, but the general thrust towards looking inside the 'black boxes' and examining the ways in which schools and classrooms were organized and teachers and pupils interacted became very popular. Sociology of education had become institutionalized mainly within college and university departments concerned with teacher education rather than sociology departments. The sociology of the staffroom and classroom gave these educators a direct justification for the inclusion of the sociology of education within teacher preparation courses. Case studies and micro analyses of teachers and pupils have thus flourished at the school level, yet there are very few similar studies within institutions of higher education. More importantly, while there are now many case studies of how changes at the macro level have affected schools and classrooms, there are very few which have studied the effects and processes of change within higher education. The only book length case study that I know which has examined the dramatic changes in universities following the 1981 cuts is my own *Restructuring Universities: politics and power in the management of change* (Walford, 1987), which looked at Aston University and the closure of the Department of Educational Enquiry within it. In its limited way, this book attempted to explore the nature of power and micropolitics in that institution at a time of rapid change.

There are several possible reasons why sociologists of education may have been reluctant to conduct case studies about higher education. First, the sociology of school education has a ready audience and justification within teacher education. There is no such direct audience for research on higher education. Second, it is far more difficult to hide the identity of an institution of higher education in any publication, such that the anonymity and confidentiality usually granted to schools, teachers and pupils is not possible. In such a situation, case studies of change, for example, run the risk of writs for libel. Third, given the larger scale and complexity of higher education organizations, sociologists of education wishing to look at higher education, would be most likely to examine their own institutions. Those looking for promotion might thus think twice about the wisdom of such a research project. Whatever the reasons, the fact is that there are few case studies of the major changes that occurred during the 1980s.

Broadly, the main area of strength within the sociology of higher education has continued to be research using the framework of the old sociology of education. There have been many studies of the relationships between social class, educational opportunity and attainment, and a regular flow of studies on undergraduate students, postgraduate students and academics (for example, Brothers & Hatch, 1971; Kelsall et al, 1972; Welsh, 1979; Rudd, 1975, 1985; and Becher, 1989). There has been a growing acceptance of qualitative data in addition to quantitative data, but the search has been for broad generalizations rather than specific instances. These survey studies have furthered our knowledge of the importance of social class as an indicator of acceptance into various forms of higher education, and described and analysed the experiences of those who are selected. They have provided information and analysis on the nature of both undergraduate and postgraduate education, and investigated the differing cultures of various academic disciplines.

Over the years the sociology of higher education has also broadened its interests from class inequalities to include gender inequalities and the experiences of women both as students and academics (for example, Acker, 1980, 1981; Acker & Warren Piper, 1984; Sutherland, 1986; and Thomas, 1990). This has been a particularly productive area of study, and one where the researchers have been prepared to move away from a purely political arithmetic framework and examine the structure of knowledge in higher education and the processes at work within institutions which lead to the inequalities found. Researchers such as Dale Spender (1987, 1981, 1989), for example, have examined the ways in which language use structures and restricts our understandings, and how male academics have constructed academic subject areas to exclude the contribution of women. She shows that changes in the structure of knowledge are occurring in many fields, but that there is still a long way to go before women's academic work and women's experience are fully accepted.

As with research on schools, the gender balance of students within different subject areas has been a particular focus of attention. A recent study by Thomas (1990), however, extends this interest into higher education by exploring the ways in which subject areas are constructed by academics and students and the relationships between these constructions and the social constructions of gender. Her interview study of undergraduates studying English and Physics leads to a consideration of beliefs about masculinity and femininity, and the ways in which subject loyalty can be challenged or reinforced by a student's sense of gender identity. Although not always successful, this study is thus one of the few which moves towards integrating the concerns of the 'new' sociology of education with quantitative indicators of inequality.

The 1988 Education Reform Act

The 1988 Education Reform Act brought a major restructuring of higher education, the effects of which are so far almost completely unresearched. A series of major changes were designed to reduce government expenditure, to make individual institutions more competitive, and to bring them into a closer and more dependent relationship with industry and commerce. In the years since their creation, the polytechnic and major colleges had become mature institutions, performing on a national stage. Many were far larger than the smaller universities, and the controlling links to local authorities had become anachronistic. The Lindop Report (1985) recommended that many of them should be granted greater freedom from the CNAA, and the 1988 Education Reform Act led to the 29 English Polytechnics and about 50 of the other large colleges becoming autonomous independent institutions, each with its own business-led Board of Governors.

The 1988 Education Reform Act also replaced the National Advisory Body by a Polytechnics and Colleges Funding Council (PCFC) and the UGC by a Universities Funding Council (UFC), each of which was to have strong representation from industry and commerce. There was considerable debate as this part of the Bill passed through Parliament. The Committee of Vice-Chancellors and Principals was able to rally ex-colleagues and others in the House of Lords to make changes in the Bill such that the government's intention to promote a full contract basis for financing teaching and research was somewhat modified. In practice, however, both the UFC and PCFC have moved towards a far more competitive system.

The government's determination to make higher education more responsive to the pressures of the market led to clauses within the 1988 Act which removed the possibility of tenure for all future university employees. 'Flexibility' in the workforce was deemed to be so important that there had to be ways by which universities could make academics redundant if their expertise was no longer fashionable. The Vice-Chancellors were not particularly opposed to the greater managerial flexibility that such a clause in the Act would give them, but there was some discussion about how this might conflict with academic freedom. There was concern that academics should still be able to research and write about whatever subjects they wished without fear that they might loose their jobs if their ideas were unpopular with government or fellow academics. This became a major issue of debate as the Bill passed through the House of Lords. An amendment was eventually passed which gave academic staff the 'freedom within the law to question and test received wisdom, to put forward new ideas and controversial unpopular opinions, without placing themselves in jeopardy of loosing their jobs or privileges they may have at their institution'.

It is worth noting that the amendment only applied to universities and not to the polytechnics and colleges. Prior to April 1989 academic staff in the public sector were employed by local education authorities often on contracts similar to those for school teachers. Their teaching loads were far higher than those of university academics and there was no tenure of office.

The 1988 Act made the polytechnics and major colleges into autonomous institutions, and many have since introduced new contracts with longer working hours and more weeks contracted per year. Equally worrying for academic freedom is the increasing competition between institutions such that academics are encouraged to apply for 'appropriate' research contracts and to publish particular forms of work. Academics are only truly able to question and test received wisdom if this is an activity which is valued and supported within the institution. The new competitive institutions, increasingly dependent upon industry for research funding and image consultants to attract students, require submissive, compliant academics, not ones who might rock the boat. Where the 'good of the institution' is given precedence over the good of the academic discipline or an individual's academic work, self-censorship rapidly becomes the everyday reality and academics freedom becomes a myth.

Since the 1988 Education Reform Act became law there have been further changes which are likely to have dramatic effects on student participation rates and subject choice. In order to further introduce the 'discipline of the market' into higher education, the government announced plans for a mixed grant/loan system for student maintenance in 1988 (DES, 1988). These were implemented in September 1990 with only slight modifications having been made, even though no substantial research had been conducted on the nature and extent of possible effects. In practice, the proposal's hidden agenda of removing students from the social security benefits framework, has actually made many students far worse off than before, even if they accept the full loan available.

Changes have also been made to the level of student tuition fees in higher education. Since about 95 per cent of home students have their fees paid by their local education authorities, the level at which they are set has little direct effect on students, and has often been used a blunt policy instrument. In the early 1980s, for example, the government halved the fees in order to give higher education institutions less incentive to accept extra unplanned student numbers. In the new competitive system, however, it is seen as desirable to set fee levels nearer to the actual costs of tuition, such that funding can more closely follow student demand (DES, 1989b). Much higher fees were thus introduced in 1990, with differential fees for the various subjects in the following year.

A Programme for the Sociology of Higher Education

Government policy for change in higher education has run far ahead of research on likely effects. If informed and critical research is to influence the future policy of the next government it is vital that a wide programme of research be quickly launched. This is not the place for a detailed agenda, but the broad outlines might be seen in terms of three major strands. First, there is a need for further, more detailed, work in the political arithmetic tradition to look at the effects of recent changes on student intakes, on academics and on institutions. Will the working class be more reluctant to take on loans than the middle class? Will loans be a greater disincentive to women and people from ethnic minorities than to white men? What will be the effect of these changes on subject choice, or choice of institutions? There needs to be close monitoring of the social, ethnic and gender composition of subject areas and institutions, but there will also be a need for sample surveys of people going into higher education and of similar aged people not choosing to continue with their education. Additionally, surveys of academics could yield information on changing work-loads and work conditions, as well as an indication of the changed cultures of various institutions.

The second strand to the broad outline of research required in the sociology of higher education is a great number of case studies and more qualitative investigations of the lives of those involved. There needs to be case studies of student life to examine such questions as: How do students actually live on such low levels of support? What are their survival strategies? How do these survival strategies interact with their higher education learning? How do they perceive and react to the more 'market led' system? Similarly, academics need to be the subject of intensive study to answer questions such as: How has the nature of academic activity changed? How do these changes relate to the perceived quality of teaching and research activity? How have they adjusted their activities to meet new demands from students and the institution? How has the nature of subjects and of subject knowledge changed? What is quality of the new relationships with students and with colleagues?

Alongside these first two strands is a need for many more case studies of institutional change as such, looking at the micro-politics of each institution and the way in which adjustments have been made to deal with external pressures. These should examine the ways in which policy changes at government level have actually been implemented within institutions, and aim to understand the effects of these changes on the teaching and research activities for which those institutions were created.

This outline programme could be extended, but it is already far wider than can be expected to come to fruition. The basic problem with the sociology of higher education is that there are too few sociologists of education who have been prepared to examine their own situation. In the short term, there is safety in exploring the sociological consequences of other people's problems, but in the long term, the survival of sociology of education itself required the study of the higher education institutions in which it is institutionalised. It is also only through detailed study of these institutions, and those who work in them, that we will be able to see new ways in which they might be changed in order to further the aims of a truly democratic society and to allow more people to benefit from the experience of higher education.

References

Acker, S. (1980) Women, the other academics, *British Journal of Sociology of Education*, 1, pp. 81-92.

Acker, S. & Warren Piper, D. (1984) (Eds) *Is Higher Education Fair to Women?* Windsor: SRHE/NFER-Nelson.

Albrow, M. (1986) The undergraduate curriculum in sociology, *Sociology*, 20, pp. 335-346.

Becher, T. (1989) *Academic Tribes and Territories*. Milton Keynes: SRHE/Open University Press.

Bourdieu, P & Passeron, J.-C. (1977) *Reproduction in Education, Society and Culture*. London: Sage.

Bourdieu, P. (1971a) Intellectual field and creative project, in Michael F.D. Young (Ed) *Knowledge and Control: new directions for the sociology of education*. London: Collier-Macmillan.

Bourdieu, P. (1971b) Systems of education and systems of thought, in Michael F.D. Young (Ed) *Knowledge and Control: new directions for the sociology of education*. London: Collier-Macmillan.

Bourdieu, P. (1988) *Homo Academicus*. Oxford: Polity Press.

Brothers, J. & Hatch, S. (1971) *Residence and Student Life. A sociological enquiry into residence in higher education*. London: Tavistock.

Croham Report (1987) *Review of the University Grants Committee*, Chairman Lord Croham. Cmnd. 81. London: HMSO.

Department of Education and Science (1988) *Top-Up Loans for Students*. HMSO.

Department of Education and Science (1989a) *Statistical Bulletin 4/89, Student numbers in higher education - Great Britain 1975 to 1987*. London: DES.

Department of Education and Science (1989b) *Shifting the Balance of Public Funding of Higher Education to Fees. A Consultative Document*. London: DES.

Floud, J. & Halsey, A.H. (1958) The sociology of education: a trend report and bibliography, *Current Sociology*, 7, pp. 165-235.

Glass, D.V. (1954) *Social Mobility in Britain*. London: Routledge & Kegan Paul.

Halsey, A.H. (1972) *Educational Priority, EPA Problems and Policies, Volume 1*. Report of a research project sponsored by the Department of Education and Science and the Social Science Research Council. London: HMSO.

Halsey, A.H. (1977) Towards Meritocracy? The case of Britain, in J. Karabel & A.H. Halsey (Eds) *Power and Ideology in Education*. New York: Oxford University Press.

Halsey, A.H. (1979) Are the British universities capable of change?, *New Universities Quarterly*, 33, pp. 402-416.

Halsey, A.H. (1982) The decline of donnish dominion?, *Oxford Review of Education*, 8, pp. 215-229.

Halsey, A.H. (1988) Higher education, in A.H. Halsey (Ed) *British Social Trends since 1900*. London: Macmillan.

Halsey, A.H., Floud, J. & Anderson, C. (1961) (Eds) *Education, Economy and Society: a reader in the sociology of education*. London: Free Press.

Halsey, A.H., Heath, A.F. & Ridge, J.M. (1980) *Origins and Destinations*. Oxford: Clarendon Press.

Halsey, A.H., Heath, A.F. & Ridge, J.M. (1984) The political arithmetic of public schools, in G. Walford (Ed) *British Public Schools: Policy and Practice*. Falmer.

Halsey, A.H. & Trow, M. (1971) *The British Academics*. London: Faber & Faber.

Henry, M. & Lingard, B. (1989) The rise and fall of a promotions committee: some reflections on the interrelationship between micro and macro machinations of power, *British Journal of Sociology of Education*, 10, pp. 335-350.

Jarratt Report (1985) *Report of the Steering Committee for Efficiency Studies in Universities*. London: CVCP.

Karabel, J. & Halsey, A.H. (1977) (Eds) *Power and Ideology in Education*. New York: Oxford University Press.

Kelsall, R.K., Poole, A. & Kuhn, A. (1972) *Graduates: the sociology of an elite*. London: Tavistock.

Kogan, M. & Kogan, D. (1983) *The Attack on Higher Education*. London: Kogan Page.

Kogan, M. (1989) Managerialism and higher education, in D. Lawton (Ed) *The Education Reform Act: choice and control*. London: Hodder & Stoughton.

Lindop Report (1985) *Academic Validation in Public Sector Higher Education*. Report of the Commission of Enquiry into Academic Validation of Degree Courses in Public Sector Institutions. Cmnd. 9501. London: HMSO.

Lockwood, G. & Davies, J. (1985) *Universities: the management challenge*. Windsor: SRHE/NFER-Nelson.

Miles, M.W. (1977) The student movement and the industrialization of higher education, in J. Karabel & A.H. Halsey (Eds) *Power and Ideology in Education*. New York: Oxford University Press.

National Advisory Body for Public Sector Higher Education (1987) *Management for a Purpose. A Report of the Good Management Practice Group*. London: NAB.

Platt, J. (1988) Research policy in British higher education and its sociological assumptions, *Sociology*, 22, pp. 513-529.

Reid, I., Bennan, J., Waton, J. & Deem, R. (1984) The cuts in British higher education: a symposium, *British Journal of Sociology of Education*, 5, pp. 167-181.

Robbins Report (1963) *Higher Education*. Cmnd. 2154. London: HMSO.

Rudd, E. (1975) *The Highest Education*. London: Routledge & Kegan Paul.

Rudd, E. (1985) *A New Look at Postgraduate Failure*. Windsor: SRHE/NFER-Nelson.

Sizer, J. (1987a) *Institutional Responses to Financial Reductions in the University Sector. Part 1: Report*. London: DES.

Sizer, J. (1987b) *Institutional Responses to Financial Reductions in the University Sector. Part 2: Comparative Analysis*. London: DES.

Spender, Dale (1979) *Man Made Language*. London: Routledge & Kegan Paul.

Spender, Dale (1981) *Men's Studies Modified*. Oxford: Pergamon.

Spender, Dale (1989) *The Writing or the Sex?* Oxford: Pergamon.

Sutherland, M. (1986) *Women Who Teach in Universities*. London: Trentham Books.

Thomas, K. (1990) *Gender and Subject in Higher Education*. Milton Keynes: SRHE/Open University Press.

Trow, M. (1974) Problems in the transition from elite to mass higher education, in *General Report on the Conference on Future Structures of Post-Secondary Education*. Paris: OECD.

Walford, G. (1983) Postgraduate education and the student's contribution to research, *British Journal of Sociology of Education* 4, pp. 241-254.

Walford, G. (1987) *Restructuring Universities: politics and power in the management of change*. Beckenham: Croom Helm.

Walford, G. (1988) The privatisation of British higher education, *European Journal of Education*, 23, pp. 47-64.

Walford, G. (1990) *Privatisation and Privilege in Education*. London: Routledge.

Weis, L. (1986) Thirty years old and I'm allowed to be late: the politics of time at an urban community college, *British Journal of Sociology of Education* 7, pp. 241-263.

Welsh, J.M. (1979) *The First Year of Postgraduate Research Study*. Guildford: SRHE.

Young, M.F.D. (1971) (Ed) *Knowledge and Control: new directions for the sociology of education*. London: Collier-Macmillan.

Chapter Eleven

Recovering from a Pyrrhic Victory? Quality, Relevance and Impact in the Sociology of Education

ROGER DALE

The major educational reforms of the 1980s may appear in retrospect to have shown us rather a lot about the nature of, and effectiveness of, the sociology of education, in Britain at any rate. On the one hand, they presented a series of events whose broad outlines and directions sociologists had foreseen, and for which they had equipped themselves (through an increasing emphasis on policy sociology) to analyze and understand. At the same time, however, sociologists were finding it much more difficult to get their voices heard. It has always seemed important to sociologists of education that their work be recognised and influential in public as well as in professional forum. While the 1980s have seen surprisingly little decline in professional activity, in the circumstances, those same circumstances have ensured that sociologists of education have come a very long way indeed from the times when they were used by Ministers of Education as important advisors on policy.[1] And that fact has profoundly affected the possibilities of the effectiveness of sociology of education in terms of its influence on educational policy and practice.

It may be appropriate and timely to take advantage of the opportunity provided by this paradoxical situation - clear relevance but inadequate means to demonstrate and register it - to focus a little more closely upon the present state of the sociology of education as a whole. My comments will focus particularly on work in that tradition in the sociology of education that peaked in the first half of the 1970s, work that sought to operate more or less self-consciously in the spirit of the eleventh thesis on Feuerbach.

It is difficult to label this work accurately; 'radical' is insufficiently precise, 'Marxist' both too narrow in its connotations and far from universally applicable, 'reformist' too weak. Perhaps 'socially committed' is the least inadequate way to describe it. It was not necessarily associated only with work carried out at a macro level - the 'new sociology of education' had a distinct micro aspect, for instance - though most current work in the tradition does adopt a more structural focus. Nor is it exclusively economically based; feminist and anti-racist strands are equally prominent.

I would like therefore to examine some of the issues raised by the current reforms in somewhat more detail in this chapter. I will distinguish for the purpose of exposition, three separate facets of the current state of the sociology of education (a) the quality and nature of sociological analyses, (b) their perceived relevance, and (c) the effect they have on practice. It is extremely important, however, to recognise the level of their mutual interdependence and that they are all indispensable features of sociologists of education's work. They are necessarily involved in contributing to the strength, the standing and the value of the discipline, and each of these is to a considerable extent dependent on the other two.

I will start by looking briefly at the standing of the discipline in Britain (and it is especially important to emphasise that my comments are restricted to Britain, since I shall be commenting later on the possible parochialism of British sociology of education). I have already alluded to the circumstances that have so clearly affected that standing, and increasingly so since the peak of its influence in the 1960s and early 1970s. These circumstances include the almost total disappearance of the sociology of education as a separate teaching subject from the syllabus of courses of teacher education. They include the automatic rejection of applications for initial teacher education from people holding degrees in sociology. Sociology's perceived irrelevance, even danger, is often cited as a reason for abandoning completely the theoretical study of education in courses of initial teacher education. This does not mean that the discipline has ceased to exist. This book alone is sufficient testimony to its continuing vitality. However, the strategies that have been adopted in order to retain a sociological influence on education curricula in higher education have affected the direction and outcome of the discipline's development. Rather like the Head teachers of the early TVEI schools (see Dale et al, 1990), we can justify our actions by saying that in adjusting to 'reality' we've done nothing that we wouldn't have wanted to do, or that we did not consider worthwhile in itself, and certainly nothing that we're ashamed of. It is just that, given a free choice we wouldn't necessarily have made those things our highest priority.

Perhaps the commonest strategy has been to emphasise the 'applied' aspects of the subject. There is now only a very small number of courses actually labelled sociology of education compared with those called Multicultural Education, or School and Work, or Gender and Education, or Policy Studies, or Classroom Studies or any one of a host of euphemisms or noms de plume (or de guerre) that sociologists have adopted. And these accommodations have had their effects, though not necessarily for the worse, as I shall seek to indicate below.

It may though, be worth looking a little more closely at the reasons why sociology of education has been so marginalized over the past decade and more. One reason, that most sociologists of education would accept as honourable, is that their work is considered 'dangerous' by those in power. This is evident in some of the reasons most frequently offered for removing sociology of education from teacher education syllabuses. In this view, sociologists of education are victims of their own success. They have, in essence, demonstrated that their approaches and analyses are so threatening that they have to be suppressed. This is similar to arguments used by feminists when confronted with hostile reactions, i.e. that they are challenging power relations. They are neither wrong nor irrelevant, but they do touch raw nerves. There is certainly something in this. But it is not sufficient as an explanation of the current state of the discipline. For one thing, there have been impressively few martyrs for the cause. Most of those who produced the 'threatening' analyses continue to be employed as sociologists of education, often in senior positions. Absence of martyrdom does not, though, rule out the possibility of a Pyrrhic victory, and this is a somewhat more convincing analysis. Sociology of education has proved its point but at potentially crippling cost that may ensure, through dissipation if by no other route, a prolonged impotence to accompany its marginalization. Again, though, the evidence of books like this, and of the continuing strength of the discipline around the world and of its literature and journals, must make us hesitate before accepting such pessimistic conclusions, even if they are ones that enable the discipline to emerge with some honour.

One other possibility that must not only be acknowledged but investigated is that sociologists of education may have contributed to the irrelevance that others attribute to them.[2] Sociologists of education (and not only those I referred to as 'socially committed') have typically accepted unproblematically what might be called the 'redemptive' view of education. Examples abound. Indeed, it is quite difficult to point to sociologies of education that do not embrace that view. It emerged in the wake of, and partly in response to, the social control assumptions of the 'educational sociology' paradigm that was so prominent in the first half of the century.

Education as an institution has held a central place in what has come to be called the project of modernity. On the one hand, it might almost be seen as both the dominant symbol and the dominant strategy for that mastery of nature and of society through rationality that has characterized the project of modernity from its origins in the Enlightenment. On the other hand, education has been a keystone of attempts to extend the benefits of progress to whole populations, indeed to the whole of humanity. It has come to stand for the possibility of individual and collective improvement, individual and collective emancipation.

Much of the sociology of education has implicitly but effectively taken the project of social redemption/emancipation through universal provision as a central normative guideline; that is to say that is has taken a utopian view of the possibilities of education, and concentrated its energies on identifying obstacles to the attainment of that unproblematic and unexamined goal. In its early post war history, sociologists of education seemed to offer some substance to those possibilities through their isolation of the link between social class and educational opportunity and the way that this link was perpetuated and strengthened by a socially divided education system. Unify the education system, and you will equalize opportunities seemed to be the message. In other words the solution lay in making provision truly universal. But even with a unified system of compulsory education, educational outcomes remained stubbornly differentiated on social class lines; and when we came to recognise race and gender divisions as well, our analyses seemed equally impotent in informing effective change. A succession of explanations have been offered. Some have concentrated on the different capacities children bring to school. Others have looked at how the outcomes of schooling are socially evaluated. Yet others have focused on the process of schooling itself, seeing it not as a form of redressing the various kind of social inequalities that children bring to school, but of reproducing them, of reinforcing them, and of legitimating them through making it appear that their causes are individual and not social. The universal emancipatory project of education remained unrealized, according to these approaches, firstly because of the teachers' and other education professionals' failure to recognise that education is, like all other social institutions, a social construction and that all that is required to transform it is for it to be differently socially constructed - a view labelled with exquisite accuracy, if not elegance, as 'naive possibilitarianism' (Whitty, 1974). Then it was recognised that it was not possible to reconstruct social institutions at will, because certain powerful groups and social forces had interests in keeping them as they were. The most powerful of these was the capitalist system itself, which had certain key functions it required education to fill, and which modified utopian possibilities in a most severe manner. The problem with this view, though, was that it was not clear how this capitalist system conveyed its requirements to the education system and ensured that they were met - at which point, enter the state. It was the state acting to a greater or lesser degree on behalf of capitalism that set the limits to possibilities of education. And most recently, the state's incipient partial withdrawal from the provision of education, has been seen to remove the final veil covering the modesty of the market and reveal it as having been fundamentally and all along, the force that obstructed and denied the utopian possibilities of education.

Of course, this is a parody of what sociologists of education have been earnestly working away at throughout their academic careers. Indeed, it would be equally possible to point to the achievements of each of those various approaches and to demonstrate how they have enhanced our understanding of education.

But, fundamental to them has been the view that education can and should be universally emancipatory with the consequent aim of identifying and overcoming obstacles to the realization of that noble possibility.

In this view, much of the sociology of education of the past 20 years might be seen as exhibiting a loyal but misguided attachment to a rather simplified interpretation of Gramsci's famous dictum 'pessimism of the intellect, optimism of the will'. The 'intellect' met in full the criteria of what Bourdieu has called 'pessimistic functionalism' by arguing that the world is as it is because it is designed to serve 'the interests of the powerful' in the interests of 'the system'. But the pessimism and the optimism were symbiotic. The pessimism arose from a failure to fulfil a set of possibilities that could only be seen as possibilities when they were generated by an optimism of the will that ignored the essential basis of its own optimism, which must be the concrete analysis of concrete situations. Lacking that analysis what we had was 'utopian' rather than optimistic, because the relationship between that work in the sociology of education and the changes it sought was rooted in a set of what were essentially a priori, rather than grounded, assumptions.

This set of approaches within the sociology of education also created a tendency to depreciate the importance of what actually happens in schools and the education system at large. Schools came to be regarded merely as neutral conduits for the transmission of the major themes of society. In this view, schools are only the witting or unwitting agents of social and cultural reproduction, and the best we can hope for from them, and encourage them to do, is to 'resist' in various ways their role in social reproduction. The excessive concentration on how far schools could modify processes they could never transform has involved a narrowing of perspective that shut out the other things that schools do, including many of those that are of the most importance to their various clients, customers and consumers.

It was in these ways that the sociology of education might be said to be in danger of contributing to its own irrelevance.

This may become a little clearer if we ask what have traditionally been the 'enemies' of the sociology of education. In my experience, two have stood out. One of these was psychology - or at least psychological reductionism, the attribution of all educational consequences to the behaviour of individuals. That rightly remains a key negative reference point for sociologists of education at a time when conceptions of fundamental human nature are more obviously influential in the design and implementation of education policy and practice than they have been for some time.

The other 'enemy', though was 'liberalism', interpreted as a belief that piecemeal improvements in education policy and practice are possible without structural change. Not only are such changes extremely unlikely to have beneficial long term effects, even more importantly, the view that they could do so - that piecemeal change could be as effective as structural change - itself was fundamentally in conflict with sociological analyses of education. The difference was as much one of perspective as of analysis. It is most effectively summarised by the Canadian political scientist, Robert W. Cox (1980). Cox states that all theory is for someone and for some purpose. Theory can, he says, serve two distinct purposes, what he calls problem solving theory and critical theory. Problem solving theory takes the world as it finds it, with the prevailing social and power relationships and the institutions into which they are organized, as the given framework for action. The general aim of problem solving is to make these relationships and institutions work smoothly by dealing effectively with particular sources of trouble. Since the general pattern of institutions and relationships is not called into question, particular problems can be considered in relation to the specialized areas of activity in which they arise.

Critical theory is critical in the sense that it stands apart from the prevailing order of the world and asks how that order came about. Critical theory, unlike problem solving theory, does not take institutions and social and power relations for granted but calls them into question by concerning itself with their origins and how and whether they might be in the process of changing. It is directed towards an appraisal of the very framework for action, or problematic, which problem solving theory accepts as its parameters. Critical theory is directed to the social and political complex as a whole rather than to the separate parts.

It scarcely needs saying that at least the 'socially committed' tradition in the sociology of education has adopted a critical, rather than problem solving, theoretical stance. And it scarcely needs to be added that that is unlikely to make that work appear, prima facie, relevant.

This has, of course, been recognised - as is again apparent from this book. 'Education policy' has become a much more prominent target of sociological analysis and as it has waxed, so analysis of 'education system in capitalist societies' has waned. Accompanying this emphasis has been an increasing interest in matters such as 'the state' and the 'New Right'. There are a number of reasons for this. Education policy, and how it is made, have become much more visible, much more public. The political theories underlying those policies have also become more explicit than they have been previously, particularly under Conservative governments. And 'the state' has become more prominent in explanations of how education policy is made as a result of the apparent inadequacy of pluralist theories to explain either the changes that have taken place in those processes, or their outcomes.

One view of this might be, as I implied at the beginning of this chapter, that the sociology of education finds itself in a position where all three of its central aims - quality, relevance and impact - can now be met. The immediate problems are sufficiently relevant and important in both their sources and their consequences, and they also combine 'immediacy' and 'theoretical interest' in a way that might enable the erosion of the distinction between problem solving and critical theory.

For that promise to be fully realised, however, it will be essential to hold on to a critical theoretical approach. That this cannot at all be taken for granted becomes clear if we consider the three key features of education policy analysis that I have just outlined - its increased visibility, the more explicit references to its theoretical sources and the need to introduce 'the state' into any explanation of education policy. The danger is that the increased visibility and public prominence of education policy and the 'New Right' distract us from the awareness that how education policy is made, and informed by political doctrines, have always been matters of crucial importance to sociologists of education. Their contemporary prominence does not fundamentally change that, and nor, more pressingly, does their relevance mean that theoretical explanations can be even temporarily suspended in favour of analyses whose outcomes are more immediately 'relevant, or even 'topical', which has been the case with several examples of 'New Right' analyses. The same is true of the invocation of 'the state' rather than pluralism in explanations of education policy making. The importance of 'the state' in these explanations is no greater now than it has been previously; it is not the presence of the state but its relative prominence that has to be explained, something that has not always been apparent in recent work in the sociology of education.

The danger is, then, that the opportunity for sociological analysis of contemporary education reforms may be missed if it takes the form of a series of ad hoc analyses, shaped by a problem solving concentration on a particular level of focus, rather than by a critical theoretical concentration on a more abstract level. The confusion of level of focus - macro, meso, or micro - and level of abstraction - explanation or description, for instance - is quite common, and always misleading. This confusion is most clearly exemplified by the notion of 'middle-range' theories where, because it is never clear whether it is the focus or the level of abstraction that is to be 'middle range', the two are not only confused but equated. And it is equally evident in the common-sense linking of micro and descriptive, macro and explanatory, though it hardly needs to be said that the opposite pairings are equally valid and empirically as likely.

The way that 'the state' and the 'New Right' have been used in some recent work unfortunately gives substance to these fears. Both, it seems to me, are in danger of being used to 'name' theoretical spaces - or more accurately to rename them - rather than analysing how (adequately) those spaces are currently filled. It is rather like a theoretical painting by numbers where the sections of the picture are coloured differently but where their outlines, and the overall picture, remain more of less unchanged. One set of concepts replaces what is already there without necessarily changing it. 'The State' replaces 'pluralism' but within the same theoretical space. Critical discussion of New Right ideas is critical in the sense of hostile rather than standing apart from them and asking how they came about.

What I am arguing here is at its simplest that in the present conjuncture the 'theoretical' projects dominating the sociology of education may be dominated on the one hand by ad hocery and on the other by a restriction to concept development rather than theoretical development. I have already alluded to the ad hocery. It is perhaps most clearly seen in those analyses of the 'New Right' that impute a single essential meaning to the broad range of possibilities that might be assembled together under that umbrella, a single meaning that takes its substance from the particular 'New Right' strand most prominent locally. This not only misidentifies the local variant in ways that it makes both difficult to identify and to overcome. It also obstructs an adequately critical analyses of what is occurring, essentially by transforming a piece of sociological analysis into a political rallying cry. These are by no means necessarily mutually exclusive, but it is crucial to appreciate their difference.

The distinction between concept development and theoretical development is equally important. The difference between the two is one of scale. Theoretical development relies on and requires concept development, but concept development is not sufficient to produce theoretical development. Rather, theoretical development requires the articulation of groups of concepts rather than their development in isolation.

This can perhaps best be explained by a comparison between the way that sociologists of education have made use of the concept of 'New Right' ideas, with the analyses offered in Peter Hall's (1989) collection of essays about the different ways that Keynesian ideas were developed and implemented (or not) in different countries. Hall distinguishes three theoretical approaches used by his contributors. These are what he calls economist centred, state centred and coalition centred approaches. The first of these stresses the impact of expert advice on policy and traces the way professional economists were won over to Keynesian ideas. Its focus is on the ideas themselves, though it also involves examining "the institutional parameters that structure communication within the economics profession and between economist and policy maker" (p. 9). The state centred approach emphasises the importance of the "institutional configuration of the state and its prior experience with related policies... some states will have the bureaucratic capacities to implement a new program quite readily ... (some) will be predisposed towards policies with which they already have some favourable experience, and even the demands of political parties and interest groups may be based on their conceptions of state capacities and existing policy legacies". The coalition centred approach focuses on the broader political context and on the "ability of politicians to forge a coalition of social groups that is large enough to sustain them in office and indeed to regard Keynesian measures as something that is in their interest" (p. 12).

What is important here is not the relative adequacy of the three approaches, but the fact that (a) they all start from attempting to explain the differences in how Keynesianism was interpreted and taken up and (b) that none of them, even the economist centred, assumes that those differences can be explained by the nature of the ideas themselves. Though there are clearly very important exceptions (for example Stephen Ball's (1990) analysis of New Right ideas and their influence) it does seem that much sociological work has been on the development of the concept of the New Right almost as if that would in itself explain the different, even contradictory, policies whose provenance it is alleged to be. The way that the concept has been developed often seems to operate by cataloguing the alleged purposes and outcomes of a policy, which is taken almost a priori to be of New Right provenance, and then using these purposes and outcomes to give substance to the concept.

Only rarely are we offered a comparative analysis that would at least have the virtue of demonstrating that things (in this case, the New Right) could be otherwise and consequently requiring us to make problematic, rather than taking for granted, not only the ideas themselves (i.e. to deepen our conceptual analysis) but also the particular sets of historical, social, political and economic conditions under which one or other interpretation of those ideas became installed. An interesting example of this is Susan Bassnett's (1986) account of the different interpretation put on feminism in different societies, which though it does see an essential core to feminism, finds that the forms taken by feminist thought and action owe a very great deal to the political traditions of the countries in which they are created. In education, a comparison I have carried out with Jenny Ozga between the uses of ideas labelled 'New Right' in the educational reforms in England and Wales, and in New Zealand, shows very little overlap between them, either in the selection from the New Right that they embrace, or in the intensity and extent to which they are implemented (Dale & Ozga, 1992). Assuming that 'New Right' in itself told us something significant about either or both those sets of reforms, then, would have been quite misleading; it would have obscured far more than it would have revealed. This is confirmed by the experience related to me by one non UK based Anglophone sociologist of education, who found attendance at a sociology of education conference in Britain 'almost a total waste of time because all they wanted to talk about were *their* problems'.

What the Hall examples, and the England/New Zealand comparison demonstrate above all is the relative poverty of theoretical development as compared with conceptual development. The same is, of course, true in the case of 'the state'. It is difficult to see how the state can be conceived of at all outside its relation with the economy and civil society, but it is becoming increasingly commonly offered as an explanatory variable in itself (see Ramirez & Boli ,1987).

How, then, if at all, might concepts like the state and the New Right be employed in a theoretical analysis of contemporary education reforms? One useful starting point would be to take what is common to all the three approaches explaining the policy impact of ideas that Peter Hall outlines, i.e. that it is the institutional and political structures through which they are passed that explains the use made of those ideas rather than the ideas themselves. Very crudely, that means that in order to understand the impact of the ideas we need first to understand the state. And I have already suggested that the state cannot be seen in isolation but that an adequate theory of the state must situate it in relation to the economy and civil society. The state both mediates the relationship between the economy and civil society (though of course it does not do so alone) and relates directly to each. In particular it lays down key parameters (but again not the only parameters) of what is possible, for itself and for its relationship with economy and civil society. State institutional structures are a key means of translating and specifying the shape of economic, political and social problems. Further, what both Hall's example of Keynesianism and Bassnett's of feminism demonstrate is that the sets of ideas, too, not only contain 'nationally specific' (rather than 'essential') solutions to economic and social problems but also affect the interpretation and the formulation of the problems to which they are solutions. 'Objective' economic changes, then, impact differently on different countries. What becomes, or are seen as, key educational *issues* have their sources in local interpretations of 'objective' economic problems; and these interpretations in turn have their sources in the institutional structures of the state, in the various discourses of national civil societies (especially the discourses of race, gender and class), and in the various ways that they intersect and interact on the terrains of national politics.

The following figure sets out this framework.

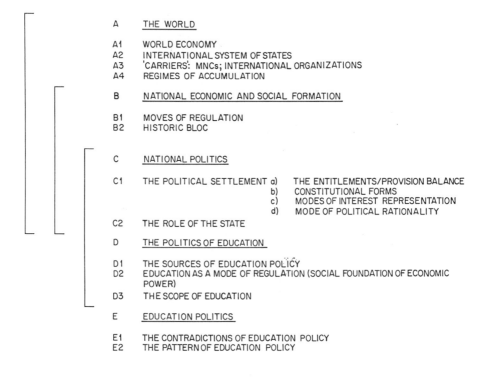

FIG. 1. *Levels of analysis (for an elaboration of this figure see Dale, 1990).*

This figure also indicates the different levels at which sociology of education might have an impact. This is particularly useful for the third purpose of this chapter - determining what and where the impact of sociology of education is and might be. It is also particularly important because while sociologists of education have been keen to influence education policy it has not always been clear what the relationship was between the analysis and its intended influence, or how that influence was to be brought to bear. The figure distinguishes between the politics of education, education politics and educational practice. It is intended also to imply that these levels are differently constituted, and that different forms of analysis would have different effects upon them. In particular, it might be argued that sociology of education has tended to move directly from analyses of levels A and B, essentially the analysis of the relationship between education and the economy, to level E, the framing of educational practice, as if the former 'determined' the latter, in a more or less immediate way. Indeed, the assumption that the relationship between education and the economy maps directly on to the relationship between school and social life (including work) appears to be very deeply ingrained within the sociology of education. The 'discovery' of the importance of the state has done much to soften the starkness of this assumption and to add complexity to it, but as I suggested above, it has both come to be seen as sufficient modification of that assumption, and to be in need of little continuing elaboration, especially in the form of articulation to what appear in the diagram as levels B and C - i.e. the relationship between the state and civil society and the nature of the state apparatus itself, as well as the relationship between the state and the economy.

The figure suggests that the school-social life (including work) relationship cannot be inferred direct from the education-economy relationship but that three distinct levels intervene between and mediate them to each other. It suggests that the education-economy relationship is determined at what is called the level of the national economic social formation.

That relationship is shaped by the response to problems and possibilities 'delivered' by the world economy and the country's place within it contained in the 'modes of regulation' prevailing within the country, and the historic bloc that dominates it. Put very simply, modes of regulation may be seen as "the institutional forms, procedures and habits which either coerce or persuade private agents to conform to (the) schemas (of a regime of accumulation)" (Lipietz, 1987, p. 33). An historic bloc is "the particular configuration of social classes and ideology that gives content to a state. It is what the state is in a concrete historical instance" (Cox, 1980, p. 402). Or, as Jessop et al (1989) put it, "An historic bloc is an historically constituted, socially reproduced structural ensemble characterized by a contingent correspondence between the economic 'base' (with its specific accumulation regime and mode of growth) and the political and ideological institutions (state form, civil society)" (p. 163).

211

If we accept that this is the level at which the fundamental relationship between the education system and the economy - how education is to 'fit in' to the social formation as a whole - is very broadly laid down, it becomes obvious that any attempt to 'read off' from this broad determination what happens in schools and classrooms, even in education policy, is bound to be misleading. The figure suggests that that relationship is mediated at three broad levels, national politics, the politics of education and education politics.

The first of these levels, 'national politics' is the arena where modes of regulation and the historic bloc are given concrete form and substance. At this level the local direction of education and the framework for the development of education policy are set. The entitlements - provision balance is an effective way of encapsulating the broad direction of social policy (see Dahrendorf, 1988). Modes of interest representation lay down which 'voices' are considered legitimate in policy formation. Modes of political rationality determine whether education policy, for instance, is to be 'supply' or 'demand' led (see Offe, 1981). Both these are related to constitutional forms such as the relationships between central and local government, labour regulation and so on. All of these, and especially the overall balance sought between the state and the market, are intimately bound up with the role of the state apparatus, the means by which they are put into effect.

The next level, what I have called the politics of education, is where many recent analyses of education policy have been concentrated. This is quite appropriate, since it is at this level that education policy is largely formulated. The more effective of those analyses have recognised that the problems that education policy is intended to address - and redress - do not come ready formed, but as a result of the processes in the prior levels. However, those levels do not determine either the forms the problems take or how they will be addressed, and such analyses are essential if sociologists of education are either to understand education policy formation adequately, or to seek to comment on it, or contribute to it. Three aspects of this issue feature in the figure. The first, the sources of education policy, has been more widely recognised than the other two. In essence, it refers to the shifting prominence, both collectively and separately, of three major items on the agenda of education policy makers, supporting the accumulation process, providing a context for its continuing expansion and legitimating that process and the state's role in sustaining it (this is elaborated in Dale, 1989). These shifts occur under the influence of shifts in the mode of regulation; though the shifts in the sources of education policy - the increasing importance of support at the expense of legitimation, for instance - have been noted accurately in much of the literature, their origins have not always been as adequately investigated.

In particular, the place of education in the overall mode of regulation - how it relates to and integrates with (or not), for instance, the industrial relations framework and other aspects of social policy - has not been as fully appreciated as it might have been. This is one of the clearer consequences of what has always seemed to me (or what has been greatly reinforced by living on the 'other side' of the world) of the insularity, even parochialism, in discussions of education policy and practice in England that I have already alluded to. This parochialism is not only 'national', but also disciplinary. It is revealing, for instance, to note how few references there are in recent sociological analyses of education policy to theoretical work in other disciplines, or even in mainstream sociology. The starkness of the exception to this general stricture, the use of feminist work, makes the point clearly. Of particular interest in this area is the work of the Aix group on the social foundations of industrial power (Maurice et al, 1986 - the French title of this book, significantly, is 'Politiques d'education et organisation industrielle en France et Allemagne'). This describes the very different production methods and processes involved in making the same industrial products in France and Germany. These include major differences in both the nature of supervision and control, and of the levels of 'skills' deemed necessary in the production processes in the two countries. These are then linked to, and located in, broader national ensembles of industrial relations framework, the nature and extent of its legal regulation, the role of trade unions, the nature and place of national systems of industrial skill training, the qualifications they provide, the 'portability' of those qualifications, and so on. What this demonstrates is that both the problems that education policy is to tackle and the solutions that it might offer cannot be seen in isolation from the whole ensemble of social foundations of industrial power and that this is especially important if sociologists of education are to suggest alternative forms and direction of education policy as a result of these analysis.

The comparative approach is also central to the notion of the scope of education (this is elaborated on in Dale, 1989 and Dale & Ozga, 1990). It involves asking what it is considered that education should and can achieve, respectively its 'mandate' and its capacity. This again varies very considerably between societies and this variation should alert us to the need to establish the existing national parameters, their history and the sources of influence upon them. This is clearly important, both in analysing the fate of reforms and in suggesting alternatives.

I can be much briefer discussing the level of 'education politics' than I have been in discussing the earlier levels. On the one hand, I hope that the foregoing discussions make it unnecessary to elaborate on its location in the overall schema. On the other hand the level of the context of policies and their relationship with practice is where the sociology of education policy has probably been most effective in its analyses and discussions of the current educational reform, as other chapters in this book demonstrate.

Looking at 'education politics' and seeing it as the most effectual level of sociological analysis does though raise the questions of audience and impact. In its heyday, the main audience for sociology of education, and the main recipient of its impact, was teacher education, both initial and in service. Today, that audience has not so much disappeared as 'been disappeared', if not in its entirely, then to a very significant degree. It takes us back to the second and third questions I raised at the beginning of this chapter, of relevance and effect; I have tried in the foregoing sections to show how those questions are related to the issue of the quality of the work. An important part of the quality of the work, I suggested, was the effective recognition of different levels of analysis. And part of the reason for the emphasis on levels was that it also clarifies and informs the issue of relevance and impact. That emphasis is intended both to indicate the kinds of analysis required to make worthwhile contributions at each level, and to provide one criterion for analyzing the worthwhileness of those contributions and the reasons for 'success' or 'failure'. That it is to say, the effectiveness of the analysis has to be tied to the appropriate level for its relevance and input to be apparent and exploited.

For instance, while sociologists of education have analysed policies and practices for their assumptions, intentions, contradictions, likely social effects and so on, they have rarely looked at how likely they are to succeed and why. That is, those analyses have sometimes missed the most important single component that binds together the issues of quality, relevance and impact, that is, the analysis of where change is possible and it is the centrality of this question that makes the distinction of levels so important, as a key means of addressing it.

The clearest illustration of this is the relative lack of impact of most sociological work in education over the past decade and more. I think that the reasons for this are different in the cases of policy-oriented and classroom-focussed sociologies of education. Very crudely, in the former case the quality and relevance of work failed to have much impact because they were aimed at a level where - as the analyses themselves demonstrated - influence leading to change was almost impossible to achieve. In the latter case, the relative lack of impact is not due to major resistance to sociologically informed change, so much as to a lack of perceived relevance; what sociologists were interested in looking at was not what most concerned practitioners.

Though the two sets of reasons differ, they may have the same origin. That origin is the fall from grace and favour that sociologists of education began to experience from round the middle of the 1970s. As I indicated at the start of this chapter, the reaction to the rejection of sociology of education was to try as far as possible to continue it - or at least its principles - under new headings. Thus there was a growth in policy studies, multicultural education, qualitative research methods, gender and education, classroom studies and so on. However, it was not possible - or even desirable - to disregard the label under which the activity proceeded, and there was a consequent emphasis on a series of *issues*, such as those signalled in the categories I have just named. At the same time, there was a continuing attachment to those fundamental principles of sociology of education that I mentioned above - a 'redemptive' view of education and a rejection of anything that might smack of 'liberalism' or psychologism.

The best illustration of some of the reasons for this general 'failure' is a relatively 'successful' research endeavour in the sociology of education in the 1980s. The TVEI research was generally of good quality, relevant to those involved in it at several levels, and effective because it raised issues at points and in ways that they could be acted on. There were, though, a number of unique conditions that made this success possible. The research was comparatively well funded. Researchers had, on the whole, excellent access. The situation was sufficiently fluid for change to be made, with vested interests in the 'success' of the project at least as a strong, as well funded and as well organised as those whose interests might have led them to obstruct it. The research was carried out in a very large number of sites, enabling effective comparative work to be done, and some possibility of explaining, rather than merely drawing attention to, features apparently associated with 'successful' outcomes. The significant point is that few of these characteristics of the TVEI research projects were found, and certainly not together, in any of the other major pieces of research into policy and practice over the same period.

Where this matters most is at the level of the school. This is because that is a level at which it is possible, as well as desirable, for sociologists of education to have some input if their work is of sufficient quality and relevance. That has always been the case but considerable fluidity has been introduced into the situation in which schools find themselves by the measures included in the current package of educational reforms. The National Curriculum, national testing, local management of schools, schemes of teacher appraisal and so on, have removed many of the old certainties and props and left schools not only in greater need of the kind of help that sociologists of education might claim to offer, because of a need to understand the new situation, but also more likely to act on it, because of the concomitant dissipation of the old certainties.

Finally, I might suggest an example of how sociology of education might continue to realize its promise. One medium through which this might be attempted is that of the study of school effectiveness. Existing studies in the area have effectively established two major facts - that schools do make a difference and that we cannot explain how or why. Recognizing the first of these does enable the retention, at least in part, of the redemption project and the maintenance of an anti-liberal stance since it shows the limits of system level change. It also allows, or even requires, the use of a critical theoretical approach. Much of the school effectiveness literature demonstrates very well the intrinsic shortcomings of the problem solving approach that it has implicitly adopted. Without probing farther beneath the surface are we bound to be left with precisely the kind of tantalising outcomes of much of this work - the isolation of a set of features that are associated with school effectiveness, but insufficient understanding of how the association works (or even in which direction) to allow for confident replication of those features in other schools.

What these studies do mean, though, are a change in the dominant foci of the sociology of the school, which are essentially legacies of the assumptions associated with the redemption project. In particular, they would require some modification of the assumption of the central importance of the formal curriculum, and of the study of teachers rather than teaching. They would require two new emphases - the replacement of the banalities of many popular organisation theory-based approaches to school organization, and a revitalization - for instance, along the (different) lines suggested by Clem Adelman and Basil Bernstein - of the study of pedagogy. Such studies would it seems to me enable the ample filling of the promise of sociology of education, by combining quality, relevance and impact through the possibility of informing change.

NOTES

[1] The work, position and influence of A.H. Halsey in the 1960s is the outstanding example. See Flude (1974) and Kogan (1971).

[2] The following paragraphs are adapted from my inaugural lecture at the University of Auckland, which is published under the title 'The Limits and Possibilities of Education' in *Access*, 1990, 9 (1), pp. 1-18.

BIBLIOGRAPHY

Adelman, Clem (1988) *Looking at Teaching*, Course EP228, Unit C1. Milton Keynes: Open University Press.

Ball, Stephen J. (1990) *Policy and Policy Making in Education*. London: Routledge.

Bassnett, Susan (1986) *Feminist Experience: The Women's Movement in Four Countries*. London: Allen & Unwin.

Bernstein, Basil (1990) *The Structuring of Pedagogic Discourse. Class, Codes and Control*, Volume 4. London: Routledge.

Cox, Robert W. (1980) Social forces, states and world orders, *Millenium: Journal of International Studies*, 10, pp. 126-55.

Dahrendorf, Ralf (1988) *The Modern Social Conflict*. Berkeley: University of California Press.

Dale, Roger (1989) *The State and Education Policy*. Milton Keynes: Open University Press.

Dale, Roger (1990) Regulation Theory, Settlements and Education Policy. Paper presented to Conference on Education Policy, Massey University, July.

Dale, Roger & Ozga, Jenny (1990) *Introducing Education Policy: principles and perspectives*. Course E333, Module 1 (2nd Edn). Milton Keynes: Open University Press.

Dale, Roger & Ozga, Jenny (1992) The 'New Right' in Educational Reform in New Zealand and England, in R. Lingard et al (Eds) *Labour and the Reconstruction of Schooling*. London: Falmer Press.

Dale, Roger et al (1990) *The TVEI Story: Policy, Practice and Preparation for Work*. Milton Keynes: Open University Press.

Flude, Michael (1974) Sociological Accounts of Differential Educational Achievement, in M. Flude & J. Ahier (Eds) *Educability, Schools and Ideology.* London: Croom Helm.

Hall, Peter A. (Ed) (1989) *The Political Power of Economic Ideas: Keynesianism across countries.* Princeton: Princeton University Press.

Jessop, Bob, Bonnett, Kevin, Bromley, Simon & Ling, Tom (1989) *Thatcherism.* Cambridge: Polity Press.

Kogan, Maurice (1971) *The Politics of Education.* London: Penguin.

Lipietz, Alain (1987) *Mirages and Miracles.* London: Verso.

Maurice, Marc, Sellier, Francois & Silvestre, Jean-Jacques (1986) *The Social Foundations of Industrial Power.* Cambridge: MIT Press.

Offe, Claus (1981) The Attribution of Status to Interest Groups: observations on the West German case, in S. Berger (Ed) *Organizing Interests in Western Europe: Pluralism, Corporatism and the Transformation of Politics*, pp. 123-158. Cambridge: Cambridge University Press.

Ramirez, Francisco & Boli, John (1987) Political control of mass schooling: European origins and world-wide institutionalization, *Sociology of Education*, 60, pp. 12-17.

Whitty, Geoff (1974) Sociology and the Problem of Radical Education Change, in M. Flude & J. Ahier (Eds) *Educability, Schools and Ideology*, pp. 112-137. London: Croom Helm.